SAVING THE OLDEST TOWN IN TEXAS

Linda Thorsen Bond

STEPHEN F. AUSTIN STATE UNIVERSITY PRESS
NACOGDOCHES, TX

All rights reserved. For information about permission to reproduce
selections from this book write to Permissions:
Stephen F. Austin State University Press
PO Box 13007, SFA Station
Nacogdoches, TX 75962
sfapress@sfasu.edu
936-468-1078

For information about special discounts for bulk purchases, please contact
Texas A&M University Press Consortium
tamupress.com

ISBN: 978-1-62288-214-4

Cover and book design by Sarah Johnson
Cover art by Tristan Brewster

To my mother, the inspiration for Peggy Jensen:
an irrepressible woman who tackles projects that would terrify most people
and doesn't believe in the concept "too far gone"

Saving the Oldest Town in Texas

Based on the true story of Benjamin S. Wettermark who emptied his own bank and skipped town in 1903, leaving his wife, his children, and his mansion behind.

1. Too Far Gone

All the things that make a Victorian home beautiful were gone. The mantles had been torn off the fireplaces. The bullseye molding above each of the door-frames, gone. Most of the hand-blown glass windows had been replaced with Plexiglas or boarded over with plywood.

Peggy Jensen stepped around a stained mattress sprawled in the middle of the front room. She turned slowly, taking in the crumbling, decaying house. Her foot caught on a broken floorboard and she lurched forward.

The real estate agent reached out to steady her. She was, after all, probably 40 years older than he was, and he was worried that she would trip, fall and crumble to dust before him.

"Why don't we go back to the house we were looking at," Tyler Pate said nervously. "I didn't get to show you the kitchen. It's all redone—everything new, gas stove like you want, refrigerator with the ice and water on the door-- it even has a spigot for hot water, right there on the door."

She looked at Tyler, at the grimace that passed for a smile pasted on his face.

"For your tea.   Tea without even turning on a burner," he added.

The house he had shown her was very nice, she told herself. The floors were engineered hardwood, permanently shiny and carefree, swept clean of any traces of a sagging, crumbling past. She was willing to bet that the faucets were as lovely as the open-concept front room, as the double-pane windows, as the ceiling fans already spinning in anticipation of her visit. It was just the right size for one person who was alone for the first time in almost half a century.

"I just love looking around historic homes. Don't you?"

"This town has plenty of them," Tyler said. "Have you restored a house before?"

"Well, no, but I've always thought about it. There weren't any houses like this where we lived," she said as she looked closely at a splintering windowsill.

Tyler nodded. "We could find you one that's all fixed up. There's some historic beauties not far from this neighborhood. This is one of the original old streets here in the oldest town in Texas."

He reached out his hand again to steady her as she walked near a pile of soggy rags on the floor. They both looked up at a rusty brown water stain high on a wall.

"Not this one, though," he said. "I think this is too far gone."

A couple of months ago Peggy would have said the same thing about herself. Just past 78, stiffening up in all her joints, too far gone to start again. She had spent seven years taking care of Bill, watching his brilliant mind deteriorate, following him as he walked round and round the townhouse, shuffling from the kitchen to the living room to the dining room and back to the kitchen. Round and round, like the hands on the relentless clock, stealing his wits every second, every minute, every hour.

When Bill died, Peggy sat in the living room, wondering what to do next. Her daughter called everyday, relentless.

"You'll love it here in Nacogdoches," Erin said. "I'll come up and help you move."

"I don't want to be any trouble," Peggy told her. "I want to get my own place."

"That'd be fine. You can live with us until you find something," Erin promised, driven to accomplish, to get things done.

Peggy sold the townhouse and pocketed more than she expected. Apparently, these little two bedroom places with the attached garages were all the rage. Everybody's getting older, everybody wants to simplify. She wasn't the only one who had to sell the family home so she could take care of her faltering husband. Then later sell again to move near family.

Erin and her son-in-law Jackson were the only people she knew in Nacogdoches. She had left behind nearly 50 years worth of friends, people who had helped her with Bill, church friends, library friends, club friends, fellow antique collectors. She felt she was ready for a brand new start.

Peggy put a hand on the crumbled wallpaper. Tyler followed her to the wall. She peeled off a tiny strip of the paper, revealing another pattern beneath it. Beneath that, the wood might be crumbling, pitted by termites or the mold that haunted east Texas.

"It can cost a fortune, fixing up these old wrecks," Tyler said, reaching out to pull off a little of the paper himself.

"I haven't got a fortune," she admitted.

"Who does? But we can sure find some good buys walk-in ready," he said, nodding sagely.

She had seen the motto "The Oldest Town in Texas" above the door of the Convention & Visitors Bureau, printed on the stationery, italicized on every brochure and flyer that promoted the town of 30,000 people.

The first Spanish Catholic mission was founded in Nacogdoches in 1716, over 300 years ago. Nacogdoches was over a hundred years older than Peggy's previous hometown. It was, of course, a hundred years younger than Boston and wasn't even a twinkle in the eyes of the Spanish explorers when New York City was born.

But this was Texas, and Texas was young. Therefore while little ole Nacogdoches was a toddler compared to the rest of the US, history seekers came from all over to see this town between Houston and Dallas. But they didn't see much that was old in the oldest town.

Right after she moved to Nacogdoches, Peggy went looking for its history. She didn't find much of it. There were a couple of historic sites, like the Stone Fort and Millard's Crossing. On North Street, most of the big historic homes had been torn down and replaced with McDonald's, Chili's, Jack in the Box and Starbucks. Some of the historic buildings now held attorneys' offices or struggling secondhand stores.

Tyler shrugged his shoulders impatiently.

"I promised your son-in-law I'd show you the best we've got, and I feel like we better get going," he said. "You get tetanus from a rusty nail, Jackson will have my head! I'm pretty sure he didn't mean a falling-down old wreck."

Her son-in-law Jackson Vance was the CEO of the Nacogdoches Chamber of Commerce. He was protective of her and her daughter Erin. He was protective of the town, too, working hard to make it prosperous. He was known as a mover and a shaker in a town that had barely moved for over 300 years.

She gave Tyler a quick defensive look, then nodded. "Erin and Jackson would be happy if I'd settle down in their living room and collect stamps," she said.

He grinned, as if he understood what that might mean to her.

She headed to where the kitchen might have been, before the cabinets, counters and sink had been stripped away. Patches of peeling dark green linoleum were the only hint that this was where the Thanksgiving turkey had been prepared.

"What's the story with this house?" She looked at him steadily as she asked.

"Pretty much lost," he admitted. "Well, there was something, but I don't know enough to tell you. Some kinda, I don't know, some bad business, I guess. It's been here since around the late 1890s. It was the Wettermark house, at least that's what the old-timers say."

She turned over a broken picture frame with the toe of her shoe. The glass was so grimy she couldn't tell if it held a picture. She slowly picked it up, careful of a shard of glass still in the frame. The frame was empty—no photo, no family smiling at the camera. There should be something left, she thought, of the beautiful home, the family gathered at the dining table, sipping lemonade on the wrap-around porch, hanging Christmas stockings in the parlor.

She looked at the discolored mattress, then at the rusty streak where rain had eaten down from the ceiling.

Tyler opened the cheap hollow-core front door. "Well," he said, "we better get back to it. I've got some really beautiful places to show you."

Peggy set the frame back down on the pitted plank floor and stepped over a pile of rags that might have been used to clean a carburetor.

She looked at Tyler, waiting expectantly for her.

"I'll take it," she said.

2. Hell Either Way

July 14, 1893

The Pullman porter swayed down the aisle toward her berth. He stood outside the curtain and said quietly, "Miss? Miss Sutton, we're about 15 miles out of Nacogdoches."

"Thank you," Daisy whispered back.

"Yes ma'am," he said.

Daisy was wide-awake, even after traveling five days to get here from New York. She couldn't even dream, she was so anxious. Clara Johnsdotter was sound asleep in a berth across the aisle.

She whispered to the porter, "What time is it?"

"Almost midnight. You got about an hour," he said. "It'll be about 1 a.m. when we pull into the Nacogdoches station."

"Thank you, George," she said as he staggered down the aisle.

When she first heard Mrs. Johnsdotter call the porter "George," she asked the older woman, "Did you meet him when you took the train up to New York?"

Mrs. Johnsdotter laughed. "No. Every porter is called 'George' because of George Pullman who invented the passenger train car. You can't go wrong calling him that."

She was glad she was traveling with someone who knew what to call the porters and how to change trains. Daisy considered herself a modern woman—she was willing to travel alone but she was glad Mrs. Johnsdotter was with her.

When she got Ben's telegram asking her to come to Nacogdoches to marry him, she had rushed in to read it to her mother.

Her mother had been aghast.

"Daisy! How could you even consider it? Let him come back here. No young woman takes a train by herself to marry a man—and all the way to Texas, at that!"

But Daisy was 24 and determined to get married as soon as possible. She had ridden around Manhattan in hansoms by herself, and she had walked to the markets on 14th Street unaccompanied. She was not going to be held back by old-fashioned restrictions on women and she knew Ben needed her as soon as she could get there.

Her mother and father would not let her travel alone and they did have a good point that without a traveling companion Daisy wouldn't have been allowed to eat in the dining car. And Mother would not go to Texas with her.

When she was convinced Daisy wouldn't rest until she gave in, Mother had asked all of the women of her club for help finding a companion for her. They found a respectable woman, Mrs. Johnsdotter, who would welcome a companion on the trip back to Houston. There was a large community of Scandinavian immigrants who were very prosperous in their new Texas home. Ben's father, Alfred Wettermark, lived among them. He had established four banks north of Houston and made Ben the president of the Nacogdoches branch when he was only 21 years old.

Daisy couldn't wait to go.

What a long train trip this had been.

Mrs. Johnsdotter said she'd overheard some men laughing about this rail line from Shreveport to Houston. "They call the Houston East and West Texas—the H.E.W.T. —Hell Either Way Taken!"

Daisy had been a little shocked, but she had to agree, it was primitive. However, this train was taking her to her new life.

From New York to Texas the two women talked and talked. Mrs. Johnsdotter reassured her, in a lovely Swedish accent, "Don't be afraid, Daisy. There are shops and schools and even a library in Nacogdoches."

That was a relief. Daisy's mind had created Wild West saloons and shoot 'em ups. Though she'd never admit it to her mother, she was just a little terrified about the trip. And a little about getting married.

Mrs. Johnsdotter smiled and patted her hand. "I've known the Wettermarks ever since Ben was a little sprite and they are the best, most respectable family I've ever known."

'We're getting married the day after I get to Nacogdoches. I had to promise my mother and father that," Daisy told her. "I still don't know if I have everything I need. I agonized over every decision and I don't know if I packed enough."

Daisy even spoke aloud of her biggest worry: "I hope Ben's four children can love me as much as I love their father."

"I am sure they'll love you." Mrs. Johnsdotter was the most comforting, kind companion Daisy could have ever had. She was also disparaging about the well-meaning New Yorkers who took pleasure in telling Daisy stories of the untamed west and dangerous Texans in the wild, wild frontier. They were no wilder, she assured Daisy, than the Swedes and Norwegians where she had come from.

The final night on the train Daisy was a little weepy that her new friend would continue on to Houston. But Mrs. Johnsdotter said they'd get together someday soon and then Daisy could tell her all the wonderful new things that had happened to her in Nacogdoches.

And now Nacogdoches was the next stop. Daisy hoped she would have enough time to get fancied up before her husband-to-be helped her from the train. She would be glad to get her feet on the platform—the Houston East and West Texas rail line was the roughest she'd experienced since they left New York.

In the curtained berth, Daisy had slept in all her underthings, not even taking off her corset. She couldn't ask Mrs. Johnsdotter to help her get into it, of course. Now she sat up in the berth, pulled her bodice over the chemise, struggled with the double rows of hook and eyes on the front. She had spread her skirt on the empty upper berth and she stood up and wiggled into it. She worried that the rustle of the heavy green silk would wake Mrs. Johnsdotter, asleep in the berth across the aisle. She was glad at least not to be struggling into a bustle. Her mother had tried to talk her into packing one but Daisy had actually laughed at her.

"Oh, Mother, I know they'll be behind the fashion, but not that far behind," she said indulgently. "Nacogdoches isn't the end of the world."

Her mother, teary-eyed, shook her head. "It seems like it, Daisy. So far away."

Nacogdoches would be the end of her journey. She would be with Ben, soon to be her husband. She smiled to herself as she struggled into her boots and hooked the laces, no mean feat in the dark.

She had met Ben Wettermark April 6, 1892 at a private party for the Metropolitan Opera.

He was in the city visiting the financial district with a group of other bankers. When the men entered the lobby, they swept in like a flying wedge, all dark tailcoats and white shirts, pushing in like they meant to take over.

"Bankers. Texans," her mother had whispered.

There are certain things New Yorkers thought when they heard either of those words. "Banker" meant cold-hearted and money-grubbing. "Texan" meant bank robbers rather than bank presidents. Those two words together drew a collective gasp from the aristocratic gathering.

Daisy couldn't take her eyes off of the Texans. Well, nobody could, but her mother was staring because she feared for the silver wine goblets the waiters were passing.

Ben was the youngest in the group. When he turned his icy blue eyes toward her, she felt a physical jolt. Their eyes held, for perhaps a moment more than was seemly. Then he and the pack moved on toward the bar on the other end of the lobby.

Her mother shook her head, causing Daisy to laugh out loud. She tried to listen to the eligible young man beside her, something about real estate on the west side of Manhattan. When the chimes rang, Daisy and her mother headed to their box. She forgot about the Texans in anticipation of an interesting evening, because the Metropolitan Opera had a policy that all the operas had to be performed in Italian. Even the Faust opera, which had been written in French.

"Excuse me, excuse me," a deep voice said, as the people in her box popped to their feet to let the young man by.

"Daisy Sutton," he said, "I'm Ben Wettermark." He plopped down beside her, and from that moment her fate was sealed. He said he had asked people in the lobby for her name, until someone finally told him.

In the next few days she discovered he was not only handsome but widowed with four young children, born in Houston to Swedish parents and the president of the only bank in Nacogdoches. He loved the opera. He loved Faust.

And it wasn't too many days before he told her loved her.

When he went back to Texas they wrote each other for months. Daisy was so love-struck, she waited each day for his letter. Their love, Ben told everyone, was like a house afire. That seemed prophetic when August 27, the day his proposal letter arrived, the Metropolitan Opera House burned to the ground.

She and Ben were engaged much longer than he wanted, but the niceties had to be observed. She had from August, 1892 to July, 1893 to think of how it would be to be Mrs. Benjamin Wettermark.

She wished Mrs. Johnsdotter could stand up with her at the little marriage ceremony so she wouldn't be so alone. Ben had written her that his father Alfred and his brother Carl wouldn't be able to join them. And, he said, his children were too little to attend a wedding.

It would just be the two of them in the judge's chambers.

This would not be the fancy wedding her mother and father had hoped—but her mother had changed her wedding plans because Ben had been married before. Mother insisted on respectable rather than extravagant.

Daisy had packed both a silk dress and a lightweight muslin dress for her wedding. Everything she thought she'd need was here on the train.

The cars rattled on the narrow-gauge rails. Daisy panicked for a moment when she could only find one of her kid gloves, but snared it on the floor at the edge of her berth.

When the brakes started their high-pitched squeal, she was putting the final hatpin into her broad feathered hat. Her valise was closed on the berth waiting for George.

Daisy was ready, as ready as possible, to step down out of the train and appear before her husband-to-be, Mr. Benjamin S. Wettermark.

Mrs. Johnsdotter peeked out of the curtains of her berth. "Daisy? You're all right?"

"I am. I think I am."

"Well, good luck, sweet child. I know you'll love Texas, and Texas will love you." The older woman smiled up at her. "I'll tell everyone in Houston what a joy you are and how lucky the Wettermarks are to have you join their family."

Daisy lurched toward the door of the compartment and tried to peek into the darkness. Finally, she could see a light beside the tracks, the only light, it seemed, in all of East Texas. The train ground to a halt at a platform and George opened the door. He hopped down and put a little stool under the stairs. Then he offered a white-gloved hand to her. She took a deep breath and stepped onto the platform. It didn't seem cool enough for such a dark, dark night. The light from the station dropped off immediately into the blackness.

A tall clock on the platform showed 1 a.m. Just as she was wondering where Ben was, a man stepped out of the darkness with his hat into his hands.

"Miss Sutton? I'm here to drive you to your new home."

Daisy froze. George was piling her bags and trunks onto a big wooden handcart.

"Where's, where's Ben? Mr. Wettermark?" she sputtered.

"He said to tell you he thought it would make the children feel safer if he was home in case they woke up," the man said. "He said to tell you he's sorry not to meet you."

George was still pulling trunks from the train but paused to reassure her. "Mr. Dilsell drives everybody from the station," he said.

"Here, let me help you with that," the driver said to George. The two men stacked the trunks, one after another, onto the handcart. "Somebody else getting off?"

"No sir, just the one," George said.

"Well, I'm moving here, it's not just a holiday visit," Daisy said, defensiveness rising in her voice.

"No ma'am, it's not a holiday. You're moving here all right," George said. He and Mr. Dilsell wrestled the handcart to the edge of the platform. The two horses looked over their shoulders at her. Accusingly, Daisy thought.

"Lucky I got room for six in this cart. You got trunks for that many," the driver laughed.

Mr. Dilsell helped her into the cart and Daisy sat on the seat behind him, her wide-brimmed feathered hat perched on her dark curls. The full moon was brilliant, not a cloud in sight. Huge trees blocked the light as they passed in and out of their shadows. The horses clopped along the dirt street, leaving the lone light of the depot far behind.

"Not a creature is stirring, not even a mouse," she said to herself. In the humid night air, that made her smile. Bravely, she thought.

Not far after the station, there were no lights at all but the moonlight, blotted out by the huge trees as they drove under them.

"There aren't many houses here," she said carefully. "Are we, are we leaving town?"

"No ma'am. We're headed downtown."

The full moon highlighted the narrow street and the emptiness of the night. She thought they must have gone a half a mile when she saw a house on the east side of the street. There was a light glowing in a downstairs window.

"There you are, ma'am," the driver said. "The Wettermark house. I mean your Wettermark house. Your new home."

It was a Victorian two-story wooden house, right on the dusty street. It was silhouetted against the moon and the one light wasn't enough to warm the window.

A chill passed over her and she shivered.

"I imagine Mr. Wettermark is looking out that window right now," the driver tossed back over his shoulder.

The horses plodded down the main road. As the driver reined in, the front door opened and Ben stood in the doorway.

"Daisy. My Daisy," he called out. "You're here."

Ben hurried down the stairs, helped Daisy from the cart and put his arms around her. She was unable to keep tears from running down her face. Ben tried to hold her close and they both laughed as he dodged around her feathered hat. He helped take the hatpins out, then pulled her to him, holding the hat behind her back.

The driver was pulling trunks out of the cart and piling them on the ground by the front steps. He cleared his throat. "This where you want these?"

Ben looked as if he just remembered the driver was there. "Uh, could you carry them in?" Ben asked.

"There's a mighty lot of them," Dilsell said with a slight whine. "Nobody else here?"

Ben shook his head. "Of course there will be extra for you," he said.

The driver struggled with a trunk that tipped over the side of the wagon and dropped to the ground with a thud.

"My books," Daisy said, looking apologetically at Ben. "I couldn't leave them behind."

Ben smiled down at her, as if a trunk full of books was a very acceptable addition to the household. "Just leave that one. I'll have some men come over from the bank in the morning and carry it up the stairs."

Ben walked Daisy into the parlor as the driver grappled with the trunks, bumping them up the stairs and dumping them unceremoniously in the parlor.

"The children are all asleep," Ben said. "They can't wait to meet you. We marked your trip on a map so they could see where you were. We've been thinking of you every mile of your trip, thinking of the train bringing you along from New York to St. Louis, to Kansas City, to Shreveport to here."

She smiled up at him and then looked around the room. The house was modest and the furniture was old, as if it was hand-me-downs from an older family. It occurred to her that the deep Brussels carpet beneath her feet was a real prize, though, and showed that Ben was not afraid to buy quality pieces.

"The trip seemed like five months, not five days," she said, smiling up at him. "I thought of you every mile, too. And nothing could have kept me from coming here to you. Not the distance, not wild outlaws, not even packing everything I own."

The day after tomorrow she would be Mrs. Benjamin S. Wettermark. Her life in Nacogdoches would begin. A husband, four children, a house in the middle of Texas. It was a lot to take in.

There would be time to make this family hers, this house her home, she thought. Time to turn life in Nacogdoches into their own story together.

3. A Nice Pot Roast

"Great dinner, Peg," Jackson said. He had worked his way through two plates of roast beef, potatoes, carrots and roasted onions, covered with brown gravy.

"Did you have enough?" Peggy tilted the platter toward him. "Here, finish this up." At 6'3", Jackson was a foot taller than Peggy and Erin. He was so grateful for Peggy's good cooking and he always had seconds—and thirds. But even he had his limits.

"I can't eat another bite," he said. "Erin, how about you?"

"I'll take that little piece of potato. And some gravy. This is sooo good, Mom."

Erin had never met a potato she didn't like, and then complained because she outweighed her mother by 20 pounds. People said they looked alike, but Peggy couldn't see it—she had short curly gray hair and Erin's was long and straight and blond. She wore glasses; Erin had contacts. Erin wore business suits; she wore polo shirts, slacks and tennis shoes.

This was the first time Peggy had lived with anyone, except Bill, in almost 50 years. She worked hard at being the best guest, the most prolific cook, the most attentive listener anyone could ever want. She had been here almost a month and Erin and Jackson didn't seem tired of her yet. Every day, Erin told her how much she appreciated her good old-fashioned dinners, the kind Peggy had cooked when Erin was growing up.

"I'm glad you like the roast," Peggy said, putting her napkin by her plate. She was nervous about telling them about the house. Why should she be? They couldn't tell her no, of course. But...what if they thought she was foolish? Or impulsive? Or just plain stupid?

Yesterday after she found the house, she had opened a search engine on the computer. She typed in, "Restoring a Victorian house." From the long list of titles, she picked "Before buying a historic home." She read, "Historic homes are a labor of love. Discover what it takes to buy, and maintain one:

The landscape of America is dotted with historic residences - Thomas Jefferson's Monticello, William Randolf Hearst's Castle and our own Mark Twain Homestead in Hartford, Connecticut. There are also hundreds of lesser-known buildings that are significant to their local history, many of which are still being used as private homes today. But while it's a fun idea to own and inhabit a piece of American history, historic residences like these present a unique set of benefits and challenges" www.realtor.com.

Peggy was realistic enough to know there would be challenges. Shoot, she had seven years of challenges keeping Bill at home while his mind slipped away. She knew she could be strong when times got tough.

Now she strengthened her resolve; there was probably no good time to tell them. While her daughter finished her dinner she said, "Well, I, I found a house today."

'So soon? That's wonderful!" Erin covered the last bit of potato with gravy.

"That Tyler Pate, he's a top-notch agent," Jackson nodded. "What'd you find?"

She hesitated, for a beat, then: "It's a historic house. Near the university." Peggy started to clear the table.

"Here, Mom, I'll do that. You know the house rule--you don't have to clean up if you cook." Erin jumped up and took the plate from Peggy's hand.

"A historic house in a historic town. Perfect." Jackson smiled at her. "That's the beauty of living in the oldest town in Texas. As we've written on our website."

"We love historic houses," Erin said as she ran her hand over the beautiful quartz countertop, the centerpiece of the gleaming kitchen in their new modern home. "But it's so nice to have efficient central heating, and everything new and working perfectly."

She smiled at her husband, who was as proud of this new house as Erin was. They had plenty of room for Peggy. She had moved into their guest room and her big bulky items of furniture and boxes were in a rented storage unit.

Jackson and Erin often told her she was no trouble and they loved to have her in their house. But Erin understood that her mother wanted something of her own.

"Want to show us the house you found tonight? Just let me get this cleaned up..."

"No, let's go tomorrow. I, uh, it'll be easier to see tomorrow." That was a sure bet, since there was no electricity in the old house. Much less central heating or quartz countertops.

When she got back to her bedroom, Peggy breathed a sigh of relief. She had started the conversation, anyway. But it was a restless night. She could see the house as it could be, a beautiful relic of history. She would become a part of the history of this town by restoring the home. But what if Erin and Jackson saw it as a wreck rather than a relic? Renovating meant she would have to stay here with them longer than she planned. And what would they think of all the work that had to be done—and the expense?

If only the house hadn't completely captured her, she could just let it go tonight, before they saw it and thought she was crazy. Well, maybe she was a little crazy. But standing in that house, she had been transported to the future when the home would be beautiful again. And she had become convinced she was the person to restore it.

The first challenge, of course, would be convincing her daughter and son-in-law that she knew what she was doing. And of course, she didn't. She looked at the article she had printed out to prepare for her "dream home."

There were seven points:

1. *Thoroughly research the home.*

2. *Determine its historical designation.*

3. *Make a conditional offer.*

4. *Order a home inspection.*

5. *Finalize your offer.*

6. *Renovate with care.*

7. *Consider resale value.*

This was the plan, then. In the morning she would begin to thoroughly research the home at the Nacogdoches library. The first point suggested she look at the National Registry of Historic Places for the history of individual properties and rules and regulations governing ownership, renovation and tax incentives. Then she would determine the historical designation. One step at a time, that's the way she'd do it.

In the morning Peggy started to the library but turned on Wettermark Street and pulled up in front of the house. The old structure was so sad and shabby she felt bad just looking at it. It looked vulnerable and fragile, two stories tall with peeling paint on the garrets and plywood over most of the windows. The wide front stairs made a semicircle and the wraparound porch was missing so many rails it looked like broken teeth.

But Peggy was captured by its charm. She got a thrill looking at it, thinking of the "after." The proportions were good, width to height. She could see small tooth-shaped blocks along the roofline. The front of the house wasn't centered, and there were two gables on the second floor. One of her favorite features was the porch wrapped around the front and side.

Peggy didn't know what the style was called, other than Victorian, but she would research it. She would find out who built this magnificent house and how they could have let it turn into this crumbling hull.

A chill passed over her and she shivered.

The library parking lot was full—surprising for a weekday morning, she thought. As she got closer, she realized people were entering the library and recreation center through the same front door. The tan brick building had been a superstore that was donated to the city 20 years ago.

She walked through rows of computers, each one with a person studiously working. She passed a glass case with a sign, "Nacogdoches Authors," and knew she'd have to come back sometime and look at those.

She stopped at the reference desk. "Excuse me, I wonder if you could help me?"

The librarian looked up from her computer and turned her black eyes on Peggy. "I would be glad to. Do you know the title or the author?"

"Oh, no, I need more help than that!" Peggy laughed. "I'm planning to buy a historic house here in Nacogdoches and I want to thoroughly research it, if I can."

"You've come to the right place. Research is my middle name. Not really, I'm just playin'. My middle name is Marita. But research is my favorite thing to do."

Peggy read the nametag and put out her hand: "Wynona Hopkins? Wynona? I'm Peggy Jensen."

"Wynona's what my mama calls me when it's time for supper," she smiled as she shook hands. "You call me Nona. I'm the archivist for the East Texas Historical Collection. So if it's here in the city or the county I can find the information you need. What's the address? Is it in Nac or outside the city limits?" She clicked to an information page on her computer.

"It's right up the street, 211 Wettermark."

"211? You sure?"

"I wrote it down," Peggy held a little piece of paper up for Nona to see.

Nona took the paper as if she was willing it to reveal some other number. "Hmm," she said. "I think I know this house. I've been by it." She typed in the address and waited while her computer churned through its memory bank.

Peggy wanted to show she wasn't just some yahoo in off the street but a person who had already gotten one important piece of information. "Is that the National Registry of Historic Places? The article I read said to start there."

"I don't think that house is on the registry," the librarian said. "There'd be a lot to do to get it listed. And I'm not sure there's enough left of that house to list."

"So a house isn't automatically on the registry just because it's historic?"

"Just being old doesn't make a house important," Nona studied her screen. She read out loud:

> "The National Register of Historic Places is the official list of the Nation's historic places worthy of preservation. The list is part of a national program to coordinate and support public and private efforts to identify, evaluate, and protect America's historic and archeological resources."

She glanced up at Peggy. "And that house isn't on the list."

"Well, shoot," Peggy said. "I think it's worthy. So you can't find anything about it?"

"I didn't say that. I know exactly where you're looking." She clicked one more time then turned her monitor to show a hand-drawn map of Nacogdoches. Peggy leaned in.

"There," Nona said. "See right off North Street? That's the house. This is the map from 1900."

"There it is! That's my house!" she exclaimed. "Well, it will be my house."

Nona wasn't as excited as Peggy. "Have you seen it?"

"Yes, and I can imagine how beautiful it can be," Peggy said. "Right there, right there on the map! It's all by itself, it looks like. Nothing even close. It's not like that now. There are houses right up next to it."

"I guess the family had to sell off pieces of the land," Nona said thoughtfully. "There were still people trying to get paid."

"What?"

"Why don't I do some research and see what I can find out? I don't want to tell you anything that might not be true." Nona took Peggy's phone number and said she'd call when she'd done some more research.

"And I know you're going to want a copy of the map," Nona smiled up at her.

"Of course! That's the first step of my thorough research."

Peggy left the library with a photocopy of the map of 100-year ago Nacogdoches. How handy to meet a librarian who loved research, and who wanted to help her. Nona might be the first person beside Erin and Jackson who could be a friend in her new town.

Peggy drove back to Erin's and was waiting, map in hand, when her daughter picked her up at 2 p.m. Erin chatted cheerfully as she drove to the house.

"Here it is," Peggy said. "Stop."

"Here? You don't mean here?" Erin's voice had risen an octave. "Oh, Mom, this is a mess!"

"It's all potential."

"Potential? It's rubble!" Erin didn't make a move to get out of the car. "You're joking, right?"

"Like Jackson said, a historic home in a historic town." She was beaming.

As if on cue, Jackson drove up and parked behind them. Peggy and Erin got out and the three of them stood in front of the house.

"Mom was just quoting you," Erin said.

"I hope I said don't do anything stupid today." Jackson couldn't take his eyes off the house.

Peggy shook her head. "A historic home in a historic town."

"I'm sorry if I gave you the impression any old house would do," he said. "A historic house that's already restored. Or with a little work to do. Not a tear-down."

"Did you already go in? Can we get in?" Erin walked slowly toward the house as if it might collapse before she got there.

Peggy climbed the cement steps and crossed the porch. As if nothing worse could happen to the house, the flimsy hollow core door was unlocked. She pushed it inward.

She called back over her shoulder, "Be careful, some of the floorboards are rotten." In the dim interior Peggy once again had the feeling this house was waiting for her. She stepped inside, looking up at the high ceiling. This wasn't just a house, it was a bona fide, hundred-year old historical mansion, just waiting to be restored to its former glory.

Erin and Jackson were quiet at first, walking around the first floor, stepping over piles of trash, carefully looking at the fireplaces, the windowsills, the walls. Every once and awhile Erin said, "Uh huh" and "Hmm" but the only noise Jackson made was the thump of his black wingtip shoes on the floor.

Peggy pointed out the ceiling height, the winding staircase, the shape of the few antique windows that weren't covered with plywood.

Finally the three of them stood in the middle of what could loosely be called the living room.

"I'm going to have to talk to Tyler Pate," Jackson said. "There must be 30 houses that would be perfect for you. What came over him?"

"Tyler was afraid you'd blame him," Peggy said. "This is all on me. I saw it and the minute I got inside I knew it was just right."

"Mom, you haven't ever done restoration. You've painted walls and moved furniture, but this is way beyond that," Erin said. "Redecorating is not restoration. I can't fathom why you would even think about something this big."

"I can imagine what it will look like—" Peggy started.

"You probably don't realize how expensive it would be to put this place back together," Jackson shook his head. "It's not just the cosmetic things like the floor, but the wiring and plumbing—and heating and air conditioning…"

"And the foundation, Mom. There might not even be a decent foundation," Erin chimed in.

"I want to get my own place," Peggy lifted her chin and straightened her shoulders. "Just think how beautiful this house can be, how historic, how elegant…"

"Well, sure, but you don't have to rush into anything. We love having you stay with us. You haven't even had time to make friends, and you want to jump into a big project like this. You haven't joined a club or walked through the Azalea Garden or gone to a concert at the university…"

"The minute I walked in this house I felt it calling my name—calling me to make it beautiful again." Peggy pulled the map from her purse. "I've already started the research at the library. I'm working with the reference librarian, and look, I've already got a copy of the map from 100 years ago."

Erin and Jackson looked at each other over her head.

She realized they probably thought she was crazy. "I'm going into this one step at a time, doing the research as I go," she said. "I'll use the money from the townhouse carefully, and I'll be restoring a piece of history. When I'm through, this will be a showplace."

"A showplace," Jackson repeated. "Well, I can't wait to see that."

"Mom," Erin sighed. "You've got to really think about this carefully, all right? Sleep on it. This is huge. We can talk about it."

Peggy nodded. She swept her eyes upward and saw a pressed tin ceiling under a coat of dingy white paint.

There would be time to make this house her home. To bring it to life. Time to turn it into the showplace it should be.

"There's a story here, and it will unfold as I put the house back together." Peggy smiled at her daughter and son-in-law, still excited. She nodded her head and put the map back in her purse as if that sealed the deal.

This house would reveal its secrets as she brought it back to life. Renovated, it would be a beautiful part of the oldest town in Texas. She could see it. A new start, a piece of the past restored.

And she could see that renovating this house would bring with it the renovation of her own life. Her new challenge, her new start.

4. The Colonel

July 15, 1893, the next morning

The sun was already high in the sky when Daisy woke up. She lay in bed for a few minutes, listening to the sounds of the house, trying to decide if she was alone. Her bedroom (their bedroom!) was warm and she pushed back the thick down comforter. Here she was in Nacogdoches, soon to be a married woman in her own home, about to greet her new life.

Sleep had helped repair her nerves. The further she had gotten from Manhattan, the more ragged her thoughts had been. She had looked out the window as the train plummeted thousands of miles away from civilization, thousands of miles from her home, far from everyone and everything. And all for the love of a man she hardly knew.

There was a little knock at the door.

"Yes?"

"Miss Sutton, I brought you some coffee."

"Oh! Please come in."

A dark young woman, about Daisy's age, brought in a silver tray with a china cup and a silver coffee service. She placed it on a table by the bed.

"How you doing, ma'am? You have a good sleep?"

"I'm embarrassed I slept so late. I—I want to meet the children."

"Most everybody's gone but they're real excited about meeting you. Little Lenore's here—she's sleeping now but even that baby's excited about you coming. Her daddy told her you were coming to live here."

"I'll get dressed and come down. Could you—do you—I'm sorry, I don't know your name."

"Alita. I'll be glad to help with whatever you need."

"My corset…"

"I can do that. I always did help Mrs. Lenore, before she passed."

Daisy nodded. Ben had told her his wife died when the baby was born, but she hadn't pressed him to tell her more. Were they still in mourning? Was two years long enough to dull the pain of losing the woman who died giving birth to a daughter?

"Have you been with the Wettermarks a long time?"

"Since Carl was born in '88. He's five now so I've been here pretty long. I reckon I'm the only mama Little Lenore ever knew. So far, I mean. Now you're here, you'll be the mama."

The mama. Now she would be the mama. Daisy hoped she'd be a good one, despite having no experience or training.

She and Alita tiptoed into a downstairs bedroom. And there was the little girl, looking like a sleeping angel. Her skin was translucent, her blonde hair curling around her face. Her breathing was ragged and rough and her cheeks were flushed.

"Little Lenore's got herself a little croup," Alita whispered.

Daisy noticed she was called "Little Lenore," as if she would forever be a small version of her mother. Alita told her the two-year old was often sickly, awake nights struggling to breathe and worn out during the day. Little Lenore walked and talked, but hesitantly, reluctantly. Alita said she carried her from room to room as she cleaned the house.

As they stood by her bed, Little Lenore opened her eyes. She stared at Daisy for a good long minute but didn't make a sound. Then she held her arms up for Alita.

"She'll get used to you soon enough," Alita said. "Then you'll be carrying her from room to room yourself."

While Alita dressed and fed the little girl, Daisy wandered through the house. Ben had told her they it built the year before his wife died. Some of the rooms were almost empty, some had piles of trunks and crates and even broken furniture. Ben and Lenore were married in 1883, but the furniture seemed much older. Daisy wanted to ask if it was hand-me-downs from Lenore's parents. Witherspoon, her maiden name was. She'd have to find out about the family.

There was floral wallpaper on the downstairs walls, but the upstairs walls were bare. The wood floors were smooth beautiful wood. There were rugs on some of the floors, like the beautiful carpet she had noticed last night.

But the children's rooms were so bare it made her sad just to look into them. The two boys shared a room, with just two small beds and a wardrobe. The girl's room was about the same—one bed, a wardrobe, a small bookcase.

Daisy went back to the bedroom where she had slept under the fluffy white comforter last night. Ben had led her to the bedroom then left her to go sleep in the parlor on the settee. She didn't think she would sleep, for all the excitement, but she hadn't even opened an eye after she lay down.

She looked around the room now. Except for the trunk he had dragged upstairs for her, this room was so plain she wondered if all the photos and personal things might have been packed away to keep his memories at bay. She vowed to fill these rooms with things that would make Ben and the children happy.

The rest of her bags and trunks were on the parlor floor. She carried the small bags up to the bedroom. The trunk full of her books was still outside where the driver had dropped it.

If she were back in Manhattan, this would be her book club day. She had all the newest books and it would be nice to start a club here and share fine literature with the local women. She probably had all sorts of newfangled notions that would surprise them but they'd be grateful to learn what women were discussing in the big cities.

That gave her a pang of remorse. Her life, rich and full in Manhattan, so far away. The suitors who were appropriate and predictable. The theatres and shops, the charities and intellectual pursuits. Back home she would be sitting at the breakfast table waiting for the Irish maid to bring her tea and scones. Her mother would be talking on and on about the opera guild and she would be feeling—what? Bored? Impatient? Aggravated? Probably all three.

By the time the three older children came home, Daisy was sitting in the parlor in a rocking chair, Little Lenore wrapped in a light blanket on her lap. The children trooped in and sat down on the worn red velvet settee. They all looked like their father, dark blonde hair, fair skin, clear blue eyes. Daisy thought they could use a little sprucing up, newer clothes, nicer haircuts. The boys, in particular, were kind of shaggy. The daughter's dress was plain and, Daisy thought, very dreary.

"Hello there, children. I'm Daisy." All three seemed to take that in and think about it.

"Let's see now," she said. "I'm sure you're Minnie and you're nine years old." Minnie silently agreed. "And you must be Ben Junior."

"Benny," the seven-year-old corrected her.

"Therefore you are—Carl," she smiled at him. "And you're—let's see—"

"Five!" Carl looked at her solemnly. "You were sleeping when we left. We came in and looked at you but you didn't even open an eye."

Minnie nodded. "We didn't want to wake you because you came so late in the night."

"I did get off the train in the middle of the night. But I thought about meeting you all the way from Manhattan to Nacogdoches. Your father told me all about you."

"Like what?" Benny tilted his head to the side.

"Like what?" Daisy looked at the three children sitting up so straight across from her.

"Like what did he tell you about us," Carl completed Benny's sentence.

"Well, he told me enough so that I could bring you presents." She smiled as all three jumped off the settee and gathered around her.

The presents were a big hit—a music box for Minnie, a baseball for Benny and a harmonica for Carl. Little Lenore hugged the teddy bear as Alita took her to lie down.

The cook, Mrs. Hamlin, came not long after and started preparing supper. Neither of the women let her know before they entered; they'd spent two years in charge of the household and she was the newcomer. Daisy stood in the door of the kitchen, not sure if she should get involved in the preparations.

"We already agreed what to make for your first dinner," Mrs. Hamlin pulled out a cast iron skillet. "I'm frying chicken and making mashed potatoes. That all right?"

Daisy assured her that sounded fine. She wondered if she would be making the menus but decided she'd talk to Ben about it.

The children, without a word from her, went to their rooms. She peeked in at Little Lenore, sleeping again. Then she sat out on the porch, watching the road that turned off North Street and led right to her.

She thought about the future, about walking to the market or visiting the library or even having tea with a neighbor.

The town was surrounded by trees—the tallest trees she had ever seen. Ben had told her Nacogdoches was in the Piney Woods, but she had imagined prairie land, cactus and sandy plains. Like penny novels about cowboys. She couldn't even see the tops of the trees because they came right up to the house. The January wind blew the pine needles around, making a whispering, shushing sound. Under the pines there were other trees, creating an impenetrable wall that blocked the view beyond the houses. Who had been brave enough to step into the forest and try to make a home? What would possess these people to willingly plunge into these soaring trees?

She sat very still and listened as the pines whispered. She felt she had moved to an ancient land, where pioneers had carved out a place for themselves in an old powerful forest. And she was the newest pioneer of all. Never in her life had she been this close to a forest. It looked dark and dangerous and as if it might close around her if she ever stepped into it.

The sun could rise, the sun could set, and she would hardly be able to see it. Well, she told herself, she hardly saw the sunset in Manhattan because skyscrapers and brownstones stood shoulder to shoulder. But she could take a carriage to the East River or the Hudson and watch the sunset. Or a ferry from Battery Park to the foot of the Statue of Liberty.

This was different. In Manhattan she lived with history all around her. But here trees shrouded the history. She would have to look through the ancient sky-high pines and find the mysterious Nacogdoches hidden deep within them.

Minnie, Benny and Carl filtered out to the porch and sat on the wicker chairs. They snuck looks at her but didn't seem to know what to say. She made a few fumbling attempts then, "Do you know what we're going to do tomorrow?" The children nodded their heads.

"You're going to marry our father," Benny said flatly.

"Yes, then I'll be here with you, with your father, to help you, to—read to you…" Her voice dwindled down to silence as the children sat very still and looked toward the road. She knew this wouldn't be easy but she would try to find the words to reach these silent children.

When Ben rode up to the house, she was so glad to see him she practically wept. He was the reason she was here, the only person she really knew in this town. He kissed her on the nose, right in front of the children, who seemed to be watching everything she did.

When Mrs. Hamlin announced, "Col. Wettermark, supper's ready," Daisy realized she didn't even know he was a colonel. Of what, she wondered?

The fried chicken was wonderful—crispy on the outside and tender under the crust, a little salty and dotted with black pepper. The children all ate heartily, except for Little Lenore, who sat in a high chair squishing the mashed potatoes around the tray.

"You're a colonel?" she smiled at Ben. "You didn't tell me that. I'd have called you Col. Ben if I'd known."

Benny answered before his father had a chance. "He's Lt. Colonel, Field & Staff, in the Stone Fort Rifles."

Ben clarified, "The Texas Volunteer Guard. But most people still know us as the Stone Fort Rifles."

"Did you fight? Did you use your rifles?"

"We were formed in '87 so we weren't in any of the big battles. Carl, here, was born the next year, and our bank made some big loans, so I didn't feel I could leave Nac."

"But everybody calls you Col. Wettermark," Minnie looked at him proudly.

"Should I call you Colonel?" Daisy teased. "And you can call me Mrs. Colonel?"

"No, I haven't called anyone that since Lenore…since she passed away."

Together, Ben and the children put their heads down as if saying a prayer. Daisy realized two years wasn't yet enough for the family to get over their loss. What if they never did?

After a respectful silence, she asked: "Do you think we could get out of the house tomorrow before we go to see the judge? I haven't seen anything of the town except for the train station. In the dark."

He looked surprised. "Of course. We'll take the carriage downtown. I can show you my bank and the shops. There's so much history—Nacogdoches was founded in 1716 when the Spanish priests started a mission here. Some people say they can still see the holy fathers in their rough robes, ropes tied around their waists. They say there are ghosts here, if you know where to look."

Yes, Daisy could believe that. She thought she knew where to look, right here in this big house. The memory of Lenore was like a presence, still causing Ben and the children to feel their loss as if it happened yesterday.

Daisy would drive the sorrow out of this house. She lifted her head and smiled at Col. Ben Wettermark. She was ready to bring the joy back to this good man and his children. And to make fresh memories for her new little family in this house surrounded by an ancient forest.

5. Ten Ways to Tell

Peggy wanted to get big black garbage sacks and huge trashcans and start shoveling all the junk out of the house. She wanted to sweep away the piles of debris and the shards of broken glass and toss out the stained mattress. The house would look better immediately.

But it wasn't her house yet. All she had was a copy of a 100-year old street map. She hadn't talked to the realtor since she startled him by declaring she wanted to buy the house.

She'd start with one thing she knew she was good at. She went right to Nona's desk the minute the library opened. "Nona! I brought you some cookies."

Nona laughed. "That is one sure way to get your research done! But you know we do this work for free, right?"

"I do know, but I want you to know I appreciate it. They don't have nuts or chocolate in them in case you're allergic."

"There's absolutely nothing that I can't or won't eat," Nona took the plate. Her big black eyes sparkled and she laughed out loud. "I'll put them in the break room. Everybody's going to want some, even though I'm doing all the work!"

"You're very important in my step-by-step process. The top two items on my list are 'thoroughly research the house' and 'determine its historical designation.' And I'm looking for your help on both those things."

Nona pulled a paper off the top of a stack with Peggy's name on top.

"I found this article from the National Park Service for you. It's 'How old is your house' and it will walk you through the steps of figuring out what style the house is. I'll bet you'll be able to tell the style right away."

"All right. Thanks."

"I've got the real deal right here, though." Nona turned her screen toward Peggy, who leaned in to read it through her bifocals.

> *"Benjamin Wettermark established his home in a large 12 room, Victorian mansion on 14 acres, facing North Street, on the north side of Nacogdoches in 1900. Colonel Benjamin S. Wettermark was a Civic leader in Nacogdoches. The home was located between North Street & Raguet."*

Peggy practically danced in place. "Oh, my gosh, we've got it! It was built in 1900!"

"Well, we know the year it was built," Nona corrected her. "But you have to find out if the house has been designated as a historic structure. There are lots of restrictions on historic renovation you'll have to know before you get into it. The house probably wouldn't have gotten so run down if it were designated. You'll need to find out if there are any general historic restrictions in this area of town."

"We've got a name and a date, and it even tells us how many rooms it had. I think that's enough to start with."

"That and these cookies. That'll keep me looking for a while. Oh, I thought you might want to check this out." Nona handed her a book. "It's about a fairly famous poet who lived here at the turn of the century. She'll give you a good feel for the local history."

As soon as she drove up to the house, Peggy called Tyler Pate and asked for the price. She wanted to get a baseline before she moved onto step three, which was "Make a conditional offer."

He sounded anxious. "Jackson's not going to throw me out of the Chamber, is he? I know he's not happy about that old house."

She took a deep breath and heard Tyler say, "Mrs. Jensen, are you still there?"

Peggy assured him his place in the community was safe, and Tyler actually sighed with relief. He said he'd check on the price and call right back.

While she waited for him to call she leafed through the book Nona had recommended, "Texas Woman of Letters, Karle Wilson Baker" by Sarah R. Jackson.

The poet had written:

> *"Nacogdoches in 1900 seemed like a mystery to solve. It was wrapped in tradition as in a garment, permeated—not to say—drugged—by the perfume of the past. Yet the tradition was vague and nebulous; it was almost impossible for the inquiring newcomer to put his finger on a fact. Nacogdoches, sitting beside her dusty streets, beneath her immemorial trees, was so proud of being 'historic' that she had forgotten her history."*

Over a hundred years ago, Nacogdoches felt the same way it did now. It was as if the oldest town in Texas, sitting beside her dusty streets, beneath her immemorial trees, had forgotten her history and needed someone to help her remember. She thought restoring the 1900 Wettermark home might be just the start it needed.

There were a couple of small bungalow-style houses on either side and a four-story 1950s brick apartment on the corner. She figured students who couldn't afford dorms came here for the cheap rent close to the university. Nothing on this block was as nice as her house.

Her house! She shook her head; she already thought of it as her house! She'd better hold off until she got further down the line. The whole block was a good example of what the poet had written about—tradition was vague and nebulous; but it was clear that this house was deteriorating.

When Tyler called, she was so deep in thought the ring startled her.

"Tyler! What?"

He laughed. "What you asked me. The owner would like $100,000."

It was lucky she had stopped the car. She took a deep breath and heard Tyler say, "Mrs. Jensen, are you still there?"

"$100,000! It's a wreck!"

"But it's a historic wreck. The owner lives in Houston and figures the land alone is worth that."

Peggy was stunned. That wasn't a lot for a house, but it really was a wreck. What if Jackson was right and she had to redo the plumbing and electric? And who knows what else? "I have to think about this," she said, though she had made up her mind. She started to hang up. "Wait, wait. What do you think would be a good counter offer?"

"Uh, I can't tell you what to offer, but I can do some work on the comps in the neighborhood."

That was good news, she thought. The comparable buildings in the neighborhood were little shabby places that reminded her of the old cowboy saying about old worn-out horses, "This horse has been rode hard and put away wet," since most renters wear out a house and have no plan for the future of it. Maybe these smaller comps would bring the price down.

She walked west on Wettermark Street and past what looked like a local hangout, the Flashback Café. Within two blocks she was looking at North Street, the busiest street in town. There was a vintage clothing store with Hawaiian shirts flapping in the breeze on a rack in its parking lot. A convenience store had cars line up at the gas pumps. This was what happened to historic towns when prosperity came to them. People came for the historic qualities of the town, then the history was razed and paved over in the name of progress.

Peggy had read an article by a woman with the National Trust for

Historic Preservation who said, "You can see when each town got a wave of prosperity, because the old buildings were torn down and replaced with whatever was modern at the time. That is, unless someone interceded and insisted on saving the historic structures."

In this town there hadn't been many people who interceded.

Peggy could see where the first wave of prosperity started as she looked around. In 1923, when Stephen F. Austin State College was founded as a teachers' college, the Victorian homes on North Street began to be chewed up, and businesses that would cater to students' desires were spit out. Bookstores, fast food restaurants and convenience stores now stood shoulder to neon shoulder where beautiful turn-of-the century mansions had once lorded over North Street or *Calle del Norte*.

The Wettermark house wasn't torn down because student-friendly businesses wanted land right on the main drag and it was two short blocks away. That was its saving grace, and its doom.

Peggy got the library book and papers and a notepad out of her car. She went back to the house and sat on a step. How had this area looked when the house was built? She opened the book on Karle Wilson Baker and read what the poet had written in 1900:

> "I shall never forget how father met me at the train, in a hot September night of brilliant moonlight, about half-past one o'clock, and brought me up through the sleeping town in the rattling old 'depot hack.' And I remember most the feeling of wonder—almost awe—the majestic old trees as we drove beneath them—into their great blots of shadow and out again into the moonlight."

That was what was missing—the majestic old trees that had been in East Texas since the beginning of time. This was a true piney wood forest and the house would have been surrounded by the tall loblolly pines that reached to the sky. Just like historic houses, there weren't many of the trees left either.

Peggy felt an aching sense of loss for what the house could be, for what it had been. She had to save it, to bring it back to the land of the living.

She looked at the article Nona had given her about how to figure out the style of the house. It looked like one of those quizzes from Cosmopolitan Erin used to read—10 ways to tell if he loves you, 10 clues to the style of the wreck you want to renovate.

The first step she already knew. The house was built in 1900, which put it in the Victorian period between 1860-1901. The article said Victorian houses have steeply pitched roofs of irregular shape, usually with dominant front-facing gable; textured shingles (and/or other devices) to avoid smooth-walled appearance; partial or full-width asymmetrical porch-es, usually one story high and extended along one or both side walls; asym-metrical facades.

Yes, this house had all of those things, so even if she hadn't known the date she might have been able to pinpoint it. The trick would be figuring out which of the seven Victorian styles the home had been. Was it Sec-ond Empire, Greek Revival, Gothic Revival, Queen Anne, Stick, Shingle or Richardsonian Romanesque?

She decided to create a chart of features on the list from the library and eliminate the styles that didn't fit. Two clues were if the house was colorful or ornamented but this was too faded and battered to use those features. She could tell this house was very clearly not symmetrical. So she wrote "Asymmetry" first.

Asymmetrical styles were Queen Anne, Shingle, Stick, and Gothic Re-vival. Symmetrical styles were Greek Revival and Colonial Revival so she eliminated them.

Gothic Revival sounded like the houses in horror movies with steeply pitched roofs and exposed rafters. Windows and doors often had pointed arches or gothic molds, so she eliminated the style that sounded like Dracula's house. The house she had fallen in love with looked rundown but not creepy.

She read, "The Richardsonian Romanesque style, named after architect Henry Hobson Richardson (1838-1886), is characterized by heavy, rock-faced stone, round masonry arches." Not stone, no arches. This house was definitely not Richardsonian Romanesque.

The style called Second Empire had her looking up the word "mansard" on her mobile phone. That meant a roof with four sloping sides, each of which becomes steeper halfway down. Nope. So she eliminated Second Em-pire.

That left stick, shingle and Queen Anne.

Shingle style sounded likely but it usually had eyebrow dormers. She looked it up and found those were long, narrow slits with short windows peeking out of the house with undulating curves on top of them. Like an actual eye. She walked into the yard and looked up at the second story. And—no.

Stick style had extensive porches and that was certainly true of this house. But the rest of it sounded too ornate--complex gable roofs, usually steeply pitched with cross gables and overhanging eaves, decorative trusses and wooden wall cladding (either clapboards or board-and-batten siding) interrupted by patterns of horizontal, vertical, or diagonal boards (stick work) raised from the wall surface for emphasis and meant to represent the underlying framework.

So Queen Anne it was, more or less. There were some things she

couldn't be sure about, like patterned shingles, lacy and decorative orna-
mentation and rich, bold paint colors. But the roof was steeply pitched,
with a front-facing gable and bay windows. There were projecting upper
floors and she could see that the wrap-around porch still had a few remain-
ing turned porch posts and spindles. If the house had leaded or colored
glass, it was long gone.

She felt like she was interviewing the house. Anyone driving by would
have seen a slim, short woman whose grey hair curled like a poodle, staring
at a notepad. She was wondering what she could bring to this Queen Anne,
besides the limited money she had from the sale of her townhouse. She
made another list in her beautiful Palmer Method handwriting:

What I bring to the table (or the house):

- *I'm not afraid of hard work—I painted lots of walls for Habitat
  for Humanity.*

- *I'm tenacious—I kept Bill at home seven years when lots of
  people thought I should put him in a nursing home.*

- *I've renovated chairs, chests, lamps that some people would
  have thrown away.*

- *I've collected and appraised antiques for the "World's Largest
  Garage Sale" to benefit Meals on Wheels.*

- *I still have my old skills—whittling, soldering, gluing.*

- *I'm an optimist. I can see possibilities other people might miss.*

She read back over the list. What else could she do? "I can cook," she
added. "That's one thing you can say about me."

Jackson drove up and parked behind her and a moment later Tyler
pulled in. They both got out of their cars and headed toward her.

She stood up and smiled, though it looked like they had bad news.

"Mrs. Jensen," Tyler said. "I've got the comps."

"And he called me to tell me the seller's price." Jackson looked grim.
This was not good, she could tell. She closed her notepad, hiding the list
she had made.

"There's not much in this area that's as high as the seller wants, but
there aren't any historic houses left in a three block radius." Tyler fidgeted
with the paper he was carrying. He looked from Jackson to her. "The highest comp is a two-bedroom that sold for $125,000 five years ago. It's rented
out all the time. In fact almost everything around here is rental."

Jackson was looking at her closely. "Do you know how much work this would be? You might not be able to imagine what you're getting yourself into."

"I can imagine," she said, thinking of her list.

"Peggy," he hesitated. "Erin and I—we want you to know we believe in you. And if you want this house, we'll do everything we can to help you get it."

She was stunned. She sat back down on the step. "You will?"

"If you want, I'll help you make a counter offer. We should be able to knock something off that price." He smiled at her.

"There hasn't been an offer on the house in—well, in all the time I've been a realtor." Tyler nodded at Jackson.

"It would cost you to get a full inspection, but I know a builder who might take a look and see what's worth salvaging."

She nodded at Jackson, tears stinging her eyes.

How long had it been since someone said they believed in her? Probably as long as it had been since someone believed in this house.

Erin and Jackson believed in her. That's what she needed to hear to get started renovating her Queen Anne home in the oldest town in Texas.

6. WEDDING DAY

July 16, 1893

Daisy got up early and went to the kitchen. Mrs. Hamlin was already there, frying bacon and saving the grease for the eggs.

Daisy hesitated in the door. "I thought perhaps I could help."

Mrs. Hamlin looked her over. "There's an extra apron on the back of the door. Do you want to make the biscuits?"

She hadn't ever made biscuits but how hard could it be? "I do." She hesitated. "I don't know exactly how you make them in Texas. Could I use your recipe?"

"It's real easy, ma'am. 'Course I don't have it written down."

Mrs. Hamlin rattled off the measurements and Daisy scrambled around looking for flour, baking powder, salt and sugar. The milk and butter was already out so she moved a bowl near them and dumped everything in it.

"Now I just stir it, right?"

Mrs. Hamlin looked over at her, surprised. "Well, I reckon that will do." She sprinkled flour on a board and stood back. "Now kneed that for awhile. Then roll it out on the flour. I'll get you the biscuit cutter."

Alita arrived and got Little Lenore out of bed. When Ben and the children came down to the table, Daisy had biscuits, butter and preserves set out for them. Mrs. Hamlin put bacon and fried eggs on each plate.

"Your bride-to-be made the biscuits," she said.

"I see you're wearing flour just to prove it," Ben laughed. The children giggled as she wiped her face with a kitchen towel. She could tell she was blushing.

"You're smearing it all over yourself!" Carl thought this was hilarious. "And my biscuit is hard as a brickbat!"

Mrs. Hamlin jumped to her defense. "This is the first time she's made 'em Texas style. We're going to be teaching her the way we do things here, and you're going to eat those biscuits and you're going to tell her thank you for jumping in and trying something new."

"Yes ma'am. Thank you, Miss Sutton," the children all chimed in. Even Ben joined the chorus.

"Please, call me Daisy," she said and Ben nodded at the children.

Minnie spoke up. "Are we coming downtown with you, Father?" All eyes turned to Ben.

"I don't think so."

Daisy looked at the three little faces. "Can't they come?"

"We're going to the courthouse. They're not set up for children."

The children looked so sad that Daisy spoke up. "Could we all go out in the carriage and drive around then bring them back before we see the judge?"

Ben looked at her then at the children and nodded.

The children were ready to go before she could even get her hat pinned on. Mrs. Hamlin was still sweeping up flour and washing dishes. Alita said she'd stay with Little Lenore and everyone else piled into the carriage. There was a squabble over who sat where, but Ben said the only rule was that Daisy sat next to him.

They went south on the road she'd come in on. It didn't seem as long as it had on that lonely ride in the railroad hack and the trees weren't so mysterious in the daylight. Yes, there were sky-high pines, but they were mixed with the fullest, glossiest magnolia trees she'd ever seen. The Victorian homes facing North Street were ornate and handsome.

The children pointed out Sturdevant's Cotton Yard, a bustling company near the train tracks. Men were throwing heavy bales of cotton from wagons onto an open train car.

They turned onto dusty unpaved Main Street. Two-story businesses crowded shoulder to shoulder, their doors opening onto the busy street. They were small and most were brick with large front windows. There were general stores and a couple of barbershops, even a decent hotel at the corner of Main and Church streets. The town looked busy and prosperous, and she sighed with relief.

"That's my bank," Ben gestured toward a small building at the corner of Main and North with "Wettermark & Son" above the door. "My father started banks all throughout East Texas and put me in charge of this one when I was only 21."

"I do look forward to meeting your father."

"You'll meet him soon. Alfred Wettermark can't come today but he'll be in town next week checking on the bank. And he wants to meet you, of course. He's quite the patriarch, running the banks, making sure I'm taking care of business. I'm sure you'll like him. Everybody likes my father."

"I'm sorry your mother's passed on—Mrs. Johnsdotter said she was the loveliest, sweetest woman she knew."

"My father's married again—she's a nice enough woman. They live in Henderson. I don't imagine she'll come over. She doesn't travel with him very often."

Ben drove around the square, the *Plaza Principal*, and pointed out a corner site. "I'm going to build a larger bank there—without my father's name on it. It'll be the finest bank in all east Texas."

She saw the children looking at him with pride. He was so handsome. That dark blonde hair, the mustache, those blue, blue eyes. And that look of determination when he talked about his plans.

He saw her looking at him and reached across to hold her hand. "We're going to have a great life together."

Daisy felt as if lightning spread from his hand to hers. She was so flustered. After a minute she stammered out, "I don't know much about this town."

Benny leaned forward from the back seat of the buggy: "I can tell you about it. The Spanish Expedition headed by Domingo Ramon came here in 1716 to counter the French movement into Louisiana. They brought in the priests who established six missions, including this one, *Nuestra Señora de Guadalupe de Los Nacogdoches*."

"I'm impressed you know that, Benny." Daisy turned in the carriage to look at him.

He smiled shyly. "We learned it in school."

"Benny's very smart," Minnie said. "He knows lots of facts like that."

Not far off the main street was Nacogdoches University, a stately building with two huge columns flanking the door. Ben told her it wasn't being used as a school since it had been turned into a hospital during the Civil War, but it housed the library the women's club operated. Daisy made a mental note to go there as soon as she could.

On the corner of Old San Antonio Road and North Street (or *Calle del Norte*, as Benny explained), there was a large pile of dirt on an empty lot. Ben told her Gil Y'Barbo, the Spanish impresario, had built the Old Stone House there in 1779. In 1848, it had become the Old Stone Fort Saloon and had still been the center of everything in Nacogdoches. Just last year it was demolished to make way for another business. The women from the Cum Concilio literary club had convinced the owners to donate the stones and the workers to mark them so they might eventually reconstruct the historic building.

"The club name means 'with wisdom,'" Benny explained.

That sounded like a project for Daisy. "I would love to get involved with that. I've always been in women's clubs that do projects to help the city."

"You should," Ben agreed. "It would be good for the bank for you to be a part of the town."

"I know a good story," Minnie piped up. "Want to hear it?"

"Of course." Daisy smiled encouragingly.

"Father Margil was one of the priests in 1716, and he stayed in Nacogdoches when the troops left. A year later, all the springs went dry, and everybody was dying of thirst and he prayed about it, and God told him to stand on the banks of the dry LaNana creek and bang his rod on the rocks. So he did and a stream of water gushed out and saved everybody. It's called the Eyes of Father Margil. The stream is still there." Minnie looked around the carriage at her family, proud that she had been the one to tell the story.

"Minnie, that's a wonderful story! Could we see that creek, Ben? Is it around here?" Daisy looked the direction Minnie had pointed.

"We'd have to go through the cemetery. We can go there some other time."

"No?"

"You shouldn't have to go through the cemetery on our wedding day."

The ride back to the house was subdued, as if any reference to their mother brought all their grief back into the present. She realized she didn't know much about children. Did children respond to adults' expectations of them, or did they really mourn for two years? She didn't know any children who had gotten a new mother one day after they'd met her.

It was already hot and humid and Ben said the temperature would continue to rise. The children went to their rooms, careful not to awaken Little Lenore. They didn't appear disappointed to miss the wedding ceremony.

Daisy could barely believe she was getting married. She changed into her lightweight muslin dress and looked at herself in the full-length mirror. What would her wedding have been like in Manhattan? Extravagant, elaborate, in a beautiful ballroom, maybe in the new opera house. Her white silk dress would have had an "S" shaped corset to show off her tiny waist, a pouter pigeon bosom and mutton chop sleeves. She'd have had a high, stiffened collar of white lace and a veil that swept over the long train. Her mother would have cried; her father would have bragged that the wedding cost him a fortune but that she was worth it. She could see it as clearly as if it had happened.

Instead, her mother cried from the moment she heard Daisy's plans and her father protested and argued that she was ruining her life.

The humidity had made her hair curly and frizzy. She picked out a straw hat with full-blown red and white silk roses. Black lace, tulle, and soft ostrich plumes flowed around to the back of the hat where there was a huge bow in sheer white net and a black velvet ribbon trailing down over the wide brim.

Now she looked like a bride. A bride who was getting married all alone in the oldest town in Texas wearing a big fancy hat to cover her wayward hair.

They went back down North Street and Ben tied up the horses in front of the three-story stone courthouse. He helped her down, swinging her through the air as he did. They were both breathless when they rushed inside.

"Judge Bennett Blake is going to do the ceremony for us himself," Ben told her as they hurried down the corridor to the office. "He's been married three times so he ought to know how to make a good marriage contract."

That didn't fill her with confidence.

"He's been chief justice for 22 years and he's decided 7,000 civil suits and 500 criminal cases. He doesn't do weddings very often anymore but he's doing this for us."

"He's a friend?"

"Well, he's a Mason. That's very important in Nacogdoches. You'll soon learn that being a Mason means I have brothers who will do anything for me."

The ceremony was fast and simple, nothing like a religious ceremony. It was mostly about signing papers and legally swearing to put their property together. Judge Blake seemed nice enough but he had obviously done so many of these ceremonies that this one wasn't very important to him. After they signed he shook Ben's hand, nodded to her and wished them good luck.

Luck. Is that what it took to make a good marriage?

When they walked out of the courthouse, Ben asked if she'd like to walk for a while. They pulled into a grove of trees by Banita Creek. They strolled a little trail beside the creek, holding hands. It was cooler under the trees and she loved the feel of his strong arm making sure she didn't slip.

"Well, Mrs. Wettermark, how do you feel?"

"Like the luckiest person in the world, Mr. Wettermark. So I guess the judge gave us a good send-off. I am sorry none of our families were here."

"Houston's pretty far for my dad and brother to come.'"

"Not as far as New York! My parents said they would come sometime. Now that I've proven the train ride is not so awful."

"No train robbers."

"And decent food."

"I've got a lot of plans for us." Ben took both of her hands and looked into her eyes.

"I want the bank to be the largest and finest in East Texas. I'm going to start making loans to farmers and businessmen. And anyone who has enterprising ideas."

"That will be wonderful."

"It will. I'm going to run for county treasurer and earn the trust of everybody here. People will know they can grow their money at Wettermark. There won't be any reason to go to any other bank. Just us."

"I want to help you anyway I can." Daisy looked up into his eyes and remembered he had earned her trust the first moment he sat beside her at the opera.

He looked determined. "We can have big parties and meetings at our house, and invite everyone who might possibly bank with us. And you will be the center of it all, bringing New York style to East Texas."

"We have to fix up the house—it looks like it's been waiting for some- one to take charge of it." Daisy hated to mention it, but it was true. The way the house was now wouldn't inspire anyone to invest with them.

"Your job, my Daisy. Anything you want, you can have. Go to Houston or New Orleans—get whatever you need to make our house a showplace. Hire anyone you need. I trust your judgment completely. And meet the local women, let them know what you bring to the town. You are going to be the belle of East Texas, I know it!"

The belle of East Texas? Daisy took a deep breath. Ben already had her work cut out for her. She was to be the good luck charm, the person who would turn his life into a dazzling success. He wanted her to turn the house into a showplace, make his bank the only bank in East Texas. Throw parties, join clubs. Show little Nacogdoches what Ben had brought to town.

She thought she knew how to do that. If that's what Ben needed her to do, she'd dazzle this little town. That she could do.

It would be much easier than making biscuits.

7. BAD NEWS

Peggy sat in her car in front of the house. Jackson had warned her his contractor friend Scott McCullough was very busy, which she thought might be code for "always late." And he was.

She drank a cup of black coffee and leafed through the papers Nona had given her the other day. She found a quote from a writer who agreed with poet Karle Wilson Baker:

> **Deep east Texas is an old, quiet land. Ancient trees, winding roads, moss and vines offer a sense of timelessness. A mysterious and almost mystical beauty prevails....over and over I sense this...land is about trees...I felt the power of tall pines and saw the exotic sculptures of cypress trees draped in Spanish moss. Somehow...[the] trees [felt] imbued with a special magic.**
> **--David H. Gibson, 1993**

Old, quiet land? There was a steady stream of traffic on North Street, complete with pick-up trucks and motorcycles. The university, just two blocks away, was filled with 13,000 students, who rushed to class, shouted to each other, laughed loudly. The only thing quiet on this street was this old house, which didn't say a mumblin' word. Out loud, anyway.

Nevertheless, the house spoke to Peggy, called her, filled her thoughts with what it could be, rather than what it was.

When Scott pulled up in his huge truck she greeted him with an outstretched hand and thanked him for coming. His hand felt as big as a baseball glove, rough and strong.

"I always wondered what this house looked like inside, but I never got around to looking." He tilted his head back to look at the second story. "These old houses, we ought to be saving them rather than tearing them down."

"I agree! I'm hoping you'll say this is a saver." She crossed her fingers behind her back for luck.

She followed Scott into the house and stood just inside the door as he looked around. He scribbled notes to himself on a little pad he pulled out of his shirt pocket. She didn't talk, not wanting to interrupt him. The contractor looked at every windowsill, every fireplace, and into each room up the rickety stairs. He pulled up a corner of the wallpaper and he looked closely at the floorboards. He stomped through the main floor in his big work boots searching for decayed spots.

When he went outside, she sat on the edge of the porch. Although he seemed too big for it, he crawled into the little space under the house to look at the foundation. She knew there were very few basements in these East Texas houses, just crawl spaces. She had the feeling that there were spiders and creepy things she didn't want to meet in the dark. Creepy crawly spaces, she was thinking.

Once she heard a thump and figured he must have bumped his head on something down there. There was a muffled voice—probably contractor curses--and she was glad it was muffled.

When he finally came back to her, he had dirty hands and a sheen of sweat below his ball cap. "Well," he said.

"Well?"

"It's not as bad as it looks, and not as good as you probably wish it was." He dusted his hands on his workpants. "Parts of it you can't tell until you get into it. Some of the wiring that was done by whoever lived here last could be usable, but you'd have to get an electrician to look at it. And the plumbing is ugly old galvanized pipe that's not worth much."

"Can you tell anything about the walls and floor?"

"There's not nearly as much termite damage as you'd think. There's mold everywhere but it's just the good old east Texas kind, not black mold. Some of the floors and walls are usable but I'd put siding over the whole exterior, if I were you."

He kicked dirt off the soles of his boots. "The foundation's got to be propped up all over. There's nothing but stacks of cement blocks holding up the house. I've seen worse, though. And of course the roof's shot."

"Do you have any idea how much it might cost to fix it up?"

"It's the kind of a project you work on 'til you run out of money, then you wait till you get money again and work on it some more. There are people who might be able to pay for it to be done all at once..." he looked at her, a question hanging.

"No, I'm not one of those people. But I can do some work myself, and I can take my time."

"Well, this house isn't going anywhere. If you got time, maybe you can get the money. Or if you got determination, maybe you can find a way."

"The next thing I have to do is make a conditional offer. Could you maybe write up a ballpark figure of what the house might be worth? There aren't any comps in this area that are relevant."

"I'll do that." Scott smiled down at her. "I got to give it to you, you've got gumption. Not many ladies would want to take on something like this."

"Thank you for not saying 'little old ladies.'"

"Little—old—even men--nobody's taken on this house at all. I'm pulling for you." He patted her on the shoulder, nodded and got back into his oversized truck.

She was standing there smiling after him when her phone rang.

"Peggy? It's Nona. Could you come over to the library? I've got something you need to see."

"What, no cookies?" Nona joked when she walked in. "Everybody here wants to do research for you now."

"Sorry, next time! I rushed right over. What have you got?"

"I hate to show you this. It might cost me my future cookies. But I'm under oath to the research librarian's code of honor. I gotta let you know the bad news."

"Shoot. What? No wait, is there really a research librarian's code of honor?"

"No, I was playin' again." Nona handed her a photocopy of a newspaper article. "Do you want to sit down? I got a lot to show you. Once I pulled up 'Wettermark,' online, there was article after article. It looks as if your homeowner cleaned out his own bank and left the country with the money."

"Oh no." Peggy read a photocopy of page 4 of the Jan. 6, 1903 Houston Post. The headline screamed:

A FAILURE IN EAST TEXAS
THE WETTERMARK FIRMS HAVE GONE INTO
LIQUIDATION
Liabilities and Assets Are Believed to Be About $400,000—
A Statement Issued By the Head of the Firm.

Peggy looked at the stack of papers Nona had made for her. "The realtor said there had been some bad business, but I thought he meant bad business, not that the man was an embezzler who ripped off the bank and left town."

"I didn't want to tell you." Nona looked sad. "But of course you have to know. The bad business is a part of the story. It's probably been trailing around after that house since Benjamin Wettermark galloped out of town in 1903."

"You did the right thing. If you don't mind, I'm going to take all this home and read it until it makes sense."

"It's still history, and you love history, right?"

"Right. I love history," Peggy clutched the papers close to her chest. "I love that house, and this is its history."

At Erin and Jackson's house, Peggy closed the door to her room and stacked the photocopies on the bed. She was glad no one was there so she could process this information by herself.

All right, this certainly wasn't a picture of the happy Wettermark family gathered around the Thanksgiving turkey.

She sorted the papers by date. Nothing for Saturday, Jan 3, 1903, or Jan. 4 or 5. The article Nona had shown her ran in the Houston Post Tuesday, Jan. 6, three days after Ben supposedly left town.

She read the headlines again: "A FAILURE IN EAST TEXAS" followed by "THE WETTERMARK FIRMS HAVE GONE INTO LIQUIDATION" and "Liabilities and Assets Are Believed to Be About $400,000—A Statement Issued By the Head of the Firm."

Peggy drew a ragged breath and read:

> This morning when the note was discovered on the door of the bank of A. Wettermark & Son, 'Closed for Liquidation,' the whole community was dumbfounded. No one here knew that the bank was in any trouble. The assets and liabilities are supposed to be about equal, about $400,000 each.
>
> No one here knows definitely the cause of the suspension as Colonel B.S. Wettermark is out of the city. The books of the bank are in the hands of Branch Matthews, Harris & Beeson lawyers, and have not been posted since December 23 and the law firm will not know exactly the amount of assets and liabilities until tomorrow evening.
>
> The short cotton crop and bad collections are said by Colonel Wettermark's friends to be the cause of the failure.

The next paragraphs in the Houston Post were from a telegram written by Ben's father, Alfred Wettermark, who founded the bank in Nacogdoches and had placed his son in charge of it:

> I have been forced to suspend on account of conditions at Nacogdoches. As soon as the assets and liabilities at both Nacogdoches and Henderson can be ascertained a meeting of

all the creditors will be called and the matter submitted to
them. No assignment deed of trust or petition in bankruptcy
has been filed because I wish to save all expenses possible
for the benefit of creditors. Mr. June C. Harris is in charge
of Nacogdoches and E. B. Alford at Henderson. –Signed with
regret. A Wettermark.

Public sympathy seemed to be on the Wettermark side, at least when
that first story ran in the Houston Post on Tuesday:

The entire community greatly deplore the calamity that has
befallen the Wettermark banks. Public confidence still stands
strong and public sympathy is unbounded both at home and
abroad."

Peggy looked through the stack and found the story that the bank was
in trouble appeared that same Tuesday in newspapers as far away as New
Orleans; New York; Vicksburg, Mississippi; Indianapolis, Indiana; Kear-
ney, Nebraska; Belvedere, Illinois.

The New York Times headed their story, "Old Texas Banking House
Fails." The Town Talk in Alexandria, Louisiana, even ran a story headlined,
"Not Our Wettermark," to make sure people knew A. Wettermark, Jr., a
cashier at the First National Bank of Alexandria, had no business relations
with "those" Wettermarks.

Peggy thought the first stories showed sympathy and trust in the Wettermarks and the calamity that had befallen them. By Wednesday, Jan. 7 the
tide had turned. The New Orleans Time-Democrat wrote that the failure
was much worse than at first thought, and that B.S. Wettermark was still
absent with no clue to his whereabouts. The books were in such condition,
the story said, that no intelligent statement could be made about the bank
assets.

Nona had made a copy of a statement written by the attorney Junius C.
Harris on Wednesday, Jan. 7, 1903 that said:

The outlook concerning the affairs of the Wettermark
bank has a gloomier appearance today, and many who spoke
kindly of Col. Wettermark yesterday, expressed confidence in
him, have changed their verdict today. Nothing is known as to
his whereabouts, and it appears that the bank's affairs grow
muddier as investigation progresses.

On Friday the newspapers throughout the United States blasted the
headlines that the hunt was on for the forger, the absconding Texas banker,
the fugitive from justice. Searches were made on seaward-bound vessels but

no trace of B.S. Wettermark was found.

Peggy sat with her hand on top of the pile of papers. Did this make the house less desirable? Was it tainted? Is that why it was abandoned and in danger of disappearing?

It was odd that no one had ever mentioned this story to her. She had taken a visitors' center driving tour around the town when she first got here and heard not a word of this story. Could it be that nobody still alive today knew about it? Or those who knew thought it was too distasteful to mention? There was still a Wettermark Street and this house sat boldly on it. The home of the forger, the absconder, the fugitive.

She riffled through the stack of photocopies. Here was a real-life, legit scandal in little Nacogdoches. What would she discover as she dug through the records, through the beams, under the wallpaper of the home?

She could hardly wait to find out.

8. Meeting Father

September 5, 1893

Daisy tried to tamp down the panic she felt. Ben had gone to the train station to pick up his father, Alfred Wettermark. After two months of marriage, she was finally meeting someone from Ben's family. Two months! Where had the time gone? There was so much she needed to do. The bedrooms and the study were still pathetically barren. She had updated the parlor with furniture from the local Branch Patton store, but that was all she'd had time for.

This was fine. Everything would be fine. She wished it wasn't so oppressively hot. A fire in the fireplace would have made the parlor warmer, literally and figuratively. By now her mother and father would have the fires going in their New York brownstone. If only Mr. Wettermark had come to meet her in New York, they would have gathered around the fireplace and Father and Mr. Wettermark would have become fast friends. If only. Well, forget the fireplace, summer would last another two or three months here.

She hoped Mr. Alfred would like her. Of course he would. Why wouldn't he? She wound the grandfather clock and straightened the doilies on each of the tables. She ran her hand over the mantle to make sure there was no dust. Still, wasn't it odd that it had taken him so long to come to Nacogdoches to meet her? She told herself she had to calm down.

What else should I do? She hurried to the kitchen to see how Mrs. Hamlin was coming with dinner. The house already smelled of roast beef, and she knew that was perfume most men couldn't resist.

"How is dinner coming?" She smiled to let Mrs. Hamlin know she trusted her with the meal.

"It'll be just the way Mr. Alfred likes it," Mrs. Hamlin was peeling carrots and cutting them into slivers. "I'm putting these here in with the roast; he likes that."

"Is there anything I should be doing to help?"

"Well, don't make biscuits, that'll help!"

Daisy laughed as if she was a very good sport. Of course the cook was better in the kitchen than she was. It was laughable how few household skills Daisy had. But she was good at lots of things. She just needed to work them into conversation with her new father-in-law.

She went to Little Lenore's room where Alita had the ruffled white dress ready for the toddler.

"Mrs. Daisy, do you want to get this sweet child dressed?" Alita was carrying Little Lenore, as she usually did.

"I would like that very much," Daisy said, and held out her arms. Little Lenore put her arms around Daisy's neck and snuggled up to her and Alita went to check on the other children. They sat and rocked awhile, and then Daisy put the new dress on her. She had bought it downtown just this week and it was as delicate and beautiful as Little Lenore herself. Her second birthday would be Oct. 5, and Daisy was already planning a little celebration, just for the family. She had to think about it carefully though; that was the day Lenore had died giving birth to this baby.

She heard the horses coming up the road and carried Little Lenore to the parlor. She placed the little girl on the new settee, spreading the lace of the dress around her.

"Your grandfather is here," she said softly as she walked to the door.

Little Lenore clapped her hands and babbled.

Ben bounded up the steps, and opened the door.

"My wife, Daisy!" he announced. He turned back to his father as if he had announced the second coming. Or at least, the second wife.

Alfred Wettermark looked like Ben would probably look in 30 years. When he swept off his top hat, she could see he was very blond with thinning hair and eyes as blue as the skies of his native Sweden. He had a short grey beard and mustache. His face was pink, ruddy really, and he was what Daisy's mother would have called "portly." He was as tall as Ben and dressed handsomely in a black suit that looked hand-tailored and very expensive.

"I am so very glad to meet you," and she could hear the Scandinavian accent he probably thought he had lost.

"And I am so glad to meet you. Please, come right in. Thank you so much for coming to see us!"

"I had to come check on Ben here and see if he's taking care of the bank I gave him."

Ben colored slightly. "Of course it's fine. You don't have to keep checking."

"Ben." Albert stopped and looked at his son. "I check on all my banks. Not just this one."

Alfred leaned down to the toddler. "How's my little angel? How's my little Lenore?"

Little Lenore squeezed herself back against the settee and looked at Daisy for help.

Ben put a hand on his father's arm. "It'll just take a little time for her to warm up to you again."

"Oh, look at your pretty dress," Alfred started to touch her then thought better of it.

Daisy picked Lenore up and the child buried her head in Daisy's shoulder. Daisy moved nearer to Albert so he could put a careful hand on the child's back.

"I got that dress just yesterday, in honor of your visit." Daisy wanted him to know she'd already started caring for the children.

Alfred turned to look at her. "I appreciate that. I'm sorry I..."

Minnie, Benny and Carl all rushed into the room, and for a while talk with the children stopped all conversation between the adults. When Mrs. Hamlin appeared at the door, they all moved to the dining room where the meal was already on the table. Albert ate like he hadn't eaten in days, and then went to the kitchen to thank Mrs. Hamlin for the meal.

After dinner, Alita came to collect Little Lenore and the other children went to their rooms. Daisy asked Alfred how he ended up in Texas from Sweden. He seemed very glad to talk; Ben sat listening quietly as his father warmed up to the subject.

He was born Otto Vilhelm Alfred Wettermark in Jonkoping, Sweden. His family included accountants, assessors, military officers, Lutheran ministers and church organists. His great aunt married into Swedish nobility.

"Does that make us royalty?" Daisy was hopeful.

"Only in Sweden," Ben answered. "And it snows there 10 months out of the year."

"Is that why you left Sweden, Mr. Wettermark?"

"Please, call me Alfred." He thought for a moment before he answered her question. "There were other Swedes here before us. People used to write back about land being available and opportunity everywhere. That was what I wanted to hear. I arrived in Houston in 1853 and I had a job as a banker from that day on. From the day I arrived, Texas has been good to me. I earned the trust of Texans and I built my career on that trust."

"Tell her about Mother," Ben leaned over with his hands on his knees. He didn't look at his father.

"Well, like Ben, I lost the woman I loved."

Daisy looked at Ben. He kept his head down.

"I married Araminta Noble in Houston when I was 24. Her family lived in a big plantation style house in downtown Houston. We lived near her family in the middle of the Fourth Ward for a long time."

"She was a wonderful mother," Ben added in a low voice.

"She was. Everybody loved her. There were some years when things were tough in Houston, but we came through it all. We weathered the fire of '59, the yellow fever epidemic of '62 and the Civil War. When Houston started recovering after the war I was already an officer and director of B.A. Shepherd's bank."

Alfred looked at Ben, who still sat with his head down, waiting for the really bad part of the story to unspool.

"We had Anna Louise then Ben and two year old Wahlfrid. Araminta was expecting our fourth, but she didn't feel well. Her doctor thought Houston's heat and humidity was too hard for her and he suggested she ought to go somewhere cooler. We talked about it, and I said there's no place cooler than Sweden. You should go to my old family home."

"So we all packed up and went to Sweden. Except Father." Ben didn't look up as he spoke.

Alfred was quiet for a moment. "Ben was strong, already 6 years old. But Anna Louise and Wahlfrid weren't. There was an epidemic of diphtheria and the two children were ---gone. We buried them there. Araminta was heartbroken. She gave birth to Elise while she was there, but she didn't come home for a year."

Ben looked up at his father then. "I don't know why I didn't get sick. And I wasn't any help—I couldn't speak Swedish and I didn't know how to make Mama stop crying..."

"You were a child, Ben. Nobody blames you. Finally I went and brought them back in '69. Araminta never got over it. She was so afraid we would lose Ben, even though we had Elise and then two more. That haunted her the rest of her life, until she passed on in '85."

Ben looked up at Daisy. "We put up a monument to her in Houston. We had it engraved:

> You are not dead to us
> But as a bright star unseen.
> We hold that you are ever near
> Though death intrudes between.
> None knew her but to love her.
> None named her but to praise."

Ben looked so sad that Daisy wanted to put her arms around him right then and there.

Alfred slumped. "We added inscriptions for Wahlfrid and Anna Louise that said they were buried apart but were now united with their mother."

Ben kept his eyes on his father. "Two years later you were married and over it."

Alfred looked as if his son had slapped him. "Over it? I don't think we ever get over it. But we go on. You, of all people, should understand that."

Daisy realized she was in the middle of a battleground that had been fought before. She was that "going on" that the father and son were arguing about. "Mr. Wettermark, would you like a brandy?"

"That would be very nice. Again, it's Alfred. We are family now."

"Ben? Brandy?"

He was still looking at his father, but slowly turned his eyes to her. "Thank you, Daisy. I would like that very much."

The next day Ben drove Albert to catch the early train to his home in Rusk.

Hearing them talk about the monument to Araminta made her think about the grave of Ben's first wife here in Nacogdoches. Ben hadn't ever wanted to take her and it was time she paid her respects. She asked Mrs. Hamlin how she could get a carriage and the cook arranged for her husband to take her in his wagon. Daisy and Mr. Hamlin dropped off the three older children at the door to their school.

She walked under a wrought iron arch that said Oak Grove Cemetery and into grounds as green as a garden. Huge live oak trees sprawled over the graves.

It reminded her of her favorite poem by Dorothy Frances Gurney:

> The Lord God planted a garden
> In the first white days of the world,
> And He set there an angel warden
> In a garment of light enfurled.
>
> So near to the peace of Heaven,
> That the hawk might nest with the wren,
> For there in the cool of the even
> God walked with the first of men.
>
> The kiss of the sun for pardon,
> The song of the birds for mirth,
> One is nearer God's heart in a garden
> Than anywhere else on earth.

She walked around the ornately carved gravestones, some dating back to the early 1800s. Every plot had a memorial engraved with the family name; some plots were marked with white stone edges. There were even a few aboveground tombs, something she had never seen before.

An unpaved path cut though the center of the grounds and there beside the path was the large Wettermark plot with white granite blocks to mark each corner. The monument to Lenore was the tallest in the cemetery, easily 10 feet tall. Carved from white granite, the pedestal was topped by a granite urn, draped with a flowing stone cloth. At the base, in big block letters, was the name, "WETTERMARK." There was no verse inscribed, only, in the most ornate letters, "Lenore, Wife Of B. S. Wettermark Born Feb'y. 2, 1865, Died Oct. 5, 1891."

There was nothing else in the Wettermark plot, just empty space covered with grass, ready to receive the members of the family. Someday her name would be here too.

"I will be buried here," Daisy thought. "Far from New York, far from my mother and father, far from anyone who ever knew and loved Daisy Sutton."

She felt very alone, standing beside the towering monument to Ben's first wife. She thought of Alfred's words to Ben: ""Over it? I don't think we ever get over it. But we go on. You, of all people, should understand that."

Did Ben understand how she felt? Did he know what it meant to leave everyone behind, to move to a strange house and to a family that was haunted by a memory? He had been devastated when his brother and sister died and he could do nothing to help his mother. He never talked about Lenore, but his four children were constant reminders. And here was the first wife and her larger-than-life huge white monument.

Daisy looked up at Lenore's granite grave marker. "One is nearer God's heart in a garden than anywhere else on earth," she thought. Was she nearer Ben's heart here than anywhere else? Was his heart in this cemetery?

She didn't come all the way from New York to be an afterthought. Not Daisy Sutton. She would be the best wife a man could ever have. "You just wait, Ben Wettermark," she thought. "We are going to go on. We are going on together."

She turned her back on the monument and walked out of the cemetery.

9. BANKING ON IT

As Peggy waited at the house for Scott to bring her the unofficial estimate, she thought about Benjamin Wettermark as an embezzler. She was eager to learn more about it—why would he steal from his own bank and skip town? Was there any doubt that he did it? Was he caught?

But she was more determined than ever to buy the house and renovate it. Thinking about the shady past of the owner did not make her want the house any less. She knew Nona would call her when she had more information, but for now she had to proceed with the ToDo list. Number 3 was "Make a conditional offer." The seller wanted $100,000 but she didn't know how serious he was. Scott had said he'd give her a rough estimate of what the house might be worth.

Scott rumbled up in his huge truck. He was a big guy, with a big smile, and Peggy though, probably a big heart. He said Jackson asked him to get his assessment done ASAP, and so he had.

"Don't tell anybody how fast I can work when I want to," he joked, and Peggy promised she wouldn't tell a soul.

After reminding her this not an official inspection, Scott handed her his list:

1.   Wiring –replace most, possibly all

2.   Plumbing –replace all galvanized pipe

3.   Termite damage –not extensive

4.   Black mold–none visible

5.   Flooring–replace or refinish all

6.   Subfloor–replace some

7.   *Walls —water damage, remove/replace modern drywall*

8.   *4 Bathrooms—need all new*

9.   *Kitchen—all new counters, fixtures*

10.   *Exterior—replace or cover with siding*

11.   *Foundation -stabilize*

12.   *Roof —replace*

"In other words, Ma'am, you could tear this down and build a new house cheaper. You'll do lots of ripping out and propping up before you ever get to the point of making it look good."

Peggy thought about missing crown molding, fireplaces without mantles, plywood-covered windows and all the things it would take to make this home beautiful.

"What do you think it's worth?"

His eyes traveled over the shabby Victorian as if he could see the future. "When it's done, half a million. On the way to that, you could spend $300,000 easy."

"Well, that's grim."

"Yeah, I guess it is. There isn't much time left for this house, unless somebody jumps in now and saves it. The longer it sits here, the more it gets et up."

"Et up?" Peggy looked at his big, friendly face.

"My gramma used to say that. Time's just eating it up, before our eyes. It's already on the verge of being more valuable bulldozed than renovated."

"I can relate to that."

Scott looked down at the list he had made. "I don't know what the realtor will say, but tell him I said if you pay more than $50,000 you're getting robbed."

Hmmm. That might be appropriate for the Wettermark house, she thought.

Tyler Pate wasn't exactly excited to hear her offer, but he was game.

"$50,000? I don't know, Mrs. Jensen, but I'll put it in front of the seller. He doesn't know much about Nacogdoches; he's used to the Houston market."

"Thank you, Tyler. I appreciate you giving it all you're worth. You can tell him what the contractor said."

"Uh, I will do that, ma'am. But he knows you're the only one who's wanted it in a long, long time."

Tonight she would tell her daughter and son-in-law about her progress. She took the pork chop casserole from the oven. She had topped each browned pork chop with a slice of onion, a mound of rice and chopped stewed tomatoes. It was the meal she used to make when Erin came home from college. Her welcome home meal every time.

The aroma drew Erin to the table. "My favorite!" she exclaimed. "Jackson, we're sitting down!"

When Erin was scraping the last spoonful of tomato-y rice from the dish, Peggy unfolded Scott's estimate.

"That sweet Scott and I met over at the house today."

Jackson nodded. "Sweet Scott. He actually is sweet, for such a big ole boy." Erin laughed.

"He is very supportive about me renovating the house. But here's his estimate of what it needs."

She handed the paper to Jackson and he and Erin read it.

"Phew," Jackson whistled.

"Mom." Erin looked appalled. "This is bad. Really bad."

"I've given that estimate to Tyler Pate and asked him to put in an offer of $50,000."

Erin and Jackson looked at each other. Peggy hated it when they did that—they were communicating with each other silently. Probably that she was old and foolish. She knew she wasn't foolish, anyway.

"I just hate to see you tie up all your money," Erin was shaking her head. "There are such cute condos..."

"I want to save that house. It's part of Nacogdoches history. And I love it."

"You say that now, but when you're knee-deep in plaster and plumbing problems, you'll wish you never started."

"Erin Louise, when have I ever given up on a project I started? The credenza you moved into your living room—you said it was a pile of junk and I scrapped and sanded and glued and painted—"

"And now it's the most beautiful thing we have," Jackson finished her sentence. "It's just, this is so much and you'd be starting from almost nothing. We'd hate for you to get underwater on this thing."

"If the seller agrees to $50,000 or $60,000, I'll have a running start."

"Mother." Erin sighed. "Mom."

"Erin."

"Mom!"

Jackson looked from his wife to her mother. Stubbornness seemed to be part of their DNA. "Next step, why don't you and I go visit a bank and see what they say?"

"Should we wait until we hear from Tyler Pate?" Peggy fixed her eyes on him. They were green behind their bifocal lenses and there was the same look he often saw in Erin's eyes. No-nonsense. Direct. Determined.

"You're right. We'll go when we have something definite to ask." He looked at Erin, more of that silent communication. This time, Peggy thought, the look might say the banker would do the dirty work so they didn't have to.

"Fine," Peggy said.

"Fine," said Erin.

"As soon as Tyler gives you an answer, I'll set up an appointment at the bank." Jackson slapped his hands together to close the case. "Is there any dessert?"

The banker was another one of Jackson's friends. Forty-ish, earnest and well dressed, Neil Huckabee was a BIN—Born in Nacogdoches. His family had been here since the 1800s and in the manner of most BINs, he considered anyone who was not a BIN a newcomer. Didn't matter if they had been here 50 years, if they weren't born here they weren't really Nacogdocheans. Even people born here recently weren't really BINs, as far as the real BINs were concerned.

Neil's office was in the historic Stone Fort Bank across from the site of the original building Gil Y'Barbo had built in 1779 on Main Street. The bank building itself was mid '70s modern. Only the name of the bank was historic.

Neil and Jackson talked about the pavilion the Rotary Club was building and he recruited Jackson for a workday. Apparently they could have gone on all day about their volunteer activities, until Peggy leaned forward and put a hand on the desk.

"We hate to take up too much of your time," she started. "I'm hoping you can help me."

"I would be delighted, Mrs. Jensen. Any mother-in-law of Jackson is a friend of mine!"

They all laughed.

"I'm planning to renovate a house and I would like to get a loan."

The look that passed between Jackson and the banker told her they had already had a discussion. She really hated these silent conversations. She wasn't blind.

Tyler had gotten back to her with a counter-offer of $75,000 and reminded her that was $25,000 off the beginning offer.

She told Neil, "I'm offering the seller $60,000 and I'd like a loan that includes as much money as I can get for renovation."

Neil smiled at her. "You're taking on quite a project there."

She was glad he didn't add the words, "Little lady."

"It's the Wettermark house. I understand Benjamin Wettermark robbed his own bank and skipped town."

Jackson turned to look at her. "What?"

"The Wettermark bank is that empty bulding across the street from your bank here. I've been doing the research. In 1903 he cleaned out the coffers and bankrupted the bank. He took off, a fugitive in the night, and people all over the United States were looking for him."

Neil looked confused. "Why would you want the house of the man who almost single-handedly destroyed Nacogdoches?"

"It's the kind of historic home that people want to see in the Oldest Town in Texas. Something with a story. A scandal. A real legacy behind it."

Neil looked out his plate glass window toward the corner where the Wettermark Bank had stood empty since 1903. "Every BIN knows that story. And none of us talk about it."

"Real stories like these, that's what people want when they visit a historic town." Peggy slid the contractor's estimate across the table. It was a black and white admission that there wasn't much left of the house. "I can turn that house into the showplace it was when Wettermark lived in it. People will want to see the home of the man who broke the bank in Nacogdoches. It could be a real attraction."

Neil read Scott's assessment then sat silently, tapping the list as he thought.

"We've lost so many of our great old buildings. People come to see our history and there's not much to see." Neil turned his full attention to Peggy. "Why you?"

"I'm the only one who wants it. I can see it, the way it could be. I'm a hard worker and I never give up."

"And you have unlimited funds?"

"Limited funds, unlimited determination."

"I don't want to insult you, but you're how old?"

She straighten her shoulders and sat up straighter. "Old enough to re-paint but young enough to sell. To quote Neil Young."

"There it is. That's why my mother named me Neil." He tapped the paper again. "Jackson, I can't believe I'm saying this, but I'm inclined to grant your mother-in-law a loan. I would love to see the Wettermark house restored. If only as a cautionary tale."

Jackson looked at Neil as if he couldn't figure out how their silent communication had gone awry. He sighed. "I have heard some rumblings that one of the restaurants is going to restore the empty Wettermark bank building across Main Street."

"That would be something for downtown, wouldn't it? Now that would be a story—the house and the bank restored. That would be a story, all right."

Neil took a form out of his desk drawer and gave her a long look. "Now, Mrs. Jensen, let's talk numbers."

10. Little Lenore

October 1894

The library she created in their home was Daisy's favorite room. Over the last year, it had become her castle with the children.

Every evening after dinner they picked a book and she read to them. It was a blissful, quiet time when there was no other sound but their slowed breathing and her own voice weaving through the stories.

Little Lenore, just turned three years old, curled in her lap, her head in the hollow of Daisy's shoulder, always asleep by the end of the reading.

Minnie laughed aloud, gasped, worried with each part of the plot. She would listen to Mark Twain every night if her brothers hadn't wanted to hear other books. Alice's Adventures in Wonderland delighted her. Of course she could read herself but she loved to hear Daisy read the words of Lewis Carroll. If Daisy wanted to make her laugh, she had only to read out loud:

> `Twas brillig, and the slithy toves
> Did gyre and gimble in the wabe;
> All mimsy were the borogoves,
> And the mome raths outgrabe.

Benny often took a book to his room to read ahead or re-read parts he particularly liked. Sometimes he quoted lines back to her. Walt Whitman's 1865 poem about Abraham Lincoln was his favorite. She often heard him in his room reciting the mournful lines:

> O Captain my Captain! Our fearful trip is done,
> The ship has weathered every rack, the prize we sought is won,

The port is near, the bells I hear, the people all exulting,
While follow eyes the steady keel, the vessel grim and daring;
But O heart! heart! heart!
O the bleeding drops of red,
Where on the deck my Captain lies,
Fallen cold and dead.

Carl leaned on her arm while she read, watching the words as she said them aloud. She and Carl sounded out words together after school each day from the primers he wanted to understand.

"I'm never going to get it," Carl would say as understanding eluded him, his eyes filling with tears.

"You are already doing so well. You'll be reading in no time," Daisy assured him. "We're going to read together until one day—Poof! —it will suddenly be clear to you."

"Poof? You promise?"

"I promise, Carl. Poof, and you'll have it."

Sometimes Ben stood in the door of the library, smiling at them as Daisy read. Then it felt as if these were her children and this was truly her home.

October 5 was Little Lenore's third birthday. They had a family-only party after dinner for her, but it was a low-key affair. Her birthday was the day her mother died. For Ben and the three other children, the day was as sad as it was sweet. They seemed guilty if they acted too delighted about the birthday, then they were guilty about not acting happy for Little Lenore.

Alita, who had spent the last year serving as Little Lenore's mother, had relinquished her gradually to Daisy. At first she had to encourage Daisy, telling her how much the child wanted her, showing Daisy how to teach her to feed herself and how to bathe the child.

Alita started telling Little Lenore, "Here's your mama, sweet chile! Go to your mama," and Daisy began to feel, in her heart, that she was the mother of this golden child.

Each day Alita left the child more and more in Daisy's care. Now when Little Lenore awakened, she called out "Mama!" and it seemed sweet every time Daisy heard it. The child held her arms out to her so that Daisy could carry her from room to room as Alita had. She was a sweet three-year-old, but she was still walking hesitantly. Daisy thought, how could the child learn when she was so delicate everyone wanted to carry her? Daisy encouraged her to walk whenever she could.

During the day when Ben was at the bank, Daisy spent all her time with Lenore. She no longer called her Little Lenore—she was not just a miniature version of the woman who was gone, but a lovely child who deserved her own identity. Lenore giggled when they played peek-a-boo, laughed out loud at patty-cake. She was putting full sentences together and she loved to sing along with nursery rhymes. Daisy held her hand as Lenore worked hard to master walking, never crying when she plopped down on her diaper-clad bottom.

Ben hired the cook's husband, Mr. Hamlin, to take Daisy to town in his buggy at least once a week. She and Lenore went in and out of the shops and she bought colorful quilts for the older children, books for each child and shelves to hold their books. She couldn't resist toys and soon their rooms began to look as if happy children lived there. She had put Benny and Carl in separate rooms rather than together, so she needed twice as much bedding and furniture. She didn't see any reason they should have to share a room. Most mornings, though, she found Carl asleep in Benny's room.

"I got lonesome," he would say.

The women shopping downtown always stopped to admire Little Lenore. They usually said something like:

"She looks just like Lenore."

"That golden hair is Lenore's for sure."

"My oh my, Little Lenore is her mother's daughter, that's the truth."

If the women heard the child call Daisy "Mama," they looked shocked. Daisy never made excuses; she just hugged Lenore close. If the women said they were the wives of Ben's partners or friends, Daisy told them she was getting the house fixed up and they must come for tea sometime. Not one woman responded by inviting her over.

And people said New Yorkers were unfriendly, she thought to herself.

When the children were asleep, Daisy and Ben sat on the porch and watched the moonlight on the trees. They could hear barred owls and sometimes the faint rustle of deer that would come out of the forest and almost up to the porch.

It was cool in October and they wrapped blankets over their shoulders.

"Will we have snow this month, do you imagine?" Daisy was thinking of the white Christmases back home, of ice-skating in Central Park.

"Probably not," Ben said indulgently. "I've only seen one snowfall since we moved here. It was late in January, and everybody rushed outside to make snow angels and throw snowballs."

"That would be fun. We used to run around in the snow in the city. We'd stay out until we were frozen through, then we'd buy hot chocolate from corner vendors."

"Do you miss Manhattan?"

"No, not really. Just remembering. I've been too busy to miss anything."

"You don't have to do so much for the children—Alita is used to doing it all."

"I want to. I like to be here when they get home from school and I love for them to tell me about their day. I want to spoil them with a cookie and a glass of milk."

"I'm sure they appreciate it."

"I'd like to hear about your day, Ben. I'd like to spoil you too."

Ben laughed. "You don't want to hear about my day. We try to get new accounts, we make loans, we attempt to get paid what we're owed. I don't think that even earns me half a cookie."

"Lenore named her new teddy bear today. It's now Daddy."

"Daddy! What a little sweetheart." Ben leaned back and smiled.

"She tells him all about her day—but only the teddy bear can understand most of what she says. Lenore and I had a lovely time today. We walked all the way to North Street. Well, we walked part way, and I carried her the rest and she carried the teddy bear."

"You know I didn't bring you all the way to Nacogdoches to be a nanny for my children."

It felt like a physical blow, it hurt so much. She thought she was becoming a mother and he thought she looked like a nanny?

"I know I'm not their nanny. I hope..." She sat very still and took a slow, deep breath. "Why did you bring me here, Ben?

He turned to see if she looked as cold as she sounded. "Well, of course I loved you from the moment I saw you. A beautiful woman at the opera, dressed in that blue silk gown with those diamond earrings, your hair so—dark and glamorous."

She was silent.

Ben went on: "And then we started writing and you were so brave, willing to hop on a train and come all the way across the United States for me...you are a strong, brave woman—how could I help but love you?"

Daisy swallowed. "And what did you expect I would do here? In this big house surrounded by pine trees? With four little children?"

"I thought...I thought...we talked about...you could get involved with the women's club, entertain, help me build trust in the bank, help me make it the biggest bank in East Texas..."

"That's what you wanted. You did say that. What did you think I want-ed?"

"I thought you wanted the same thing I want. To...build a life in Nacog-doches. To make the bank successful."

"And the children? What did you think I would do with the children?"

"I know they need a woman in their life, not just cooks and housekeep-ers. I love the way you're helping with the children, Daisy. Especially Little Lenore."

"Lenore."

"What?"

"Not Little Lenore. She has her own name."

Ben shook his head. "But it's…"

"Lenore."

He looked very confused.

"I will join the women's club, Ben. And I will decorate the house and I will entertain. But don't expect me not to love your children."

She was crying now and Ben stood up and pulled her into his arms.

"I'm sorry, Daisy. I am a buffoon. A big buffoon. I don't deserve to have a teddy bear named after me.'"

"No you don't," she agreed, her tears blotting into his stiff white shirt-front.

He hugged her to him, kissed her dark hair. "I'm sorry, I'm sorry. Thank you for loving my children. Thank you for loving me. I am so lucky you came to live with us."

"Yes you are," she looked up at him, tears in her eyes. "I promised myself I would open my heart to Minnie, Bennie, Carl and Lenore. I know I won't replace their mother, but I will be here for them and I will give them all the love I can."

He lifted her chin and looked into her eyes. "Anything you need, any-thing, let me know and I will get it for you. Whatever it is you want. You just tell me."

She wondered how to tell him what she really wanted. She wanted to rebuild a home for these children. She wanted Lenore to call her Mama with-out anyone being shocked. She wanted this house to be filled with joy. She wanted to be Ben's first thought when he heard the word "family."

And she would do everything she could to make that happen.

When Mr. Hamlin brought the buggy to the house, Daisy was wearing her best dress with a gabardine traveling coat and a hat with long black feathers. Alita was feeding arrowroot crackers to Lenore.

"My, you look fine, Mrs. Wettermark."

"Thank you, Alita. I have to go downtown and conquer polite society."

"What?"

"I'm going to get invited to join the women's club."

"Well, that'll be real nice. I know they meet over to the Nacogdoches University, 'cause my sister cooks for their luncheons. She's about the best cook in town."

"That'll be worth joining for, I'm sure!"

Daisy walked from the corner of North along Main Street. She saw Lizzie Voigt Schmidt walking toward the public square. Her husband, John, was one of Ben's bank customers. John built the opera house in Nacogdoches, so Daisy thought perhaps Mrs. Schmidt might have the same love of opera she did. John was a member of the Masonic Lodge, Elks Lodge, and the Knights of Pythias. Obviously, Lizzie Schmidt was someone Ben would like her to cultivate.

"Mrs. Schmidt! Hello!" she called out as she crossed the main street. "I'm Daisy, Col. Wettermark's wife."

"Of course I know who you are, Daisy," Mrs. Schmidt said. "How are you adjusting to life in Texas?" Mrs. Schmidt looked her over, studying her hat, her coat, even her black kid gloves.

"I like it very much. I really want to get involved in the community, though. I wonder if you could tell me how to join a women's study club?"

"You can't just join the study club, of course. But you could come to a meeting as my guest."

"I would like that very much. When is the next meeting?"

"I'm not sure. Why don't I have Mr. Schmidt let the Colonel know and we can arrange to have our driver pick you up?" Mrs. Schmidt looked once more at Daisy's hat, as if to memorize the style.

Daisy walked to the Wettermark & Son Bank and stuck her head in. This was the first time she had visited the bank without making arrangements with Ben beforehand.

"Daisy--Mrs. Wettermark!" Ben stood up from his desk when he saw her. "Please come in. Is everything all right?"

"Perfect, Col. Wettermark." She walked into his office. "Mrs. Schmidt just invited me to come as her guest to the women's study club. She'll have her husband let you know when."

"Thank, you, Daisy. I appreciate that."

"You're welcome, you big old teddy bear. I'm sure it'll be a barrel of fun."

He took her hand and walked her into the main room.

"You all know my beautiful bride, of course. She has made me the luckiest man in the world."

The two young bank tellers nodded.

"Thank you, Col. Wettermark. I will see you at home." Daisy swept out of the bank, the long black feathers on her hat swinging as she walked. She glanced back and all three men were still staring at her.

She blew a little kiss at her husband and he grinned like a fool.

11. FAIR MARKET VALUE

Peggy stood on the corner in downtown Nacogdoches and let history wash over her. The town still retained elements of the past--the street paved with bricks, the small two-story shops, the dates above the entrances—1870, 1889, 1902.

But much of the town's history was left to the imagination. The words poet Karle Wilson Baker wrote in 1907 came back to her:

> "Nacogdoches has a soul, a spirit, an atmosphere. She is no raw product of today or yesterday. There are ghosts on her streets. Have you turned the clock of your mind backward for 200 years, and seemed to see the holy fathers in their coarse woolen gowns, barefooted, with the knotted rope about their waist, preserving their vow of silence?"

And Peggy's favorite lines:

> "The spirit of Nacogdoches today is a gift from the men of the past, the spirit of the future will be the gift of the men of today."

The brick building Ben Wettermark bankrupted in 1903 looked as if it could open its doors any minute. But the inside of the bank had been gutted, all the way down to the floorboards that a modern owner had torn out and thrown away. The Wettermark bank building looked as forlorn as the Wettermark house.

Perhaps to some people, renovating the Wettermark house would be all about bricks and mortar. To Peggy, it meant grabbing hold of the spirit of Nacogdoches.

The holy fathers in their coarse woolen gowns may have started Nacogdoches, but Peggy wanted to be a part of keeping it from disappearing.

At the library, Nona had another stack of photocopies on her desk. She was indignant about the information she'd found about Ben Wettermark.

"Oh, that man was a scoundrel. Listen to this, Miss Peggy: 'Ben was married and had three children and a grandiose 12-room Victorian mansion in the north edge of the city when he left town that cold January night with nothing but the cash from the bank.' From what I've found, he left his wife and kids and ran off. They stayed here alone for a year before they finally moved away."

"What kind of a man would do that?" Peggy took the paper from Nona's hand and read it herself.

"A man who's gotten too grandiose for his britches." Nona wrinkled her nose in disgust.

Peggy agreed.

Nona handed her another stack of photocopies. "Are you going ahead with the renovation?"

"Ben Wettermark has made it more interesting to me, not less. This is a house with a story. I've got the beginnings of a loan, but there's a lot of work before I can get one. I'm going to take pictures before the official appraisal."

"Seeing the before and after is my favorite part of a make-over."

"Thank you so much for doing the research. I've already got the 'after' in my head."

"I think that bank failure might have been a turning point in Nacogdoches history. I'll do more research but closing the bank seems like it broke the city's back. It took a long time to recover."

Peggy paid for the copies at the front desk on the way out. She was lucky to have met a person who was as interested in the role of the Wettermark house in Nacogdoches history as she was. It felt like she had more in common with Nona than anyone she'd met here. She hesitated, then went back to the research librarian.

"Nona, would you like to see the house now before I start?"

"You know, I would. Nothing more fun than seeing the process right from the beginning."

At ll:30 a.m., Peggy used a key she'd gotten from Tyler Pate and let herself into the house. She was standing in the living room when Nona came in.

Nona looked around, shocked. "Bless your heart, Miss Peggy, you have got yourself a heap of work. Is that a mattress? Looks like a hundred years of trash piled here."

"There is." Peggy started taking photos. "Would you stand over there by that fireplace so I can take a picture?"

Nona was a willing model and photographer, and the two worked their way through the house passing Peggy's cell phone back and forth taking pictures of each other pointing out different parts of the interior.

"This is quite a step down from grandiose, isn't it? What's next?" Nona asked.

Peggy looked at a list she'd made. "I have to get an official inspection for the loan. I'm rounding up information about my income and credit history for the bank and then they need copies of the house's appraised fair market value and qualified house inspection. I've asked the realtor to find out about deed restrictions, easements, and historic designation regulations."

"There couldn't be too many restrictions or those little houses and that apartment building wouldn't have been allowed."

"The banker said I need to decide if I'm doing a renovation, rehabilitation, or restoration." When Nona looked puzzled, she went on: "Renovation means I want to make the house like new. Rehabilitation is restoring or fixing-up a property while keeping its architectural value. Restoration brings the architecture back to a certain time period."

"Which are you thinking about?"

"I'd like to take it back to the Wettermark's time. I read that means I would 'accurately depict the form, features, and character of a property as it appeared at a particular period of time.' I would remove anything from other periods in its history and reconstruct the missing features from the early Victorian period when they built it."

"Lucky for you everything's already removed! Does that mean you can't have a current kitchen or bathroom? You have to have the same plumbing they had in 1900? Or lack thereof?"

"No. Even the US government says it's okay to keep 'code-required work.' Thank goodness for that. This house has got to have decent bathrooms!"

Nona looked closely at a wall. "That's shiplap. See this? I've read that wide rounded shiplap siding was used from 1890 to 1900. Traditional shiplap has a groove cut into the top and bottom that allows the pieces to fit together snugly, forming a tight seal."

"Nice," Daisy said. "At least that's left."

"Which bank are you working with?"

"The Stone Fort downtown. The banker is a BIN –Born in Nacogdoches--and he seemed really interested in the house for the sake of the town's history."

"That's good. This house could be really important to the town. I'd like to see that. You know, I'm a BIN too."

"You were born in Nacogdoches?" Peggy didn't mean to sound so surprised.

"My family was here from 1866 on. After the war we got land and my family's been on it ever since."

"You're part of the history of Nacogdoches yourself! Have you done research on your family?"

"I've started an oral history, saving the stories from my great grand-
mother and the oldest people I can find. There's not much written," Nona
said. "Not even all the gravestones are marked. Some of the historians at
the University found the African American cemetery near Oak Grove and
they're trying to do some identification. I've always wanted to know more
about my family."

Peggy looked at Nona with new eyes. "So you became a research librarian."

"I love finding the clues that lead to the past. I have always loved to
read, and I can dig and research and find things that are hidden to most
people."

The two women had taken photos of everything they could find, from
the lower walls where there should have been mopboard to the few bullseye decorations left.

Peggy locked the front door. "I look at this house and I can see how it
looked back then—it was grand and substantial and the family probably felt
like it would last forever."

Nona nodded. "That's how I feel when I do research. I read the words
and I can see how people felt. I can imagine how this family suffered when
that man robbed his own bank and left them with the disgrace."

They both gazed up at the gable on the second floor above them. For a
moment, they were quiet. Then Peggy promised to email Nona photos and
Nona promised to keep digging into the past and they each drove away.

Neil Huckabee was waiting for Peggy at the Stone Fort Bank. He had become very interested in her "project," and had been doing his own research.

"Miss Peggy, I've been looking into the appraisal process for this project," he
stood until she was seated. "There are four steps to determine a historic house's
value." He walked her through a document he'd pulled up on his computer:

> "First, the appraiser defines why the appraisal is being conducted (to
> determine fair market value, insurable value, investment value, or a com-
> bination thereof); what restrictions and easements are associated with the
> property; and what the current local real estate market conditions look like."

Neil explained, "Fair market value is an estimate of the highest price
the house and its land will command in the open market. Insurable value
means an estimate of the cost to replace the house and other improvements
on the land should they be damaged or destroyed and investment value is
determined by considering the rental income that could be derived from the
property and its likely selling price at some future point."

This kind of talk made Peggy uneasy. "I'm worried that with everything you list the cost for the loan goes up."

"Not the cost of the loan, but the amount I can loan to you. This is a good thing, Miss Peggy. It may help me be able to secure enough to get you a ways through the renovation. Are you planning for this to be a multi-family building?"

"It won't be an apartment building," Peggy was a little indignant.

"That would be if you actually wanted to make money on the project. It's just one of the considerations, not that you're going to do it. Sometimes people subdivide historic estates."

Peggy shook her head. "Again, I'm restoring the house, not chopping up the land for new developments. And there's not really any land left around it anyway."

Neil put a finger on the computer screen and told her the appraiser would prepare the report depending on her choice of the market, cost or income approach.

"What do you want to do with the house?" Neil looked intently at her.

"I certainly don't want to rent it, or flip it. I—I want it to restore it so it can be an important historic property in Nac. I think about living there, but that's not really the end game. I suppose, when I've restored it, I'd like someone to take it who values it as a part of the oldest town in Texas."

"You're planning to take it back to 1903?"

"I want it to look like it did when Ben Wettermark left his wife and children and took off with the bank's money."

"Well, we certainly can't use the income approach because that means you'd be getting rental payments from it. Maybe cost approach, because then we'd toss in depreciation value for over 100 years."

Peggy thought that sounded sensible, not to mention helpful. "So the next step is getting a bona fide appraisal."

"And that costs. We can ask the seller to pay for it, but it's probably going to fall on you." He picked up the phone and called Tyler, who at this point was the real estate agent for both the seller and the buyer.

Tyler told them that the owner didn't want to pay for the appraisal. After he hung up, Neil told her this was exactly the kind of thing that Peggy would find throughout the process and that she'd need to be prepared for unexpected expenses.

"If there's no way around it. I'll pay for the appraisal myself." Peggy had a look of determination that Neil suspected her daughter and son-in-law often saw. "Let's get this process started. We're losing history as we talk."

Neil laughed. "I don't know if we can lose history, but time can certainly destroy the evidence of it. "

"I'm grateful you're putting your trust in me. I didn't know if my age..."

"Age isn't important to a banker," he said. "It's our gain if you succeed and it's our property if you default."

"So the bank wins either way."

"That's true, but there's more to it than that." He smiled at her and tapped his pen on his desk. "Nacogdoches wins if you restore that piece of history. I'm banking on that, Miss Peggy. My money's on you."

12. A Dark Day

November 22, 1894

It was 11:30 a.m. Mrs. Schmidt's carriage would arrive soon but Daisy hated to leave Lenore. Alita stood with her arms out, ready to take the child.

Daisy rocked Lenore softly and ran her hand over Lenore's cheek, so pink with fever. The child looked as if she might sleep, but she would startle each time a racking cough overcame her little body.

"I'll sit with her all the time you're gone," Alita said. "I won't take my eyes off her."

Daisy was still reluctant to let go. "The doctor said he'd come back if we want. We'd better get him. I know it was just two days ago but he needs to see she's not getting any better. She's so weak and that cough is terrible."

"Yes ma'am." Alita took Lenore from her arms as the carriage drove up.

"I'll be home soon, Alita. Will you ask Mrs. Hamlin if her husband can go get the doctor?"

"Yes, ma'am."

Daisy tore herself from Lenore, so sick and so small. She hesitated before she got into the carriage and almost turned back. But this was the first opportunity she had to go to the women's club and she knew it was important to Ben.

Mrs. Schmidt wasn't in the carriage and she sat alone behind the driver. Why hadn't she come with the driver? It made Daisy feel like she wasn't worth much to Mrs. Schmidt. She turned and watched her house until they were on North Street and she couldn't see it anymore. It was chilly and damp and she pulled her coat around her.

The grey light of November filtered through the bare trees, making the town look gloomy. The tall loblolly pines still had their green needles but they were so high above the streets that they didn't soften the day.

When they pulled up in front of Nacogdoches University, she was pre-occupied and anxious about Lenore and she didn't even appreciate the tall white columns that made the building look so grand. She accepted the driver's hand and went up the steps to the front door.

One of the members opened the door and ushered her in. There were already women sitting in the parlor at little tables, drinking tea from fine bone china cups. They all turned to look at her and conversation stopped.

Mrs. Schmidt arose from her seat and said, "Please, Daisy, come sit by me." To the women at her table, she said, "Ladies, this is Daisy, Col. Wettermark's newest wife." Daisy took a seat and a gloved waiter poured her steaming tea. Then he put a small plate of cucumber sandwiches before her.

"Thank you, Mrs. Schmidt. I'm sorry I'm so distracted —Lenore is sick and I've been up with her all week..."

"Little Lenore, what a darling child," one of the women said. "How terrible that her mother left us so soon. She was the loveliest woman."

"Kindness to a fault," another said. "Lenore was too good for this world."

"Irreplaceable," another said.

The meeting started and the officers made their reports. Then the president, Mrs. E.C. Branch, called for each member to stand and give a short reading on "The First Thanksgiving." Some women read poetry; others seemed to be quoting from the Encyclopædia Britannica. The women apparently took the club's name, which Benny had told her meant "with wisdom," to heart.

Daisy tried not to fidget. She wanted to be at home with Lenore where she belonged.

After each and every woman (except Daisy) had finally said her piece, Mrs. Branch asked Mrs. Schmidt to introduce her guest.

"This is Mrs. Benjamin Wettermark. Daisy," Mrs. Schmidt stood and gestured for Daisy to do the same. "She came to us from New York, as you all probably know. She rode all the way to Nacogdoches on the train by herself."

The women nodded their heads and stared at her. Apparently they already knew that.

"Well, I wasn't really alone. A woman from Houston, a friend of the Wettermarks, rode with me." Daisy looked at the unfamiliar faces. She did recognize a few women she had met in church.

"You didn't know her, though? Goodness, you are a modern woman!" Mrs. Schmidt was playing to the audience, looking at Daisy as if she were a heathen. "And you met the Colonel...?"

"At the Metropolitan Opera. Faust. In Italian."

"Were you alone there as well?"

"No, of course not. I was with my mother, and Ben, Col. Wettermark, found out my name and came and sat beside me..."

"Daisy has expressed interest in joining Cum Concilio." Mrs. Schmidt aimed that to the president.

It seemed abrupt to Daisy but she was glad to get her intentions out in the open. "I understand that you have a library here in Nacogdoches University. That you lend books. I love to read, and I brought quite a collection that you might not have. I would be glad to donate some of them."

Mrs. Branch shook her head. "I should imagine your tastes are far too advanced for our library, Mrs. Wettermark. We have to offer what would be interesting to the people in our community. Thank you, though, for considering it." She nodded to Daisy as if to dismiss her. "Now, we have a report about the Christmas soiree."

As one of the members walked to the front of the room, Daisy and Mrs. Schmidt sat down. Was that it? Weren't they going to say anything? Acknowledge that she wanted to join? Refer it for a later vote? Daisy's cheeks were burning and she wished she hadn't come. She wanted to make Ben happy; but she had never considered that the women wouldn't accept her into their society.

Mrs. Schmidt reached over and patted her hand. "This is the last report, dear," she said. "Then we'll get you back to that house you're refurbishing."

It was 2:30 p.m. when the meeting ended and she could finally leave. Mrs. Schmidt said she would ride home with her next-door neighbor and the driver could take Daisy home.

Daisy saw the doctor's buggy outside the house and sighed. At least the doctor would turn the day around. She hurried into the house and found Ben was already home.

"Ben! You're early!"

Ben's hair looked as if he'd been running his fingers through it and his eyes were red. "Mr. Hamlin came downtown and told me the doctor was on his way. I thought I'd better come home and see our little girl."

Alita was sitting at the kitchen table, a large handkerchief in her hands and her eyes red. Daisy gave her a little hug as they went by. Alita seemed so tired she could hardly lift her head.

Ben and Daisy slipped into the room where the doctor was sitting by Lenore's bed, his hand on her forehead. The strong scent of camphor filled the room. Lenore was almost as pale as the little pillow under her head. Her blonde curls were damp and disheveled. Daisy hoped for just a moment that Lenore would look up and say, "Mama" and hold her arms out to be picked up. Then Daisy would rock her and tell her how very much she loved her.

"She's sleeping," the doctor said. "I've given her the strongest analgesic I have."

Daisy's eyes filled with tears. "She hasn't eaten, I can hardly get her to drink water even though you told me she needs it so much."

Ben put his arm around his wife. "Doc, you said it was a chest cold."

The doctor turned to look at them. "She first had cold symptoms, the sore throat, fatigue, a runny nose, chills, aches, and a slight fever. But now I think we should call it bronchiolitis. The small air passages in her lungs are filled with mucus and are swollen."

Ben pulled Daisy closer. "What does that mean?"

"There is blood in the mucus and she's gagging when she coughs. Her breathing is severely compromised." The doctor lowered his eyes to Lenore rather than look at them. "I don't think she will make it through the night."

"No!" Daisy sank to the floor by the bed.

The doctor stood and packed his case. "I've made her as comfortable as possible. She is finally sleeping."

Daisy sobbed. Ben folded himself into the rocking chair and put his head in his hands.

"I would recommend you keep the older children away from the room. This is not as contagious as diphtheria or pneumonia. You'll all probably get it, but it's more serious in little children than in adults." He looked sadly at them, then left, closing the bedroom door behind him.

Alone with Lenore, Ben and Daisy tried to keep their hopes up.

"What can we do? Is there anything we can try?" Daisy looked at Ben as if he might have some idea.

He shook his head. "We can't lose her." Tears filled his eyes; he grasped Daisy's hand.

As the afternoon dragged on, Daisy and Ben sat by Lenore. Ben looked as if he had given up; Daisy alternated between hope and despair. She put cool cloths on Lenore's forehead, whispered to her, wiped her own tears away and swaddled the heavily sleeping child in a little quilt.

When the children came home from school, they came to the door of the room and looked in. Daisy hugged each of them, and told them Lenore was so sick they couldn't come into the room. Minnie, 10 years old now, took it upon herself to comfort Benny and Carl and led them to the kitchen.

Mrs. Hamlin fed the older children then bustled them off to their rooms. Ben slumped in the chair; Daisy wept by Lenore's bedside, unable to stop. She felt broken, crushed by the weight of sorrow and love.

As night came, Lenore was still except when she coughed, and then she struggled to wake up and breathe. Every strangled cough felt like a knife to Daisy. She picked up the limp child and held her to her heart, walking slowly around and around the room. When Lenore coughed, Daisy patted her back, hoping to dislodge some of the mucus.

Ben reached out to Daisy. "Here. I'll rock her." She helped him take Lenore and he held his little girl to his shoulder, rocking and patting her back. Daisy sank back down to the floor.

There was no sound except the creak of the rocking chair for a long time. Then Ben said, "No one thought she would live through that terrible birth. She was so weak, barely able to cry. Her mother didn't even get to hold her. We hadn't chosen a name. When they asked me for her name, I just said Lenore because that's all I could think of. Lenore, Lenore, Lenore. Dying here in our bedroom."

Daisy suddenly hated this bedroom for the role it had in this tragedy.

Ben's voice was a strained whisper. "I should have thought harder, given her a better name, loved her more."

"Ben." Daisy had been so filled with pain she hadn't thought how this felt to him.

"I asked myself, why did I live? Why did Anna and Wahlfrid die and I lived?"

She raised her eyes to look at him and realized he was talking about his brother and sister who died in Sweden. His handsome face was blotched and his eyes were closed.

"You were just a child."

"Diphtheria killed almost all the children around us. I lived and they died. Mother was destroyed. I wasn't enough to stop her grieving. She told me if she died giving birth to Elise, she could be with her babies buried under the icy earth of Sweden."

"You stayed a year?"

"Until Father finally came and got us. She didn't want to leave Anna and Wahlfrid there. She hadn't wanted to go to Sweden in the first place, then she didn't want to leave."

Daisy moved closer and put her hand on his leg. He was patting Lenore, rocking—and crying. Tears rolled down his cheeks.

"My mother was the next to die. Then Lenore. Now this sweet baby."

She took Lenore gently from his arms and laid her on the bed, pulling the quilt around the child. She wrapped her arms around Ben and he sobbed into her chest. She patted him like he had been patting the three-year old.

"Ben, Ben, Ben. I love you. Minnie loves you. Benny loves you. Carl loves you. We will be together and we will be strong. I promise you, we won't leave you."

She held him until his sobs stopped. Then she sat on the floor beside him, with one hand on his knee and one hand on Lenore.

Before midnight, Lenore slipped away from them. Ben and Daisy cried in each other's arms. Then she went down the stairs to Alita, who had been the first mother Lenore had known. She didn't need to say a word, just put her arms around Alita and joined her in tears.

Oak Grove Cemetery was crowded. There were people from the Presbyterian Church, bank customers and officers, shopkeepers and wives of East Texas business leaders. Ben's relatives had come from Houston and Rusk. Some of the Wettermarks' friends were recent immigrants from Sweden.

The sky was leaden gray, and there was a damp chill. It felt as if the day was in mourning for the tiny, beautiful child. The women wore black dresses, capes or coats and most had black veils covering their faces, as if they could not take in all the tragedy. The men looked almost identical to each other in black suits, white shirts, ties and top hats.

Daisy shook her head to drive away the thought that this could be a scene from a Verdi opera, dark and grim and inevitable. She thought of *La Traviata*, of Violetta, dying of tuberculosis as punishment for her sins. Beautiful Lenore, who called Daisy mother, had no sins. Why was the child punished? How could Daisy have left her that day? What club could have possibly been more important than her own child—she sighed, her own stepchild?

The crowd filled all the space from the wrought iron cemetery gate to the Wettermark plot. Near the 10-foot tall memorial, Ben stood shoulder to shoulder with his father Alfred. On his other side, Daisy leaned against Ben. Her knees were weak and her head ached from all the tears she had cried. The children were considered too young to attend a funeral and had stayed at home with Alita and Mrs. Hamlin.

The minister of the First Presbyterian Church in Houston had come to conduct Lenore's ceremony. He started with a reading from Revelations:

> "*The Lord is the everlasting God,*
> *The Creator of the ends of the earth.*
> *He does not faint or grow weary,*
> *His understanding is unsearchable.*
>
> *They who wait for the lord shall renew their strength,*
> *They shall mount up with wings like eagles,*
> *They shall run and not be weary, they shall walk and not faint.*"

Daisy hoped she would not faint.

Clara Johnsdotter, who had come in from Houston, stepped forward to put her arm around Daisy's waist, supporting her. The grave looked heartbreakingly small in the family plot. Before the tiny wooden casket was lowered into the ground, the pastor asked everyone to bow their heads with him and he prayed:

"Merciful God,
You renew our trust in you
That by the power of your love
We shall one day be brought together again
With this beautiful child Lenore Wettermark.
Grant this we pray through Jesus Christ our Lord."

Daisy thought she had cried her last tears, but now they flowed. Ben leaned heavily against her, his shoulders shaking.

The mourners filed past, shaking Ben's hand and patting Daisy on the shoulder.

Mrs. Schmidt, a look of guilt on her face, took Daisy's hand in both of hers and said, "I'm sorry for your loss, Daisy. I know this has been a hard year for you."

Daisy looked at her steadily. "Yes, it has been very hard. I had no idea how hard it would be."

"I am so sorry...perhaps you could come to tea sometime?"

"Perhaps, when Col. Wettermark and the children and I have time to recover."

Mrs. Schmidt nodded, and had the grace to lower her eyes. Then another person replaced her, telling Ben it was a blessing that Little Lenore would be with her mother in heaven.

When everyone had finally filed out of the cemetery, Ben and Daisy stood before the Wettermark plot. There was no stone for the child yet; there hadn't been time for the engraving. Ben had been adamant that Little Lenore have her own marker, rather than adding her name to her mother's towering memorial. The short granite scroll would be placed later. It would be engraved:

BABY
LENORE
OCT. 5, 1891
NOV. 22, 1894

"Let's go home, Daisy," Ben said.

"I hate to leave her here," Daisy said. "She's so little."

Ben took her hand. "I know how our other children feel. They are probably as heartbroken as we are."

"Yes. We should go home."

Together, arms around each other, Ben and Daisy stumbled to the carriage and left the chilly grey cemetery.

13. THE FOUNDATION

Peggy sat nervously in the real estate office across the desk from Tyler Pate. She thought he looked awfully young to be involved in such an important financial transaction.

"Sign here, initial here, here...." Tyler pointed to page after page on the stack of papers that required her to practically sign her life away.

This was not the most expensive purchase she had ever made, but it was the first that she had made alone. As they moved from their first little two-bedroom to each new and bigger brick house, Bill had done the negotiating and signing. Not that he was a great negotiator; he usually just bought whatever he wanted for the asking price.

He was the most happy-go-lucky fella, an optimist through and through. He assumed everything would work out, and for the most part everything did. Until it didn't.

His Alzheimer's was cruel and debilitating. She had sold the big house because she couldn't keep up with all the doors through which he could exit. The townhouse only had the front and back doors and she installed locks he couldn't open. She lost him a couple of times when they went out—or he lost himself—and she would look frantically until she found him, sweaty and confused, angry at her for his circumstances.

Their long marriage had been the one constant of her life. They moved when he got a new job or they could afford a bigger house. They had lived throughout the southwest in Texas, Kansas, Oklahoma, Mississippi, and Arkansas. She was never afraid to make a change, even though it meant packing everything they owned and going somewhere she'd never been.

Now as she sat in real estate office, she vacillated between joy and terror. What was she doing? What possessed her to take on this debt for a rundown house in a sleepy little historic town? All alone?

She wanted to DO something, that much was true. But more specifically, she wanted to rip off old wallpaper, throw out abandoned junk and wrestle this wreck of a house into shape. It would not be easy but every step she took to restore it would be tangible proof that she was strong, she was capable and she was not all used up.

Tyler looked up with a broad smile. "That's it, Mrs. Jensen. You just bought yourself a house." He jumped to his feet and reached for her hand. "Congratulations!"

"Thank you, Tyler, thank you. I own the Wettermark house!"

"You sure do! Let's go on over and I'll pound one of our SOLD signs out front. We don't want everybody trying to buy your house out from under you!"

"Yes sir, otherwise everybody's going to try to buy it!" Peggy laughed at the idea. "I think after this long, the line of people who want that house has dwindled down to me."

"You never know." Tyler took the big stack of papers to make copies. "Maybe not now, but you're going to turn that house around. You just made the first step for saving part of Nacogdoches history."

The foundation guy, Tanner Elroy, was skinny and wiry except for a beer belly that kept his jeans well below his waist. He had a sunburned face, crinkles at the corners of his bright blue eyes and a pale line where his ball cap provided shade. He started under the house when Peggy stopped him.

"Could I possibly come look with you? I want to know this house from top to bottom."

"Sure you can. You're not afraid of spiders and snakes, are you?"

There was lattice all the way around the bottom of the house, covering the space from the bottom of the porch to the ground. Tanner moved a piece of lattice and Peggy followed him in. It was about three feet tall and even lower in some spots. The ground beneath her feet was dry and dusty. This was not something that could be converted to a basement. It was truly a crawl space. It wasn't as tight for them as it had been for big Scott McCullough, but she still bumped her head as they walked around bent over.

"It's so open to the outside," she said, peering through the lattice out to the front yard.

"That's a good thing. That way it don't get all moldy down here. And anything that gets under the house can get right back out."

He went further in. "Mizz Jensen, you want to come look at this?"

"It's not a snake, is it?"

"No ma'am." He pointed to a hollowed-out spot. "Probably been raccoons sleeping here. Or possums. That's why there's no snakes."

He shined his light on a stack of cinderblocks that went from the ground to the house. She could see that there were stacks like that around the perimeter and spaced throughout the area.

Cement blocks seemed awfully flimsy to hold up a great big two-story house. Peggy moved closer to a stack. "Is this the way this foundation looked over a hundred years ago?"

"It was probably timber back then. They just chopped the trees and propped up the house. Then when cinderblocks came available, they replaced the wood. A whole lot stronger."

He put a hand on the blocks and they moved just a little. This seemed like a very bad idea to Peggy, who backstroked out of there as fast as she could.

"You don't have to worry that it's going to fall right down." He crawled out and stretched.

"So what will we need to do to the foundation?"

"Depends. What did the inspector say?" Tanner looked like a man who was used to contingencies. And wasn't afraid to work around them.

"The report says the foundation needs 'shoring up.' I'm not sure what that means."

"It means we can pretty much do what we want." Tanner grinned. "We can do it the hard way or we can do it the easy way."

"This is where it all starts for me," Peggy told him. "I want this house to last another 100 years, so I guess I'm saying I want to go the hard way. Would you mind doing an estimate for me, writing out two or three ways to do this?"

Tanner took off his cap and wiped his forehead with his sleeve. "I'd be glad to. When do you want to start?"

"As soon as you can get it to me. "

"Yes, ma'am. I'll get on it right away."

That night after supper, Peggy sat with Erin and Jackson over decaf coffee and told them she'd gotten the loan for the house.

"So you're really doing this?" Erin looked at her over the rim of the cup.

"I am."

"Well, what's the schedule?" Jackson took out his phone and opened his calendar.

"Tanner Elroy is going to give me a bid on the foundation. This weekend I'm starting the clean-up."

"Are you getting a roll-off? A big dumpster?"

"I thought I'd just bring trash sacks. I don't think there's enough for a dumpster."

"I know for sure there's an extremely nasty mattress right in the middle of the living room. Erin, you always say my truck is like a big wheelbarrow. Maybe we can fill it up and make a couple trips to the dump."

"Jackson! You're going to help?" Peggy put down her cup.

"Mother. Of course we're going to help." Erin looked aggrieved. "We're not going to stand by and let the person we love go down into the mines alone."

"And we don't want to miss out on any of the fun," Jackson added.

Peggy was delighted. "All right, Saturday morning we'll start early. I'll bring trash sacks and donuts."

Jackson smiled. "And I'll bring the Ford 250 wheelbarrow."

"Wait a minute. Just what do you mean by early?" Erin cocked her head. "And can you make mine raspberry filled?"

When Peggy, Erin and Jackson arrived at 7 a.m. it was already light. They had a big thermos full of hot, black coffee, and of course, a box of donuts. They were all wearing old work clothes. Jackson, who always wore a suit and tie, looked more like a repairman than a chamber exec. Erin had her shoulder-length blonde hair in a ponytail and had tied a bandana around her head. Peggy wore her oldest sweat pants and tennis shoes. They completed their chic outfits with canvas work gloves and clear plastic goggles.

Jackson had brought facemasks and insisted they all wear them. Peggy thought it made them look like doctors—doctors whose patient was a big, sad house suffering from neglect and depression.

Jackson took a selfie of their trio on the front steps in masks and goggles. "Ugh," Erin said. "Maybe nobody will recognize me."

They entered through the front door and stood looking at the mess.

"Why don't we get the worst job done first," Peggy said. "Shall we get that mattress out of here?"

They waded through junk and lifted the awful mattress and pushed and shoved it out the door, down the steps and hoisted it into the pickup.

"That was so heavy and disgusting I sincerely hope that was the worst job," Erin said.

Erin wanted to pry the plywood off the windows so they could get better light, but Peggy and Jackson persuaded her to leave it since there was no glass on those windows. They left the front door open so they could get a breeze, but the back door was nailed shut so there wasn't any cross-ventilation.

They used shovels first, digging up old coffee cups, fast food wrappers, cigarette butts, broken window glass, horrible clothes and dirty rags. Peggy put each plastic bag in a big trashcan so they could shovel everything right into it. Each time a bag was filled, Jackson tied it closed and carried it to the back of his truck.

When they had gotten the piles of debris cleared, they stopped for coffee. Peggy said, "I just don't understand how this got so bad. How did the city let this happen?"

"Well, of course, it's not the city's job to maintain old houses." Jackson blew on the still steaming coffee. "It's supply and demand. Nobody wanted it, so nobody took care of it. And vice versa."

"This was a beautiful Victorian mansion. Now it's almost a trash heap. I just don't see how Nacogdoches lost so many of its historic homes," Peggy said.

Erin was searching the box for her filled donut.

"It's a sign of success," she said, "When Stephen F. Austin State Teachers' College came in, the land around here became so valuable people bought everything they could at almost any price. It was 1923 and after working for years to get a college, people were beside themselves thinking of the prosperity that would come with it. By the 1960s, new businesses offered big money to the homeowners. They jumped at the money, built new houses or moved to Houston or Dallas."

"The town was completely changed by the college," Jackson said. "For the first time ever, the BINs weren't the most important people in town. Faculty and students came from the big cities and brought their own ideas. The result, of course, was that a bookstore for the students was much more important than an old wooden home."

"There it is!" Erin looked delighted. "My raspberry donut." Jackson and Peggy just looked at her.

She said, "So these old mansions were torn down and paved over. The area around the college was the most changed. Nacogdoches started its steady growth and now there's 30,000 people including 13,000 students. The only place you can see the old houses is out at Millard's Crossing where some of them were towed and re-erected."

"So why didn't this house get swept up in that?"

Jackson looked thoughtful. "I looked into that Wettermark story after we talked to Neil at the bank. I saw that the Hayter family bought it after the scandal but then it changed hands again and again. I think there was, not a curse, but maybe like a cloud on it that just kept it from thriving. It just never fully recovered."

They tossed out junk until they were worn out and it got too dark inside to accomplish anything.

The next day, they began sweeping. It wasn't easy because old flooring was curled up and cracked and they kept getting their brooms stuck. They tried not to stir up the dust, but soon the main floor was swirling with it.

Peggy was glad for the mask and goggles. Her eyes were streaming anyway, trying to flush out the dust.

"Maybe we should try something else for awhile," she said. "We could wash the windows; there aren't many left."

Erin and Jackson agreed that would be a nice change. They had glass spray and rags, but it was slow going. The windows were so filthy that it took rag after rag to create a spot that would let the light in. Peggy went outside and worked on the other side of the windows, matching her work to the spots that had already been cleared.

The existing windows were the real thing, glass that had a slight wavy appearance with an occasional small bubble and subtle surface imperfections. It would be expensive to replace all the missing windows with glass like this, but she knew it was necessary to make the house look like it had when Ben Wettermark betrayed the town and left it.

Through the window, she could see Erin grinning back at her. Her daughter's face was lit by sunlight peeking in that window for the first time in years. She grinned back.

There might have been a cloud over this house since the bank scandal, but she was here now. She was determined to drive that cloud away.

14. STONE FORT RIFLES

June 1897

It had been almost three years since they buried Lenore. Daisy still put flowers on the tiny grave every week. Sometimes Ben went with her, sometimes Minnie, Benny and Carl. But she always went, even if she was alone. She still treasured the memory of the time she was Lenore's mama.

She watched Ben pull away from his three older children more every day, but she moved closer to them. He was so busy with the bank and he didn't seem interested in anything she had to say about the children.

One night as Ben and Daisy sat on the porch looking into the darkness, she told him how she felt.

"After the funeral," she said slowly and gently. "I vowed that I would let the children know that they were not alone. I understand I can't replace their mother, but I will always treat them as valuable and important."

He didn't answer at first. Then he cleared his throat. "They seem to have gotten over—everything—very well. They don't think about the past."

"I'm not sure of that." She looked at his profile, so strong in the dark. "I don't think they'll ever get over the loss."

"Do they say that?"

"No, but..."

"Then they're fine. Don't worry so much about them."

"I do worry about them, Ben. And you. Losing your sister and brother in Sweden made a tremendous impact on your life. It broke your mother's heart and you felt bad that you couldn't help her."

"That was long ago. If we don't talk about Lenore, they'll get over it. We don't need to remind them of it."

During the next three years, she took the children to church every Sunday. The people at the First Presbyterian were always kind to her, always complimenting the children. That led to another opportunity—she got to buy their Sunday clothes.

What fun to get dresses for Minnie, who had seemed so dowdy and plain. In the shops downtown, she bought pale blue cotton and lavender silk and floral prints with bluebells and violets. She found white lace and grosgrain trim and tiny jet beads, and took Minnie to the best seamstress in town so that the dresses fitted her perfectly. She brushed the 12-year old's hair and taught her how to braid and curl her blonde waves. Daisy planned to take Minnie to New Orleans when she turned 13 in December, and let her buy something sumptuous in velvet. Dark blue velvet, probably. That would set off her Scandinavian coloring.

Benny would be 11 years old this month and he was as handsome as his father, without the mustache, of course! He was very serious and careful, a little afraid something awful could happen any minute. Her main job with Benny was encouraging him and letting him know everything was all right.

Carl turned 9 in March and he had learned to read so well he was often asked to read in class. Even when the teacher didn't call on him, his hand was waving in the air. Just as Daisy had said when she started to read to the children, poof! one day he understood what reading was all about.

She still read to the children every evening, but she knew they didn't need her for that. It was just a nice time for them to be together. Ben no longer came in and watched them. He worked so late that he often missed dinner and their reading time. Mrs. Hamlin would wait, then finally set aside a plate for him so he could eat when he came home.

The new building for Wettermark Bank was the talk of the town. Ben had the architect Diedrich Rulfs design it so that it angled with the double front door catty-corner on Main and Pecan, He paid $2,500 to have it built, and although townspeople raised their eyebrows, they all wanted to see it. It was sienna-colored brick with arched windows and a balcony running all the way around the second story.

"It's beautiful, Ben," Daisy said as they stood before it. "You've created a landmark for Nacogdoches."

"The best part is that it's just Wettermark Bank, it doesn't say A. Wettermark & Son," Ben looked at it with pride. "Finally, I'm out from under my father's wing."

After that, they hardly ever saw his father, Alfred, who was busy with his own Wettermark branches. That didn't seem to bother Ben at all.

Although he was too busy to come home in time for supper, Ben was completely devoted to the Stone Fort Rifles. That's where he got the title Colonel Benjamin S. Wettermark. As Benny had said, Ben was officially a lieutenant colonel, Field & Staff, of the Texas Volunteer Guard, 1st Regiment, Infantry, Nacogdoches. Daisy was never sure what that long title meant, except that the Stone Fort Rifles got together once a month and wore their uniforms and rode their horses.

None of them allowed their jobs to interfere with their meetings. The men were distinguished looking; most had formidable mustaches like Ben's and long sabers clanking from their belts. They called each other by their rank, and Ben was always Colonel.

The Stone Fort Rifles (the Rifles, as they called themselves) were up in arms about the upcoming Spanish-American War, and they literally wanted to be armed. Their favorite topic of conversation was the people of Cuba being overrun by Spain. Revolts had been occurring for some years in Cuba against Spanish rule. Now US public opinion had been agitated by anti-Spanish propaganda led by newspaper publishers such as Joseph Pulitzer and William Randolph Hearst who called for war. And they sold more newspapers and got more readers.

Unlike Nacogdoches, which was solvent, the business community across the United States had just recovered from a deep depression, and feared that a war would reverse the gains. Many of the bankers lobbied vigorously against going to war. Not Ben and the Rifles.

One evening after a meeting, Ben came bounding in the door. "This is the first time since the Civil War that Americans from the North and the South will fight a common enemy."

"Spain, you mean? They're our enemy?"

"Our enemy because of their injustice to the people of Cuba. All the Rifles look at this as a way to bring the country back together."

In May, Congress appropriated $50,000 to provide food, clothing, and other supplies to approximately 1,200 destitute people living in Cuba who had both Cuban and American citizenship. On June 7 the Secretary of State John Sherman issued an official protest to the government of Spain regarding their brutality.

After that meeting, Ben came home and announced: "I think we're all going off to fight."

"You mean the United States?"

"I mean all of us in the Stone Fort Rifles! We're going to sign up and take off for Florida together to get in the fighting."

She looked at him, aghast. "You would leave your daughter and two sons and run off to a foreign war?

He looked surprised. "Well, the Stone Fort Rifles…"

"You would leave your wife who came thousands of miles for you and go to a country across the sea for people who are in no way related to you?"

"The men and I..."

"You would leave your precious daughter lying in Oak Grove Cemetery; you would leave us here alone without you?"

"I was just thinking..."

"Benjamin Wettermark, you are 35 years old. You are the head of this family, the only father these children have. The only husband I will ever have. Do NOT leave us. Or I swear to you, I will pack up everything we have and follow you across the ocean, right into the Stone Fort Rifles' camp."

Ben looked shocked. "You will?"

"I will. I took a train all the way across America to be with you, and I will not let you leave us alone here."

Ben laughed. He pulled her to him and kissed her forehead. "I believe you, Daisy Sutton Wettermark. All right, I will not leave you. Not even if President McKinley himself rides into Nacogdoches and orders me to my horse."

She put her arms around him. "Thank you, Ben. If he does, you tell him to come talk to me."

Nacogdoches was booming. There were over 24,000 people in Nacogdoches County, with 1,827 in the city. Cotton was king on 3,000 farms right near town and new businesses were proliferating. The local cotton gins processed almost 7,000 tons of cottonseed.

There was so much activity with the gins and lumber mills that the trains were running all the time transporting cash crops to the bigger cities. Ben felt personally responsible for creating the prosperity in Nacogdoches. He was in the middle of everything, making loans, supporting the farmers, helping establish mortgages for people moving into Nacogdoches.

Daisy wasn't the only person shopping downtown. New stores opened every day, shoe shops and general mercantiles and hardware stores. Everywhere Daisy went, the merchants were enthusiastic and courteous, quick to establish credit so she didn't have to pay for her purchases right away. Shop owners greeted her like a friend, showing her the latest ribbons and fabrics and unveiling the newest shipments they thought she might like.

With the Wettermark Bank so strong, rumor had it that the First National Bank that had been established in Nacogdoches in 1886 was in trouble and might close. That would mean Ben's bank would be the only one in town.

Daisy thought being the most respected banker in Nacogdoches would be enough for Ben. But he was single-minded and ambitious and wanted more. In the '80s he had been an alderman, which was an elected official of the municipal council. Before his wife died, he had been the town treasurer. Daisy thought that was about as important as a person could be without being mayor.

Ben didn't have an office or title now, except Colonel. Once Daisy made him promise not to run off with the Stone Fort Rifles, the fun had gone out of it for him. So what was left? She should have seen it coming.

"Daisy, I've been thinking. Nacogdoches needs me. I've decided to run for mayor."

"But Ben, you're so busy. The bank takes so much of your time."

"I'll hire another man. Everything's running smoothly. I just hate to see Nacogdoches without the leadership it needs. Certainly, things are going well now. But I can insure the future for this town. I know how to do it and I'd be wrong not to try."

"You will be the most handsome mayor in the state of Texas," she smiled at the enthusiasm that had brought a flush to his cheeks.

He laughed as if he considered that a fair statement. "I do have vision and I can see the greatness that could be ahead for us." He took her hand. "I need your help, Daisy. I need you to help me woo the voters. We need to be established in society, we need to have parties here at the house, we need to look successful."

So his old argument was back. Daisy tried to put out of her mind the terrible experience at the women's club the day she visited. That ended very badly last time but she wanted to make him happy.

She had to find a way to be a part of Nacogdoches society.

Over the last three years, she had become more involved with the Presbyterian Church. It was a comfortable place for their family; the women were kind and solicitous, there were children the age of Minnie, Benny and Carl and the men all knew Ben. It would be a good place for her to launch Operation Mayor.

That Sunday she approached one of the women who had brought a peach cobbler to the house when Lenore died. Mrs. Goodson was short, rounded and pink-cheeked. She had a sweet smile that showed her dimples and she often patted Daisy's hand and asked how she was doing. Although they were probably the same age, she always called Daisy "dear sweet child," and told her she had been thinking about her and "those three darling children."

After church let out, Daisy walked along beside her. "Mrs. Goodson, I wonder if we can do anything to help the poor people of Cuba, so hard hit by the soldiers from Spain?"

"Oh, you dear sweet child. I've been thinking the same thing! My husband is going off to fight with the Stone Fort Rifles and it's been laying heavy on my heart. And please call me Matty, everyone does. It's short for Matilda."

"I was wondering, Matty, if perhaps we could form a group to knit or sew for the Cubans who have been left without anything?"

A week later there were eight women knitting in her parlor. Daisy didn't actually know how to knit, but she provided tea and Mrs. Hamlin's sugar cookies and bought skeins of wool in every color she could find. She arranged for their first batch of socks and mittens to be presented at a meeting of the Rifles. There was not a dry eye in the room, especially Ben's, who was still wishing he could go fight.

Did the Cubans need wool socks and mittens? Perhaps not, but the women of Nacogdoches were doing their part. And their men would go off to war with knitted offerings for the afflicted.

Matty Goodson thought Daisy was the dearest, finest person she had ever met.

One day after the success of their knitting endeavor, Matty stopped Daisy on Main Street.

"Dear child, I don't know if this would suit you, I know you prefer to work for charity, but I wonder if you might like to join our little book club?"

Without even asking what the book club did or when it met, Daisy said yes.

The club met the third Wednesday of every month at 2 p.m. and discussed a different book each time. Daisy had joined for Ben's sake, but the club turned out to be the greatest experience she had in Nacogdoches. Daisy got to know six more women. They were different from the knitters, more outspoken, more literary.

It was in book club that Daisy learned that newspapers in New York had erroneously reported the death of Mark Twain. The women all laughed together when they heard Twain's famous statement, "The report of my death was an exaggeration."

They talked about Thomas Hardy and Henry James, about Robert Louis Stevenson and Jules Verne. They even talked about new authors like Somerset Maugham, whose novel was considered too racy for Texas. They shivered when they read Bram Stoker's Dracula. To Daisy, the group felt like a little New York City, right in the middle of East Texas.

The women introduced her to the writing of Kate Chopin, who lived across the border in Louisiana. They knew Chopin's short stories from Vogue and Atlantic Monthly, and Daisy felt the author captured the old world atmosphere that was part of this area. Even though the civil war ended 37 years ago, there was still the feeling of the Old South here, the separation of black and white, of managers and workers.

What a lovely group of women. Daisy thought. She felt confident because of her success creating the knitting group and joining the book club. Now, Daisy told herself, it was time to throw her hat in the ring at Cum Concilio, the women's club that had dismissed her so rudely the day Lenore died.

She went looking for Mrs. Lizzie Schmidt.

15. INSPIRATION

Peggy didn't have any trouble finding the fundraiser for Zion Hill Baptist Church; she just had to follow the smoke from the barbecue pits and the heady scent of pork ribs and brisket.

There were about 100 people milling around on the grounds of the old church and in the barricaded streets. Then Nona waved and hollered, "Over here!"

As she hurried into the shade of a canopy, Peggy thought she had never wanted barbecue more than right this minute. "Oh my gosh, Nona, that smells so good! Can we eat right now?"

Nona laughed. "They're just about ready. You'll know it's time when you see the line form at one of the pits. Let's get over there where the line's gonna start." On the way over, Nona snagged two plastic cups of sweet tea and handed one to Peggy, who thought it was truly southern, like Zion Hill Baptist itself.

Peggy felt lucky to be invited to the fundraiser for the historic African American church, and not just for the barbecue. Maybe she could pick up some pointers on renovation. The empty sanctuary was one of the most impressive buildings in Nacogdoches, and the community had been trying for more than 20 years to raise money to restore it. They'd already spent over $400,000 on the enormous new roof, paint, electrical wiring, and heating and it still wasn't done.

Nona introduced her to so many people, black and white, that she lost track of their names. There were pastors and college professors and women who sang in Nona's church choir. Peggy met people from the historical society and construction workers.

One of Nona's sisters, Missy, was selling meal tickets.

"You're Peggy? Nona said you're gonna redo that big house on Wettermark."

"I thought it was big until I saw this church! This is enormous."

"It is big. And we're restoring it inch by inch. I hope it doesn't take you as long as it has us. We get something done only to find something else needs doing." Missy handed her the change and Peggy stuffed it in a DO-NATE jar on the table.

When their plates were filled with ribs, sliced brisket, potato salad, barbecued beans and peach cobbler, Peggy and Nona sat at one of the tables on the grounds in the shade of the towering wooden building.

"This church is so big it makes me feel small, sitting here beside it," Peggy said. "It's beautiful."

"It is," Nona agreed. "I think of it as an architectural wonder. One of those rare and beautiful historic buildings that deserves to be preserved forever. It was designed by Diedrich Rulfs, the architect who set the style that made Nacogdoches what it is today. He built most of the businesses downtown and the most remarkable houses in Nacogdoches. He was an expert at making each of his houses look unique. In 1914 when he designed Zion Hill, he was really hitting his stride. You can probably tell that Zion Hill blends Gothic and Victorian elements."

She grinned at Peggy.

Peggy, who was learning but didn't really know styles, tried to look knowledgeable. Nona understood and pointed out each aspect as she talked about it.

"The west tower with the pointed belfry vents and shingled spire are Gothic. You can see that style on the windows on the east side. The trefoil or 'clover' designed lights over the windows on the northwest and southwest fronts, they're a Gothic touch too."

She slowed down a little for Peggy. "The Victorian style shows in the way it's shaped like an opera house. It's not completely symmetrical and there's the octagonal lantern, or dome, on the roof over the sanctuary."

Peggy looked way up at the spire. "It is impressive."

"John Schmidt, who had once been a partner with your guy, Wettermark, was right in the middle of it. He offered the services of his architect, Diedrich Rulfs. Only a person with divine inspiration could have come up with the design for this church."

"Can we go in?"

"Of course. If you've had enough barbecue?"

"Too much. It was so delicious."

Peggy was struck with the beauty of the interior of the sanctuary. It was a vast sweep of white wooden bead board, from the entrance on the first floor to the ceiling that was open all the way up to the top of the second floor. Zion Hill was designed to be one of those buildings where "there's not a bad seat in the house." Sunlight through the yellow and blue windows painted the balcony and altar with color.

Peggy was unable to speak. She felt uplifted just by standing in this 100-year old sanctuary.

Nona spoke quietly. "The congregation was here for 78 years before they moved out and went to a more modern building. It's been empty ever since. There's just not the money to renovate it the way it needs to be done. But as the choir sings, 'One day at a time, sweet Jesus.' That's the way we have to do it."

When they went outside, Peggy got her voice back. "This is just spectacular. It should be the top of every tourist map."

"It should be. It's the finest thing Diedrich Rulfs designed, and he designed some mighty fine things. And here's a real nice piece of news—he designed your house too!"

Peggy had to sit down in one of the folding chairs on the lawn. She felt as she stopped breathing. "Nona! You're not just playin'?"

"I've looked at a book on everything Rulfs designed and built. He designed the Wettermark Bank downtown in 1895. And in 1900 he built your house. The same year Ben Wettermark was elected mayor."

Peggy felt her eyes fill with tears and she took deep, steady breaths. Rulfs designed her house and Ben was mayor? That elevated her house to the status of local royalty as far as she was concerned. "Mayor Wettermark," she tried it on for size. "That's a big deal in a small town."

"To put it in perspective, this building, Zion Hill Baptist, wasn't built for another 14 years. When the Wettermark house was built, the Civil War had been over almost 40 years. Nacogdoches had grown from 500 people to 1,827 at the turn of the century. That's when downtown got all those brick buildings that are still there today. John Schmidt had Rulfs completely changing downtown, even building an opera house."

"Sounds like it was a very prosperous time in little Nacogdoches."

"And your mayor was one of the most prosperous of them all."

Peggy walked back to her car along the edge of the Oak Grove Cemetery. It had been a spectacular day. A spectacular lunch, a spectacular building. And now, another piece of information about the Wettermark House. She felt like the luckiest woman in the world.

She took a pad of paper and some pencils and hurried to her house. Zion Hill had inspired her and she was thinking, "Let the renovation begin!"

She had just unlocked the flimsy front door when Tanner Elroy pulled up. "Here you go, ma'am. Home delivery." He handed her a bill for the foundation. The work he did below the house cost more than twice as much as she had expected. And he didn't seem the least bit apologetic about it.

"Well, Miss Peggy," he drawled, "We just had to do more shoring up than I expected. You said you want it to last another hundred years."

She sighed. The first step on the renovation was already more than she'd budgeted. She thought of the renovation of Zion Hill, where this had probably happen a lot. At least now her house was jacked up, firm & level.

You had to have a good foundation to build on, she told herself.

She looked slowly around the main floor. It was definitely more promising since she and Erin and Jackson had spent two weekends cleaning it out.

She started a list:

- Front door, new locks

- Roof (completely new)

- Windows—some can be salvaged

- Flooring—can some floors be saved, wood matched?

- Fireplaces—four in house

- Staircase—all stairs, needs railing

Yes, those were definitely important. Then she thought, now was the time for vision. *What do I really want to do? I want this to feel a little like Zion Hill, open and breathtaking. Open concept? Not really, just not cramped little rooms.*

This architect was a genius. She needed to show his design but make it functional. She was restoring a mansion, she told herself. A mansion! For a moment, she was a little overwhelmed. Why hadn't she found a tiny house like they show on HGTV?

Despite that thought, she pulled out a tape measure and started writing down the measurements of the first floor. This was not easy to do alone. The metal tape wouldn't stay down. She even tried putting one of her shoes on it just to hold it in place.

Next she would hire an electrician and a plumber. Scott McCullough, the contractor who was Jackson's friend, had told her some of the electric might be worth saving, but she doubted it. She thought he was probably just trying to be nice. He was pretty definite about the plumbing though—all of the galvanized pipe would have to go. He seemed like an honest guy, and a nice guy. She would ask Scott to work with her.

Of course she needed to get this done right away. Lights and running water would make the work go so much faster. She loved the history of the house, but the basics had to be done or she had nothing.

There was a little knock at the front door, and it slowly opened. Why hadn't she locked that before she started crawling around the floor? A man stuck his head in.

"Hello? Hello? Can I come in?"

She stood up and looked him over. He stood in the doorway, not taking another step in. He was old, probably as old as she was. White hair, where there was hair.   A ruddy face, wire-rimmed glasses. He had on a short-sleeved plaid shirt and khaki slacks.

"I'm sorry to barge in. I saw the Sold sign and had to see who was taking on this house. I've got one of these Victorians and I know how much work they are."

She walked to the door, not wanting to let him come all the way in. "Where's your house?"

"Over on Virginia Avenue. There's a whole line of restored homes over there. Big as this, if not bigger. I'm William Calhoon, and I figure you must be new in town. I haven't seen you anywhere."

"Calhoon Electric?"

"Yes, ma'am. And you're..."

"Peggy Jensen. I just moved here to be with Erin and Jackson Vance. "

"Oh, Jackson. With the Chamber. Good man. How is it going?"

She moved toward the door and he backed out onto the porch. This was the kind of thing Erin had warned her about, just that morning. "Don't talk to strangers. Don't invite strange men into the house when you're alone."

"Pretty well. I just wrote a check to the foundation repairman for more than my husband and I paid for our first car."

"Woooo, I understand that. It all costs more than you expect, doesn't it?"

She and William Calhoon stood on the porch and talked, then walked to the middle of the front yard where they looked up at the house and discussing architectural features.

"My house has that same steep hip and gable roof," he pointed up. "Right on top of that you probably had a widow's walk of decorative iron. It wasn't real, it just looked good."

"It was built in 1900 for Col. Ben Wettermark."

"I know." He started to say something then thought better of it. "And I can tell it's by Diedrich Rulfs. What a waste that people let these houses just fall apart. I'm real glad you're doing this. I did some of the work on my house. I'm no contractor, but I'm pretty handy. And I'm free some days, if you need help."

He invited her to come see his house and she said she would bring Erin and Jackson over some time. By the time he left, she felt kind of silly about not letting him in, but it couldn't hurt to be cautious. That was Erin's voice in her head, she realized.

She stood on the porch and looked toward North Street, where traffic ran day and night. College students raced their motors, parents shuttled children to soccer and softball fields. Eighteen-wheelers weren't allowed on this main thoroughfare, but there were plenty of trucks almost as big. People driving from Houston or Dallas cursed the stoplights they could have missed if they had taken the Loop around town.

That made her smile and she thought of 1900 when this house was built on the far north edge of Nacogdoches. Today it was right in the middle of town, just a block away from the university campus.

According to Nona, this house established the new outer residential limits of the town at the time. There might have been a sign above the door: *Beyond here lie monsters.* Little did the people of Nacogdoches know that the monster was inside the house, in the heart of their mayor.

The architect's biographer Jere Jackson had written:

> "*Throughout Diedrich Rulf's lifetime North Street continued to be the premiere residential street in Nacogdoches. Reading between the lines, it appears that the newer and grander houses in town (especially the houses for Schmidt, Blount, Harris and Jones) were pinching Wettermark socially and psychologically, for he was a promoter and a showman.*"

Apparently, it pinched him so hard that the road where she stood right now had been named Wettermark Street by its modest mayor.

There was so much work to do and William Calhoon had offered to help. She'd check him out; she could use all the help she could get. It was a big job, the kind of job that could stretch on forever. And she had to do it piece by piece.

Peggy thought she could put up a sign of her own that would be more fitting: *One day at a time, sweet Jesus.*

Like it or not, that's the way she was going to have to do it.

16. POLITICKING

1898-1900

The parlor was crowded with men, smoking smelly cigars and talking loudly. The air rang with the clink of glasses filled and refilled with bourbon.

Daisy and Minnie were hiding out in Benny's room, eating sugar cookies Mrs. Hamlin baked that morning. Carl snuck down the stairs to see if the men were leaving anytime soon. He came back and plunked down beside Daisy.

"I don't think they're EVER gonna go home," he said. "There's still more bottles and they'll probably work their way through those."

"You are the best little spy in town," Daisy said and pulled him close. "I'll bet they didn't even know you were peeking into the parlor."

"Father knew, and he kinda jerked his head like I'd better get back upstairs."

"It's not every day your father announces he's going to run for mayor. Those men are his biggest supporters. It's a very important undertaking, and they are starting off with a bang."

Minnie giggled. "With a bang and a bottle!"

"Maybe we should read some more of 'Tom Sawyer' just to keep ourselves busy?" Daisy knew the answer would be yes.

"When Tom and Huck get to watch their own funeral," Benny said. "That's my favorite part."

Daisy pulled out the well-worn book and the three children snuggled around her. Even Minnie, who was 14, still loved it when they read together.

Daisy wanted to spend as much time with them as she could. Ben told her they'd be "campaigning hard" and she wouldn't have much time for the children once they started. Lately the house that had been the right size for them seemed too small as she and the children tried to stay out of the way of the Rifles, the businessmen and the city councilmen, planning and campaigning.

Ben seemed bigger than ever. He slapped men on the back, he laughed loudly at jokes and he shook hands in a two-handed clasp that looked like he was the best friend anybody ever had.

He had told her he wanted to be mayor more than anything he'd ever wanted. If that was what he wanted, then she could want it too.

When the men finally stumbled to their buggies and horses, she could imagine how welcome they would be at home. They all smelled terrible, like cigars and whiskey. At least their wives would know they weren't lost in the Piney Woods. Not a man in the bunch would be good for anything tomorrow, she thought.

Minnie had gone to her own room an hour ago. Benny and Carl had fallen asleep before she finished reading. She went downstairs and Ben looked up when he saw her.

"Daisy, my own little Daisy." He jumped to his feet and waltzed her around the kitchen. "We are on our way!"

"We are, Ben. You'll be the best mayor Nacogdoches ever had."

"Yes I will, my dear, yes I will. And you'll be the best mayor's wife in the history of Texas!"

Ben was very good at speeches and he gave many of them. The theme for his campaign was "trust" and he spoke of it often and well. Trust in our future, trust in our prosperity, trust in the history of Nacogdoches that led to our present.

She attended every speech to which women were allowed. She tried not to dress too ostentatiously but it was hard not to overdress when Ben appeared so proud of her. Sometimes the children came with her, and days later 10-year old Carl would still be quoting almost every word his father said.

There were so many people in and out of their house that Mrs. Hamlin took to making a cake every morning and setting it on the counter so Daisy could serve tea to whoever dropped in.

Alita was always ready to help if they needed, or walk the children to and from school. She kept the parlor neat and ready for company, and worked with Mrs. Hamlin to feed the steady stream of well-wishers. She washed and ironed all of Ben's shirts and kept Daisy's dresses pressed and hung in her wardrobe. She was there for the children when Ben and Daisy had to leave them behind in all the campaigning.

Daisy had become well known in town. She baked casseroles for pot-luck suppers (well, she brought Mrs. Hamlin's), she served on charitable committees, and she took Minnie to every cultural event.

She had been so cordial and kind to Mrs. Lizzie Schmidt that the woman probably thought Daisy had forgotten how rude she had been at Cum Concilio. Daisy had not asked again to join the club. This time they could ask her.

The day after Ben's announcement for mayor, Daisy went to Schmidt's shop on Main Street. Ben said she needed some dresses that would show the town he had married a woman with style. She was looking at fabric when Mrs. Schmidt walked in.

"Daisy! You're just the person I wanted to see."

"Mrs. Schmidt. It's good to see you—how is your husband feeling today?"

"He was apparently overcome with joy about Ben's campaign. Or overcome with something; he couldn't even get out of bed this morning!"

They laughed together, as if they were old friends and had shared many laughs.

"Daisy, I know how busy you are. You have been such an asset to our little town."

"Thank you so much, Mrs. Schmidt. What a lovely thing to say."

"You must call me Lizzie. Please." She reached out and took Daisy's hand. "I wonder if you would consider, the ladies wanted me to ask you, if you might have time to join Cum Concilio?"

Daisy made a little "O" of surprise with her mouth. "Lizzie! How nice of you to think of me!"

"I'll bring the carriage round next week and pick you up. We'll have such fun!"

Yes we will, Daisy thought. We will have such fun. She didn't want the kind of "fun" she had with Lizzie Schmidt at the first meeting with the women's club. But now Ben was running for mayor and Daisy was an asset to their little town. They wanted her now.

She picked her dress carefully for the meeting, trying to decide between the four new dresses she'd had made for the campaign. She picked the rich green one with the ecru lace around the mutton sleeves and down the pouter pigeon bodice. The hat was embellished with the same lace but didn't have any feathers that might appear too frivolous.

When Daisy saw Lizzie Schmidt's carriage out front, she hesitated just a moment. It was hard to go back to Cum Concilio and pretend the women hadn't rejected her.

Alita saw her stop with her hand on the door.

"Mrs. Wettermark, you look beautiful, far prettier than anybody else in town," Alita stood up a little taller. "I'm proud to work for you, Mrs. Wettermark. You're a real fine lady."

"Thank you," Daisy opened the door then turned back. "And Alita, so are you."

At Cum Concilio, Daisy graciously received the accolades the women heaped on her. Apparently, sweet Matty Goodson spoke so highly of her they thought they had a saint among them.

When the president, Mrs. Branch, called on Daisy to tell about Ben's campaign, she was able to quote one of his speeches almost as well as Carl.

"Trust," she told them. "Trust is the center of Ben's campaign. He feels it to the core of his being; trust in our future, trust in our prosperity, trust in the history of Nacogdoches that led to our present."

The ladies gave her a standing ovation, that's how well her speech went. She was actually very touched and felt herself blushing as she stood there in front of them. They were so nice now that she was more than just Ben's newest wife.

Although that still infuriated her whenever she thought about it.

On the day of the election, she rode downtown with Ben. Her new afternoon outfit was lavender muslin decorated with colored silk embroidery. It had a high ruffled neck with the shirtwaist bloused in front.

Ben was as excited as a child. He might have been nervous, but he wouldn't admit it. He put her arm through his and kept her close. He wore the new high-buttoned box-cut suit with peg-top pants that she'd had the tailor make for him. His dark brown derby made him look especially handsome and modern, she thought.

People were as excited about the election as Ben. They seemed to be rejoicing in a new day of prosperity, so close to the turn of the century. Men thumped him on the back, people he barely knew shouted out to him.

"Ben!"

""Hey, Colonel!"

"There's my banker!"

Daisy and Ben walked in and out of the shops, smiling and greeting everyone they saw.

"Be sure you get over to the courthouse and vote!" Ben reminded his supporters. And it seemed like the whole town was full of his supporters. "Come on over after the election and we'll get the results together!"

She couldn't resist buying enough meat, produce and staples to feed the whole town. She reasoned that Mrs. Hamlin could now have her pick of anything she felt like making. As the workers piled crates of food into the carriage, Ben pulled out a roll of money and paid the grocer with a flourish.

Ben smiled down at her and patted her hand. "Anything else you want, darlin', you just let me know."

When they got home, Mrs. Hamlin and Alita started unloading the crates, and when the children came home they pitched in.

"This is way too much, Mrs. Wettermark," the cook said. "It's not going to fit in this kitchen or the pantry."

"I'm sorry, Mrs. Hamlin, I just got carried away! I have a feeling everything you cook will be eaten over the next couple of days."

Everyone who came to the house that evening agreed, the dining room table was a splendid affair. Mrs. Hamlin had cooked hams and roasts, platters of vegetables, pies and cakes. She had been baking while Ben and Daisy were away all day, and she didn't stop until she had turned out enough food to feed an army.

"Mizz Hamlin, you cooked like a house afire!" Alita exclaimed as she carried trays and bowls to the dining room.

Thank goodness she had, because everyone Ben had invited showed up. The men came, and they brought their wives and children. Nacogdoches folk filled their plates and spilled out onto the porch and into the yard, rejoicing that there could be a new mayor in town. Ben spoke to all the people who were there, thanking them for supporting him for what he hoped would be a new era of prosperity.

Minnie, Benny and Carl ran in and out of the house, surrounded by friends. Daisy couldn't stop smiling. It felt like all the joy in the world was concentrated right here in their house.

When the polling places closed and John Schmidt rode up to announce that Col. Benjamin S. Wettermark was the new mayor, there was such hooting and hollering that Daisy hoped all the neighbors were there at the party so they wouldn't be disturbed.

"Mr. Mayor, or is it Col. Mayor?" Daisy wondered.

Ben turned to her. "You may call me 'Mayor Ben Wettermark.' Or 'my sweetheart,' if you prefer. And I will call you 'Mrs. Mayor, my own true love.'" And he kissed on the cheek, right in front of the entire town.

Mayor Wettermark was as good as his word. He worked hard to bring prosperity to Nacogdoches. If a farmer needed a loan, he had only to come to Wettermark Bank. When the lumberyard needed new equipment, Wettermark Bank would stand behind it. There was not a new idea or venture that Ben didn't sound out. He was known throughout the region as the banker to see if you needed a large loan; cotton farmers came from miles around to get his backing.

Just after the election, he came home and announced that Nacogdoches had heard the death knell of First National Bank. Chartered in 1890, it closed in December, 1899.

"Now we're the only bank in town! Not that I'm gloating; First National just didn't have the backing of the town."

"Like you do, Mayor," Daisy smiled up at him.

"Like I do. I just want to spread the prosperity around."

The wave of prosperity at the turn of the century was there for everyone to see. There were construction projects all over Nacogdoches, and Mayor Wettermark was overseeing them. He was creating rental houses and supervising a new bridge. He invested in business partnerships, sat on company boards and was one of the sponsors of city improvements.

"From our bank, I can see the change spreading like wildfire through Nacogdoches." He stood on their porch, gesturing as if the entire town was just beyond the railing.

Daisy leaned against him. "A woman stopped me downtown yesterday and said you are one of Nacogdoches' top visionaries."

"One of?" Ben looked aggravated. "ONE of?"

Daisy knew that if some people called Ben visionary, it was architect Diedrich Rulfs who could bring those visions to life. In this kind of prosperity, visions were turning into brick and mortar.

Since moving from Germany in 1880, Rulfs built a reputation by creating some of the finest homes and businesses in Nacogdoches. The architect built Ben's new Wettermark Bank in 1896 but he had been working non-stop for Schmidt since then.

Ben seemed to admire and resent Schmidt at the same time.

"All around the bank, Schmidt has got Rulfs changing the face of downtown. First it was the big two-story red brick building on Main Street. You know Schmidt's calling the company 'the Hercules of Nacogdoches business homes.' Then he had Rulfs build the Nacogdoches Opera House and the hotel."

"That's good, isn't it?"

"Yes, it's good. It's what I want for Nacogdoches. Prosperity. New businesses. Schmidt asked me if I want to be a partner in Nacogdoches Wholesale Grocery Company."

"And you said?"

"Yes, of course."

But she knew something was bothering Ben. She didn't ask, she just stood with her head on his arm, letting him work it out his own way.

"Just between you and me, I can see Mr. Hercules needs my help. He's not the most important man in town."

She stood still, waiting.

"Daisy, this house is too small for us. We need something bigger and finer. I'm going to ask Diedrich Rulfs to create something for us that will be the talk of the town. Bigger and better than Schmidt's fancy house on North Street."

Daisy thought, "Ah, yes, this is it."

"I've got my eye on some land just north of town. There's a big plot, about 14 acres. We can have a grand driveway, so you can stand on the porch and wave at me all the way to the door!"

Daisy took a deep breath. She knew 1900 would not be only a year of change for Nacogdoches but for the Wettermark family.

"I hope Nacogdoches is ready for this," she said.

"*I hope I'm ready,*" she silently added to herself.

17. Unreachable

Erin and Jackson laughed when she told them she hadn't let William Calhoon in because she thought he might be a marauder or something.

"Calhoon is a great guy," Jackson said. "He is the BIN of all BINs. Born in Nacogdoches, raised here, a mainstay of the community."

Erin patted her mother on the hand. "But I am glad you listened to my advice. First time ever."

"I just didn't like the feeling of somebody walking in while I was alone in there. I felt kind of trapped," Peggy explained. "I need to get a decent door and lock in the front."

"And you don't have to worry about the back door because it's nailed shut," Jackson said.

"Right. Now, what about Mr. Calhoon?"

Jackson walked over to the bookcase and started looking at the book spines. "He and his wife have given to every important civic project in the city. They gave the land for the plaza downtown and they paid for most of the construction. That big sculpture downtown, William paid for that. Their name, or at least their handprints, are evident everywhere."

He pulled out a book about the city and flipped through it, showing Peggy page after page of projects with the name "Calhoon" on them.

"He said he had a big Victorian house too and he'd be glad to help with mine."

Erin whistled. "That's wonderful. He's about as experienced at restoration as anybody in town. And he's dedicated to preserving Nacogdoches history."

Peggy looked from Erin to Jackson. "Do you think we could go see his house? I'm at the sketching and designing stage."

Erin seemed surprised. "Do you sketch and design? I did not know that."

"I do. You don't know everything about me." She grinned at her daughter. "I was studying interior design when I met your father. I only made it one year so there are a lot of things I don't know. But I did all the decorating on every house we lived in."

Jackson had already found Calhoon's phone number on his phone. "Since he offered, I'll bet he won't mind us coming over." He dialed. "Mr. Calhoon? This is Jackson Vance. I understand you met my mother-in-law today. Yes, she is. Yes. Yes, she's a pistol. Say, I wonder if we could come see your house sometime? It's such a grand historic home."

"Thursday?" Jackson looked at Erin and Peggy, who nodded in unison. "How about 5:30? Then I can meet them there after work. Thanks."

When he hung up, Peggy shook her head. "I am not a pistol, Jackson. That makes me sound like Annie Oakley or something. But thank you for getting it set up."

"You're welcome, Ms. Oakley," he laughed. "He said you were measuring the floor. He must have been impressed. I think that seemed very... rough and ready to him."

Peggy thought he was amused rather than impressed, more likely. "Well, I am ready to get started on this renovation, that much is true. And I'm pretty sure it will get rough before it gets ready."

Erin was off work Thursday afternoon and went with her to measure the Wettermark floors. Peggy was really glad to have her daughter crawling around on the floor with her.

"This is 200 percent easier with someone else holding the measuring tape."

"You sound like a football coach," Erin teased. "But I know what you mean. This tape measure has a rebound feature, that's for sure. Every time you let go, it rewinds and snaps me in the hand."

Peggy sketched the main floor and added the measurements. There were some walls that she considered unnecessary, but she'd have to see if they were weight-bearing. And there were a few places there should be walls, like around a bathroom pipe that stood all by its lonesome.

"What do you think about this wall going away?"

Erin knocked her knuckles against the wall. "People do this all the time," she said. "But I have no idea what they're listening for."

"I don't think that'll tell us if the wall is weight-bearing, but I can kind of tell where the studs are." She knocked across the wall. "See right there, that sound? That's where the stud is. But that's mostly to hang pictures. That'll come later."

Impressed, Erin stood in the biggest room. "Without all that junk we shoveled out of here, the main floor looks enormous. This must have been the parlor. And then there's the ballroom on the second floor. Can you imagine having a ballroom in your house?"

"Nona said Wettermark was mayor when he started building this house. I guess he had a certain standard to maintain."

"Wettermark must have been setting the standard, not just trying to maintain it."

Peggy ran her hand over a wall and thought how she would like to tear off the wallboard. "I'd like to bring it back to that."

"Because you need a house with a ballroom?"

"Nacogdoches does. This town needs a big beautiful house with a ballroom and some history."

"What next?"

"Scott McCullough's coming over tomorrow to let me know if he'll take on the contractor job. I really liked him."

Erin nodded. "Everybody likes Scott. He's a honey."

"He's a honey, all right. But he's really busy."

Erin looked at her watch. "We've got to get going. Mr. Calhoon puts a high price on promptness, from what I hear."

Mr. Calhoon was waiting at the door for them. His house was truly the most beautiful in Nacogdoches. Like the Wettermark house, it was two and a half stories tall, but it was at the top of a hill and that made it look even taller. The Victorian style was unadulterated, and the paint was perfect. All the elaborate touches that marked the turn of the century were there—balustrades on top of the balcony, Tuscan pillars on the porch, circular windows on the gables.

Looking at the house almost took Peggy's breath away. Well, that and the steep hill and stairs to get to the front door. Erin, too, was puffing when they got up to the porch. Jackson was smart enough, or experienced enough, to park on the side street and come across to the house.

"Welcome!" Mr. Calhoon opened the door, which had a big glass panel in the middle and two long glass windows on either side. "Please, come on in."

The interior was just as spectacular as the outside. Everything that was missing from Peggy's house was there in gleaming color. The floors were burnished wood. The mantles matched the crown molding. The wide staircase was the same shining wood of the floors. The wallpaper was rich shades of green, red and gold...it looked like a movie set.

Peggy felt like crying. Her job was monumental. Too much. Unreachable.

Erin must have known how she felt because she took Peggy's arm. Mr.

Calhoon showed them around the rooms, talked about the restoration and the work they had done to take the house back to the way it had looked when Diedrich Rulfs designed it.

Jackson followed closely, commenting on the workmanship, "The kind you can hardly find nowadays."

The tall windows had sheer drapes that let in the light. Chandeliers caught that light and reflected it around the big and airy rooms. The Persian rugs were sized just right so that the floors glowed in each room.

Peggy wished she could have seen it before the restoration was done.

When they got to the dining room, Mr. Calhoon pulled out a chair for Peggy and she sat down. Even the dining room was perfect. She could imagine the people around the table in the 1900s. There was ornate china displayed in the antique hutch and she imagined how beautiful it would look at a Victorian dinner party.

Erin and Jackson sat down at the table with her.

"I have ice water." Mr. Calhoon said but it sounded like a question.

"I would love ice water," she answered.

Erin and Jackson agreed.

He brought the glasses in on a silver tray.

"You don't like the house?" Mr. Calhoon was watching her face.

"Oh, I love it. It's just so much, so far from where I'm starting."

"You've done the hardest part. You made the decision to grab hold of it. I can remember how we debated and decided and worried. And you see, it turned out all right."

"Mr. Calhoon..."

"Please, call me William."

"William. How long did it take you to do this?"

"A couple years. But I was working fulltime, and there weren't many people around here who knew what they were doing."

"And there are now?"

"Well, me, for one. And I already said I'd help some."

"Thank you. I'm going to take you up on that. My next step is to hire a contractor. I was thinking of Scott McCullough."

"Good choice, nice young man. He did some of the more recent work on our house when we had to open the walls to pull out some pipes and he repaired some woodwork."

"Maybe you could give me the names of more people who are skilled in restoration."

Jackson spoke up. "We have a list at the chamber; William, maybe you could come over and we could go over them and pick out the best."

"I could meet you there," Peggy said. Jackson nodded.

"Sure, that's a good idea. And Peggy, your husband, has he ever done anything like this?"

"Well, not like restoration. He was more of a 'rip it out and put in new' kind of guy."

There was a moment of silence.

Erin filled it in. "He, my dad, died last year. That's when Mom came here and moved in with us."

"He was sick a long time," Jackson added. "Peggy took care of him –for years."

"I'm sorry. I didn't know." William looked abashed, focusing on his hands clasped on the table.

"We're just so glad she's moved here with us," Erin jumped into the silence.

"Where did you move from, Peggy?"

"We lived a lot of places. All over Texas, Oklahoma, Kansas. And we were originally from Minnesota. For a little while, when we were first getting started, we moved every couple years."

"Not me. I've only ever been here in Nacogdoches."

"I can see why. It's a beautiful town, a historic town."

"It is. "

"And this house, it is truly what Nacogdoches is about."

He looked proud. "That's exactly the way I feel. I love every inch of this house. And we repaired, repainted and rebuilt every inch of it."

"You did a lot of it yourself?"

"My wife and I primed and patched walls, we pulled out rotted boards, we even ripped out kitchen cabinets ourselves. 'Course there were lots of things we supervised. We didn't lay the floors or put in tile. Or bathtubs. We hired that done. But we did pick out every faucet and sink in the house and we worked with every person who had a part in the restoration."

"Of course. That's what I'm planning to do. Let the people who do it for a living do it." She looked around. "Where is your wife? I haven't met her."

"No, she's gone. We lost Edna five years ago."

Now it was Peggy's turn to look abashed.

"Oh, William. I'm so sorry. I didn't know."

"She was sick a long time too. It just eats you up inside. There wasn't much I could do, just try to make everything as easy as I could."

Jackson said, "I'm sorry, Peggy, that we didn't tell you. For some stupid reason, I thought you knew."

"I feel terrible about it. There are so many things I don't know. "

"You couldn't know, if your own family didn't think to tell you!" William looked sternly at Jackson and Erin, then smiled. "Sometimes I still think she's going to call me from the kitchen and we'll have a cup of coffee together."

"I understand that." Peggy was nodding. Her mind still played tricks on her sometimes.

Erin cleared her throat. "We've taken up so much of your time, we'd better get on home."

Peggy stood which triggered William to stand, which made Jackson stand. Then Erin stood and they all looked at each other standing around the table and they laughed a little.

"Thank you, William, for letting us look at your wonderful house. I can only dream of creating something this true to the history of Nacogdoches," Peggy said and smiled at him.

"So, Jackson, Peggy, before you go," he said. "When do you want to meet over at the chamber? I'm sure I can help you find people who are good at working on houses that are over 100 years old."

"We appreciate that," Peggy said.

He put his hands in his pockets and looked at the table. "It's important to save the history, if we're going to brag about being the oldest town in Texas."

Jackson checked his calendar and Erin chimed in that she wanted to come too. They found a day and time they were all available.

"What a house," Peggy said when they got to the car.

"What a man," Erin said, with a significant look at Peggy.

"Please don't get any funny ideas. I'm not looking for a man."

"Of course not."

"But it would be nice to have help from someone with that kind of experience."

"Yes. I understand. Why don't we invite him to dinner?'

"Erin! Stop it!"

Erin smiled. "Okay, Mom. But everybody's got to eat dinner, right?"

"Let's just keep this uncomplicated, all right?"

"All right."

But Erin had a look on her face that told Peggy this discussion wasn't over.

18. Make That Bigger

1900

Ben was determined that their new house be the finest in town. He told Daisy repeatedly that he had an obligation to Nacogdoches, as its mayor, to show everyone what this town was all about.

"Our house has got to be bigger than anything else in town and we need more modern features and furbelows," he announced over dinner.

"Furbelows? Is that a Texas word?"

That made Minnie laugh. "It just means fancy stuff, like bows and lace and things like that. Except on a house."

Ben often convinced Daisy to ride slowly with him down Main Street and through downtown and note the design of the most impressive houses.

Ben and Daisy took so many trips looking at houses that Lizzie Schmidt stopped Daisy during the women's club meeting.

"Daisy, dear, I see you almost everyday. I just have to wonder why you and the mayor are driving by my house so often?"

"We're looking for ideas for ours," Daisy said honestly, because that was the truth. Almost the truth, because it was a lie of omission. She didn't tell Lizzie they were looking at her house because Ben wanted to be sure his house was better.

Lizzie smiled sweetly. "You just come on over anytime. We would love to show you around the house. And be sure you bring Ben's sweet children with you."

Daisy felt a rush of heat spread over her face. She had to struggle not to say she would never, ever set foot in the Schmidts' house with HER children. She drew her lips into a narrow line and didn't say a word. She never told Ben how Lizzie made her feel.

For now, Ben didn't need to go in the houses. He was content to drive around looking at the exteriors and meet with the architect.

Diedrich Rulfs was the nicest, most modest man Daisy had met. He had moved to Nacogdoches from Germany in 1880 and had, over the past 20 years, become the darling of the moneyed set. He was courtly and polite, creative and industrious. At 52 years old, he could be trusted to design and construct the finest buildings Nacogdoches' upper crust population could afford.

Rulfs did so much work for John Schmidt that he was practically on retainer to him. But he had built Ben's first house in 1890 and the new Wettermark Bank and now he would find the time to create the house of the mayor's dreams.

The architect listened to every idea Ben and Daisy had, writing in a little leather notebook. Sometimes he would look up and question what Ben meant.

"You know, Col. Wettermark, I'm afraid that will increase your cost considerably," he would say,

Ben assured him money was no object. It was the end product that would be the bottom line.

Rulfs would come back later with a sketch that showed he had captured what they wanted. Every time he brought a sketch, Ben added on another idea that would make the house more elaborate, harder to build, and, of course, more expensive.

But the architect did what Ben asked. He would reply, in his thick German accent, that he would certainly add that, delete that, make that bigger. Then he would give a slight bow to Daisy, nod to Ben, and leave to design some more.

There was one house that Daisy just loved. It was commissioned by E.A. Blount in 1894 for his daughter Laura when she married McNeil Chapman. It was not as large as some of the houses on North Street, but Daisy thought it was lovely.

"It's not big enough," Ben said. "But I do like that steep roof. And the widow's walk of decorative iron."

"Ben, we don't need a widow's walk," Daisy tried to reason with him. "We are nowhere near the sea, and I wouldn't walk up there looking for you if we were."

"We need a widow's walk like the Blount Chapman House," Ben told the architect.

"A faux-widow's walk," Rulfs corrected. "You couldn't really walk up there."

"Faux-widow's walk, then."

Rulfs nodded and added it to his sketch.

Ben liked the more impressive Queen Anne house that belonged to one of Laura's relatives, Judge Stephen Blount. It had wooden embellishments all over and a grouping of three decorative windows called a Palladian that had become Rulfs' signature design. Daisy was able to convince Ben they didn't need all the embellishments, but he wanted Palladian windows like the Judge had. So the Wettermark house got not one but two sets of Palladians in the gables over the large two-story bays on the north and south of the house.

On Virginia Avenue, Mr. Junius Harris' house used the crest of a hill as the base line for the house. There was a large dormer under the high-pitched roof. The house couldn't have been more different from the Wettermarks'. But Ben told Rulfs his house needed the large dormer like the one that projected from the Harris' front roof.

"You know, Col. Wettermark, I added this feature because Mr. Harris' house is built on a hill. The dormer has no relevance to your house; it doesn't fit with the fundamental design."

"That's true, Ben," Daisy said.

Ben turned to her then glared at Rulfs. "Our house needs it."

Rulfs looked at him a moment then added it to the list.

And then there was the matter of the location. Ben had purchased 14 acres north of downtown. It was a mile and a half away from the train station where Daisy first alighted in Nacogdoches. There was nothing anywhere near their new house.

Once the First Baptist Church was built on Main in 1886, the Baptists gravitated toward North Street. The Methodists built their houses in the Washington Square Area so they were near their church and near each other. Roland and Esme Jones built their house downtown because it was near the Christ Episcopal Church.

There were no churches or houses near their house. "I don't want to be all jammed up next to people," Ben explained. "You know the smart money is going to follow us to the north side when they see the house anyway. We can sell off parts of the land if we want."

One addition he wanted was a fireplace in the front entry hall. Rulfs had developed that for Will and Ann Perkins in 1890 to make the front entrance more like a welcoming room than an entry. They were very involved with the Baptist Church, and often after services or church meetings, the Baptists would gather at their house for ice cream. That fireplace in a wide, welcoming entry hall worked perfectly for them.

The Wettermark house got a fireplace in a wide entryway. Daisy understood the architectural features Ben wanted weren't based on need, but on making an impression.

But the ballroom was all Daisy's idea. She would have a beautiful ball honoring sweet 16-year-old Minnie, with a quartet playing and an excited throng of young people waltzing and doing the cakewalk. She could imagine the dazzling crystal chandelier and the high sheen of the dance floor. She'd help Minnie become a debutante. She could have a grand coming out party, and Minnie would be the most beautiful girl in town in her own ballroom. Just thinking of it made Daisy breathless.

Of course, Rulfs incorporated her vision into the house plans. He didn't even mention the extra cost when he saw how excited she was about it.

Ben was content with Rulfs' designs until the day he saw the inside of Schmidt's house. During a business meeting downtown, John Schmidt had said, "Say, Colonel, why don't you and Daisy come over Friday? You haven't even been in our house."

On Friday evening Daisy changed dresses three times as Alita helped her. Her hair wouldn't do anything and all of her hats looked ridiculous and frumpy. She was infuriated with herself for wearing all of her new dresses during the campaign. She didn't have anything that would put Lizzie Schmidt in her place and show her the mayor's wife was a very important person in Nacogdoches. And in the lives of Ben, Minnie, Benny and Carl.

She pulled off one dress. "No, that looks awful."

And another. "That makes me look fat."

And a third. "I've worn that twice already."

Alita picked up each dress as Daisy tossed it on the bed.

"That Mrs. Schmidt, she's not near as pretty as you. Or as nice. She looks like she's eatin' a lemon all the time."

Daisy tried not to laugh. "Alita! That's terrible!"

"And true." Alita made a sour face, and then they both laughed until Ben hollered, "What's so funny?"

"You're gonna be fine, Mrs. Wettermark. Just let her show you her house and you know yours is going to be much, much finer. And here, try this purple faille. You're especially beautiful in that."

Ben rang the bell and Daisy smoothed the skirt of the purple dress. When John Schmidt saw her, he exclaimed, "Why Mrs. Wettermark, you are a thing of beauty! Come into this house. And you too, Colonel!"

As Mr. Schmidt took her hand, she said, "Please, call me Daisy."

"Only if you'll call me John."

"You can still call me colonel, you old scoundrel!" Ben chimed in.

Lizzie, the consummate hostess, escorted them through the house. It was the largest house in Nacogdoches with 13 rooms. Unusual in East Texas, it had a basement for John's imported wines. It felt bigger still because the ceilings were 14 feet tall.

Rulfs had often mentioned how important it was to use local materials, but he imported dark woods from Germany to trim the local curly pine wainscoting and doorframes. Lizzie told them, casually, that all the mantles came from Europe.

"And look at the clever pocket doors he had made for us." She demonstrated by pushing a door back into the wall. " They give us such an open feeling and more flexibility for entertaining."

"You'll want that, Daisy, " Ben said. "For all of our entertaining."

Daisy mentally added pocket doors to her list.

Lizzie cocked her head as she just suddenly realized her home was being mined for ideas.

Then John showed them the first indoor plumbing in Nacogdoches. Rulfs had created a rainwater collection system in the attic that supplied the house with water. The drinking water, which Lizzie demonstrated by pouring them each a glassful, was from a well built into back porch.

And as if that was not enough, John flicked on the chandeliers and wall sconces throughout the house.

Ben nodded gravely. " I see you've got the acetylene power system that Rulfs used in the Bullen Hotel that he built for you downtown."

He was so calm and off-handed, Lizzie probably had no idea he was adding the power system to his list.

Rulfs' contracting firm was working on three projects for Mayor Wettermark: the bridge, rental houses and his house. Ben didn't wait till the house was finished to throw a party for the carpenters, Rulfs and his family.

And what a party it was. The mayor had Rulfs invite all of his workers for a spread such had never been seen in Nacogdoches.

According to the June 22, 1900 issue of the *Daily Sentinel*:

> Colonel Wettermark had a party set up near the ice factory at Joe's Place: "A 20' table held roast beef, switzer cheese, salads, pickles, sliced tomatoes, rye bread, etc. while two kegs of beer, fresh and cold were on tap.

> The Colonel told the men to "eat as hard as you work and drink as heartily as you receive your pay!"

> It is needless to say that the boys obeyed to the

> letter Col. Wettermark's injunction and did ample jus-
> tice to the banquet. It was an enjoyable occasion and
> the invited guest seemed to relish the bill of fare
> as much as the crowd for whom special benefit the
> spread was given.

Daisy and the children didn't eat with the jostling crew of construction workers, but they did get to see them. Ben introduced his family to the workers and the owners of Nacogdoches businesses who were his invited guests. But once the construction workers got boisterous from all the beer, Daisy and the children were bundled onto a wagon and sent home.

They laughed and chattered all the way to the house, proud of the giddy happiness Ben had brought to all those people.

A joyous feeling of prosperity was everywhere in Nacogdoches and many people attributed much of it to their hardworking, handsome mayor Col. B.S. Wettermark. He was everywhere, on construction sites, making loans to cotton farmers, watching Nacogdoches-grown produce loaded onto trains to go all over east Texas. There was no business deal made in 1900 that Ben didn't have some sort of a hand in.

When Ben and Daisy rode down the streets, people waved and called out. Daisy acknowledged everyone with a wave and smile. Nacogdoches was the best place on earth to be.

But the downside of prosperity was that everyone wanted to get in on it.

Ben was madder than hops. A new national bank had come into town in 1901. Commercial Bank was going to try to move into the void left when the First National Bank closed in '99.

Ben took this very personally. The Wettermark Bank had been able to handle all the financial needs of the town but now there was this new usurper and he didn't like it one bit. The national banks hadn't bothered Ben too much before because they had to have a minimum capital stock requirement of $50,000 to open. But in 1900 Congress reduced the minimum capital stock requirement from $50,000 to $25,000. Within two years hundreds of new banks entered at the minimum size.

And Ben was infuriated by national bank notes. National banks, chartered and regulated by the federal government, could deposit bonds in the US Treasury. The banks then could issue banknotes worth up to 90 percent of the value of the bonds. The federal government would back the value of the notes—the issuance of which created a demand for the government bonds needed to back them.

Individual banks like the Wettermark couldn't create their own bank notes. Ben wanted to tell every person in Nacogdoches that a national bank couldn't really take care of them. But some people were disloyal enough to move their accounts to Commercial.

Ben walked out into the bank lobby when Roland Jones came into Wettermark. He and Roland exchanged the Mason handshake.

"Mr. Jones! How are you doing today?"

"I'm fine, Mayor, just fine. Working on the building fund for the new building for Christ Episcopal."

"I'll be glad to help you with that. Come on into my office."

"I'm sorry, Ben, I really am, but we're going to have to open the account over to Commercial Bank."

"Roland! We can do better by you than an out-of-town bank."

"That's what I told everybody but we're working the contract to pay for the new building through E.A. Blount at Commercial. You know he's the new bank manager. I'm going to take the church's money over there as a show of good faith."

Ben gritted his teeth. So Commercial Bank had the loan for the new Episcopal building. Roland's wife, Esme Bullen Jones, probably got everybody involved in this project. He knew there were a lot of important people on the building committee. All of them his friends.

Ben went back to his office. Was he too late to talk to the others? He figured Oscar Matthews, Schmidt's partner in M & S, was on the committee. As Roland closed the church's bank account, Ben sat at his desk, studiously carving lines on a piece of paper with his pen, while Roland betrayed him.

When Ben stomped down the street to talk to Matthews, he found out the Episcopal board of directors had already signed a contract with Commercial Bank. He convinced Matthews to show him the contract, and he laughed out loud. Commercial had required each member of the board to sign individually for any liabilities.

"Poorly written, Oscar," said Ben. "I hate to see what you've gotten into. I'm afraid your board is going to wish they had come to us."

He was still laughing after he left Oscar's office. He was laughing when he got back to his bank. Then he sat down at his desk and realized he didn't feel like laughing anymore.

19. HISTORIC TREASURE HUNT

William Calhoon was already in the chamber of commerce conference room when Peggy and Erin got there. He was looking at the ink drawings of historic buildings Jackson had found in storage and put on the walls. They showed 15 of Nacogdoches' finest old houses. Some no longer existed. Some had captions such as, "Now a funeral home," and "Now a law firm."

"You're here already!" Peggy was a little dismayed. She didn't like keeping anyone waiting.

"I can't help it. On time is late to me. " William turned back to the frames. "These drawings really showcase what we've lost."

"Isn't that the truth?" Erin agreed.

"Coffee, anyone?" Jackson brought the coffee pot from the office kitchen and poured a round for everyone.

Peggy smiled at William. "Thank you so much for coming."

"Wouldn't have missed it. I thought we should start with what kind of work you need done."

"The first step...Jackson and Erin spent two weekends helping me clean out the junk on the floors."

"Including the world's nastiest mattress." Erin crinkled her nose at the memory.

"The day you came over I was working on this." Peggy handed him the drawings with the measurements. "We finished it all up. I'm working with the reference librarian to find all the information I can about what the house looked like."

"You know about Wettermark, then?"

"I do. And I guess that might turn off some people. But it makes Nacogdoches more interesting to me."

"I just wonder...if you don't mind, what are you planning to do with the house when you finish it?"

"The minute I saw the house I felt I needed to save it. It had the look of an old dog that was right on the edge of being put away. If somebody didn't do something, it was gone. And apparently that somebody was me."

"It's a mighty big house to live in all alone. And I know a lot about that," William said.

"Well, I'll have one room for my spoon collection. And one for my photo albums. And one for my—miniature buffaloes. And every time I get a room messy, I'll just move out to another room," she laughed. "I'll never have to throw away newspapers, I'll just have an entire room full of them!"

Then she got serious. "At first I didn't think about how big it was. I just had to get it done. Lately I've been wondering if I had a moment of temporary insanity! I've been asking myself what I'm going to do with it."

"You could open a shelter for homeless historical reinactors." This from Jackson.

"Or retired chamber of commerce execs?" Erin added.

"Good ideas." She laughed with them.

William smiled too but he wasn't laughing. "I think you could get the board of the historical society involved. They might even be able to help. You bought the house yourself?"

"Free and clear. I got a loan and I had some money from the sale of my condo."

"And so far, you're doing the work yourself?"

"I'm meeting Scott McCullough there today. He can tell me what he can do and what I'll need to hire in."

"Peggy, I like your style. You've got gumption in a time when gumption is in short supply."

"Well, thank you."

"I really enjoyed all that demolishing and scraping and painting we did on our house. It's gratifying—when you renovate a house, you get to see your progress every day. You can see you're making a difference."

Erin looked at her hands. "Just shoveling out trash made a difference to me. I broke every one of my nails."

William set his jaw and looked at Peggy. "Well, you can call on me to swing a sledge hammer if you want to tear anything down."

"That's so nice of you! I will."

William looked shyly at her. "I don't work everyday at the electric company but I still own it. What do you say I get those workmen of mine over to your house to check it out for you. They can tell you what you need to do."

"I'd appreciate that. Thank you."

William was still looking at her. "You're meeting Scott today?"

"After lunch. At the house."

"After you talk to him, have him let me know if I can get my crew chief to meet with him and have a look around."

"All right, William. Thank you."

She put out her hand and shook his. "I don't want you to feel like you have to do this."

He looked her in the eye. "We got to save these great old Nacogdoches houses, don't we?"

"Yes, we do."

"Yes we do," said Erin, who seemed to want to get the last word.

Peggy and Scott McCullough stood in the middle of the first floor.

She handed him her drawing with all the measurements. "I know it's going to be a lot of work, but I hope you'll be the contractor."

"I thought you'd never ask!" Scott always sounded like he was about to laugh out loud. It made Peggy smile just to talk to him.

"Mr. Calhoon is sending his crew over to look at the electric. He said call him and he'll arrange for you to meet with his men."

Scott turned in a 360 circle. "What are we going to do here?"

"I don't have the 1900 blueprints but I have some information about the house. And here's a copy of a photo of the exterior. Let's take the outside back to the original, if we can. But I don't really want to go completely authentic inside. There were 12 rooms and lots of them were little."

Scott was studying her drawing. "Like what might you do differently?"

"Well, not all open concept, but I want to figure out if there are some interior walls we can do without. I think some of these walls were added after the original build."

Scott paced around the room, tapping on walls, looking up at the ceiling.

Like Erin, she wasn't sure what all that tapping would reveal. "I've read that there was an extra big entry hall here with a fireplace, and I'd like to see if we can find where that was."

He walked to the middle of the room and pointed up. "There was a wall here and it looks like there were two chimneys in the middle of the house. I hate that they're gone."

"Gone? Could they be hiding in a wall?"

He looked around and grinned. "A historic treasure hunt, huh? X marks the hidden fireplace? We'll go up on the roof and figure out where they started and maybe we can see where they went."

"How soon can you get started?"

"We'll be here Tuesday to make sure the walls are sound. If we don't have to replace the exterior walls yet, we'll leave them till later. We're going to do the roof right away to make sure the work we do stays dry. You're going to come work with us, right?"

Peggy nodded. "Of course."

"While we're doing the roof, you check the windows to see what you've got to replace. You want storm windows? You want to put in bigger windows?"

"I want the antique ripply glass."

"Okay, make a list of all the windows that still have, as you say, ripply glass and how many more you need. Measure each window. There are a couple of places in Houston we can get antique glass. Shoot, you might decide you want to enlarge the windows."

She pulled out her notepad and started writing as fast as she could.

"Then I'll rent a dumpster and we'll go on to some serious demolition. We'll very carefully demolish anything that needs to go away. I'll check to make sure there's no lead-based paint, and if there is, we'll have to get a remediation expert in here to remove it."

"But the house was built so long ago! Surely there wasn't lead in paint in 1900."

"There was lead in paint back in colonial days," Scott looked serious. "In 1904 Sherwin-Williams was talking about the dangers of paint that contained lead."

"All right, remediation it is."

"If it needs it. Maybe it won't.

"But it probably will."

"Yeah, it probably will." Scott sighed. "Then we'll move walls and make new walls, and maybe enlarge the windows. We'll add beams, punch in new doors. While we've got walls and the ceiling open, we'll install ductwork for central heating and air conditioning. You do want those, I assume?"

"You assume correctly. But I want it to stay as authentic as possible."

"Then we'll see about the electric. Maybe Calhoon's crew will give us the best bid."

"We're on our way!" Peggy was practically dancing.

At 9 a.m. the next Tuesday, Peggy was waiting with a big thermos of coffee, styro cups and a box of donuts. That was her go-to offering for morning work calls. Scott and his workmen pulled in right after her. There were four men with him and they all seemed to know what to do. Scott had building permits in his hand.

The men were all over the house, testing walls, pulling off exterior and interior boards, looking at, as Peggy told Erin on her cell phone, "joints and joists and *je ne sais quoi.*"

And Erin replied, "Mother! Since when do you speak French?"

Peggy measured and counted windows, checked window frames and kept a list in her little notebook. She could see ladders leaned against the house as the men climbed to the roof. She could hear the thump of their boots and she worried that the roof might crumble and one of the men would come crashing through the ceiling.

A technician came and analyzed boards all around the house, checking for lead. He had a handheld XRF analyzer that he said would provide fast, easy, accurate and non-destructive alloy identification and elemental analysis from Mg to U.

"Mg to U?" Peggy thought, but thanked him for coming so quickly. Scott came in while the technician was working and waited quietly beside Peggy. They held their breath while the man looked at the results.

"No lead," he said.

Peggy and Scott whooped with joy.

"Thank you, thank you so much," she said and thrust a donut and a cup of coffee into the technician's hands.

"That is great, great news." Scott patted the man on the back, splashing coffee out of the cup and onto the bare wood floor.

"We dodged a bullet," Peggy exulted.

Scott laughed. "A big lead bullet." Peggy poured him some coffee and he told her the crew was going to start on the roof. "I don't think you'll want to be inside here while we're working up there."

"I guess not. Oh, I'm just so happy we're getting started. This is going to be a great, great house. No lead!" Peggy felt like she was grinning ear to ear. "That's a good sign. I just know it's going to be smooth sailing from here on out!"

Scott was grinning too but shook his head. "Don't count your chickens before they hatch, Miss Peggy. We've got a long, long way to go..."

Peggy added, "I know, I know, and we don't know which way this egg will roll."

One look at her face and Scott knew she might be joking around, but the job ahead of them looked mighty big. The future held uncertain expense, intense labor, more challenges than she could imagine.

"Thank you for picking me to help you, Miss Peggy. I'm honored to work with you on this historic house."

She seemed to shake off the worry and she smiled slowly. "I am honored too, Scott. This house kind of picked us both and we've got to do it justice."

"Yes, ma'am. We've got to do that."

They clinked their Styrofoam cups together in a toast that the future of the Wetttermark house might be better than its past.

20. DAISY'S WORK

1900

Had anyone asked Daisy for advice about how to live through building a new home, she would have told them vehemently, "DO NOT DO IT."

It was the most exasperating, aggravating experience of her life.

"And that's saying something because I once rode the railroad known as Hell Either Way Taken!" she joked with Alita.

The work was delayed. The materials were wrong. The porch didn't match the drawing, the glass for the windows was two weeks late.

And making it happen, all of it, was Daisy's job.

Ben was far too busy at the bank and serving as mayor. He had to go to Masons and Rifles and a half dozen other meetings. He was now a principal in the Nacogdoches Compress & Warehouse and Nacogdoches Ice and Cold Storage Company, and he was buying and selling land throughout East Texas.

His most important venture was the Nacogdoches Grocery Company with his partners John Schmidt, E. A. Blount, B. F. Hardeman, Oscar Mathews, and S.T. King. They built a large two-story brick building on the Houston, East and West Texas, the same Hell Either Way Taken railroad that Daisy had come in on. The company was a wholesale supplier to grocery and general merchandise stores. Ben and his partners expanded its trade territory to 11 counties in East Texas, with most merchandise being shipped by railway.

Whenever Daisy told Ben about the work on the house, he would take her hand. "I'm sorry, Daisy, but I can't take time out of every day to look at the house. It is crucial, with the new national bank in town, that I let everyone know Wettermark Bank is the bank for Nacogdoches."

So Daisy went to the work site every day. She had learned to harness the horse and drive the buggy. She would drop the children at school and drive a mile and a half to the house. It was not very ladylike but it had to be done.

Mr. Rulfs was unerringly polite and calm.

"Mrs. Wettermark," he would say. "Welcome to your home! Let me show you our progress."

If there was a change to be made, Daisy and Mr. Rulfs worked smoothly together. When Daisy made a suggestion that was not in the original sketches, he would sometimes say, "I'm so sorry, Mrs. Wettermark, but that will add some cost for you."

One day Rulfs said, "I know your husband is adamant about this, but are we sure that is necessary for this house? It's already a beautiful home without adding that."

"I'm afraid we have to have it," Daisy said, but she was glad to see the architect understood Ben needed for this to be the most outstanding house in town.

Rulfs unerringly supported her and he never said, "No, we cannot possibly do that."

But Mr. Rulfs wasn't there everyday. His foreman was not nearly as pleasant. He was reluctant to show her around because he knew she could spot the mistakes he made.

"Wasn't this supposed to be curly pine?" she would ask politely, and he would consult the plans then stomp out of the room.

"Didn't we agree on Palladian windows here?" Daisy would ask, and he would yell at the workmen who were putting in the wrong windows. Sometimes her corrections meant they had to tear down and rebuild an entire wall.

With the noise and the sawdust, Daisy had a headache almost every day. When she picked up the children at school and drove them home, she would collapse on a settee.

"Alita, thank goodness for you and Mrs. Hamlin. How do women manage who don't have help?"

"Well, they probably don't go to a construction site every day and argue with the workmen," Alita answered as she brought her a glass of cool water.

It took almost a year for the house to be finished. But when it was, it was as spectacular as Ben had envisioned it, and as fulfilling as Daisy had hoped. There were 12 rooms for her to fill with her own style of fine furniture.

What the Wettermarks spent was far beyond what they had imagined. What the Wettermarks received was a house that combined the best architectural ideas from Rulfs' designs all around Nacogdoches.

It truly was the mansion of Mayor Col. B.S. Wettermark's dreams. And of course, the huge expense would have given most people nightmares.

Daisy felt she could finally relax. Each day deliverymen brought things from their old house to their new house. It seemed to take forever to move and their furnishings looked tiny and shabby when they finally moved into the big new house.

After supper she finally had a moment with Ben. The children were in bed, Alita and Mrs. Hamlin had gone. There were no deliverymen carrying their old furniture. Finally, alone with her husband.

Ben was assessing the front rooms with an eye toward inviting his partners over. The movers had put most of the decent furniture into the parlor so that's what people would see first.

He said, "All right, we have enough chairs to accommodate a group, but it just looks bad. The furniture doesn't fit the house. Why don't you go on down to New Orleans and find things you really like? Those companies'll haul it back up here for us."

"Ben, I have to slow down."

"I don't know if I've told you often enough, you did an incredible job with the house. It's a tribute to your dedication, whipping those workmen into shape. Now you just need to pick out furniture. You can go down to New Orleans..."

"Ben, we are going to have a baby."

He looked shocked. Then he put his arms around her and held her close.

"Daisy, my own little Daisy. A baby. What wonderful news."

Daisy wrote her mother and father that night and invited them to come to Nacogdoches. Her family had not visited once in the eight years they'd been married. Her parents thought, as many New Yorkers do, that there was no civilization beyond the borders of Manhattan.

The baby, however, was a bona fide reason to take that long train ride to the hinterlands.

Ben and Daisy didn't tell anyone about the baby except Alita and Mrs. Hamlin. Not even the children, who didn't need to think about things like that. When people asked, Daisy just said the construction of the house had worn her out and she wanted a little time to herself.

Her mother wrote back that they would come as soon as humanly possible. Daisy should wait to get the crib until her mother came and they could decorate the nursery together.

By then, Daisy hoped, she wouldn't feel so tired and washed out.

Mrs. Hamlin cooked her special treats and Alita made sure she put her feet up and rested. Ben treated her as if she were fine china.

Ah, she could get used to this.

When the doorbell rang, Daisy was sitting at the roll-top desk writing a list of names. She couldn't use Benjamin, since there was already Benny, who was Benjamin Wettermark, Jr. Maybe the middle name could be Sutton, her maiden name? That would be a nice traditional name for a girl or a boy, she thought.

The mailman handed her the letter. "From New York!" he said.

Her father had written:

> *Dearest Daisy. I regret to tell you we cannot come to see you at this time. Your mother has fallen ill with the influenza that is sweeping the city. The doctor does not have much hope for her; so many people have fallen all around us.*

By the time Daisy received the letter, her mother had passed away. Her father's next letter was too late for Daisy to attend the funeral, even if she could have made the train trip in her condition. She cried until she couldn't cry anymore, feeling alone and motherless in this remote town far from her childhood home.

The children were upset to see Daisy cry. Carl, now 14 years old, brought her flowers from the field by school. "I know how it feels to lose your mama," he said, and gave her an awkward little hug. "What I mean is I'm glad we got you."

When the word got out about Daisy's mother, the women started coming by, bringing cobblers, cakes and flowers. The members of Cum Concilio had an arrangement delivered to her with a nice letter about how they knew how heartbroken she was and they were sorry her mother had never come to Nacogdoches.

Matty Goodson made toffee for her and brought her a new book. She stayed for tea and they ate cherry cobbler that had been dropped off by one of the clubwomen that morning.

"Are you all right, sweet child? You worked too hard, bringing in this new house."

"I am worn out, Matty, I really am. I was looking forward to my mother coming and I...I had just told her I'm having a baby."

"Oh, Daisy!" Matty hopped up and hugged her. "A baby! How wonderful, dear child. But to lose your mother at the same time you get this good news, that is heartbreaking."

"I haven't told anyone but Ben. I'm just not ready for everyone to know."

"No, I understand. I will not say a word until you say so. But you have got to rest and get past this sorrow. How can I help? I can get the children ready for school—or organize a group so we can do that every day for you. You have help and a good cook, so that much is taken care of. Do you want furniture arranged? Books in the bookcases?"

"Maybe you could just come over every once and call me 'dear child' and drink tea with me?"

Matty smiled. "If that would make you feel better, I will do that every day."

Matty was true to her word. She came almost every day. She put the books on the shelves in the front parlor, arranged alphabetically because she said that just made her feel good. She worked with Mrs. Hamlin to plan the meals and helped Alita with the children's activities.

She and Daisy ate cakes and cobblers that the other women brought over and she arranged flowers into vases. She told Daisy they could make a list of all the furniture pieces for the new house. Daisy knew Matty was trying to distract her. It would a long time until she went shopping in New Orleans. But making lists kept her from dwelling on the loss of her mother.

"Now you know you don't need this all at once, don't you?"

"I do. And I'm not even considering it until the baby comes. But I have to have a crib."

"Don't you worry about that. I have cribs stuck in the attic that my babies outgrew long ago."

As Daisy talked about the furniture, Matty walked through the big empty house with her.

There were a few rooms that didn't need much. The ballroom, for example. Chairs, but not much more. Maybe a few little tables.

The kitchen was a cook's dream, thanks to Mr. Rulfs. Mrs. Hamlin was happy with the new stove and the icebox that Rulfs had ordered and installed. The little kitchen table from the old house was fine for now.

The children all had beds and she had bought them dressers when she first moved in. She would love to redo the master bedroom, and she was sure the "master" would say yes to that.

But it was the rooms on the main floor that needed to be richly appointed to look like the home of the mayor. The most successful banker in town needed two or three deep buttoned, chesterfield couches, made from leather, with arms and back of the same height. And beautiful armchairs to match. They owned one really nice rug, the deep Brussels carpet that Daisy had noticed on her first night in Nacogdoches. They needed carpet that nice for each room, at least on the main floor.

She wanted a big dining room table and matching chairs. And a credenza. And maybe a hutch. She really needed something new and attractive. It wouldn't do to have parties with the old furniture, even though it had been good enough in the old house.

Matty wrote down everything Daisy said, agreeing with each new item. Every day she would say, "I'd better run home now, Daisy dear, and take care of my own family. But I'll see you tomorrow!"

Daisy sighed. It was nice to have a friend who knew about her secret and wanted to help her. Someone warm and, yes, motherly, who just wanted to make her feel better.

Ben was late for dinner, and she and the children sat and waited for him, not eating their roasted chicken and mashed potatoes until he got home. Mrs. Hamlin kept everything warming in the kitchen and brought it out when he walked in, then hurried out the door to her own home.

"I'm sorry to hold you up, but Schmidt had to give me an update on our wholesale grocery business. If the train line closes down, we're in big trouble. I don't think we can find enough buggies and carts to deliver all over east Texas."

"That's not likely to happen, is it?"

"We're hoping not."

"Father, I'm giving the oration for the class assembly tomorrow." Carl stood up and started, 'Four score and seven years ago...'

Ben said, "Carl! Everybody knows you didn't write that!"

Carl laughed and pulled a folded paper from his pocket. "Don't worry, Father, I've made up an even better speech!" And then he read the entire thing to them.

They all agreed Carl had written a fine speech, worthy of going down in history like the Gettysburg Address.

Benny talked about how hard the arithmetic exam had been, then said he had made the only A in the class.

Minnie, always solicitous of her father, said, "Please eat, Father. We can all talk later."

Ben nodded and dove into the roasted chicken as if he hadn't eaten all day.

That night in bed, Daisy woke in a sweat. She had stabbing pains in her stomach and felt like throwing up. There was no way to get comfortable. She doubled over with pain.

She had never felt so miserable. Ben brought her cold cloths and rubbed her back. Finally, he was so worried that he woke up Minnie to stay with her and he rode off to get the doctor.

The doctor was too late. Their own beloved baby did not live to be born.

21. Paving the Way

The roof was done and the house felt more secure already. Scott had re-moved a modern wall between the parlor and the living room, which made the main floor feel large and open. He had pulled off some of the boards on the main floor to see if the wooden studs were good enough to keep. Some had been ruined by the roof leaks and his crew was removing the bad boards and replacing them with new ones.

Peggy proved she was an able worker by scraping off five layers of wallpaper in the main floor. This was a truly miserable job and she went home every eve-ning with her shoulders aching and her arms sore. She sprayed steaming water on each section, then scraped that off, then went back and did it again with each layer. She could see the shiplap emerging from under the old layers. She had wallpaper shards sticking out of her curly grey hair at the end of each day.

Scott said he would have one of his workers do the parts she couldn't reach and at first she was reluctant.

"I can stand on a ladder as well as anyone," she said, but by the third day she was willing to let some tall, experienced wallpaper-scraper do the walls above her head. She had barely gotten 10 feet around the wall and there were three other walls she hadn't even touched. She would continue to scrape as high as she could reach, but she had to let the rest of it go.

"Let's talk about bathrooms," Scott said.

There were the remains of a big bathroom on the main floor and one small powder room. Really, there was so little left that Peggy wondered if Scott was more of an archeologist than a contractor.

Using the sketch she had drawn, Scott had created a very neat drawing with a computer that plotted everything.

"Not that your pencil drawing wasn't a good start!" he assured her.

He pointed out the large bathroom on the drawing and walked her to the spot where it should be. "We need a four-piece here. That's a tub, sink, toilet and counter. The smaller bathroom just needs the toilet and sink. Want to pick that out?"

"Of course! That'll be our first buy. I think all the bathrooms should be similar. Same basics and we can add color and accessories to give them personality."

"You said you want a master bedroom on the first floor. Do you want a tub and a shower?"

"Let me think about it. I know I want two big bathrooms on the second floor."

She had been envisioning the design of the house since the first day she saw it. Now she went to the library to look at books on specific renovation style.

Nona was right where she should be, lighted by the glow of her computer at the reference desk. She looked so happy to see Peggy that it made her feel like a valued library customer—or a friend.

"Miss Peggy! How are you? How's that renovation coming?"

"Oh, Nona, it's the hardest work I've ever done and the best. Thank you again for inviting me to see Zion Hill. It was just the inspiration I needed."

"Maybe sometime we'll come see your house and get inspired by what you're doing."

"Come anytime. Wear old clothes. Prepare to work."

Nona nodded. "We could do that, you know. My sorority has work days where we all come out and help."

"You're a sorority girl?"

"A service sorority, Tau Alpha Sigma. We pick out projects like literacy. But maybe we could spend one day rolling paint on walls or something."

"That would be wonderful. The house is so big. Well, not as big as Zion Hill, but big for me." Peggy instantly started imagining the work group, how she would pick a project they could do in one day, if donuts would be enough or if she should serve lunch.

Nona showed her the shelves of books on renovation of historic homes. Peggy studied and took notes on the bathrooms until she felt confident she could make some choices. Obviously, the Wettermark house should have bathrooms for people who needed tubs and showers.

Peggy went alone to a home appliance store and spent about an hour making her choices. She picked footed tubs and three sets of cabinets that would hold double sinks for the bigger bathrooms. She chose four new taller toilets that were designed to conserve water. The fixtures were all from a collection that was called "historic" and had a nice solid feel.

She paid extra to have them delivered to the house and told the clerk that Scott would call to arrange the date. She told Scott about that when he called to let her know Mr. Callahan's electricians were in the house inspecting the wiring.

She and Scott had talked about repaving the driveway. He said it wasn't really something he and his crew usually did, but he could recommend a company at the end of the build.

That was why she was so pleased when a paving contractor dropped by. Scott and the crew had left for lunch and she was just about to go to Erin's to heat up some leftovers.

The man was dressed in a three-piece suit and a tie, unusual in hot, humid East Texas. He looked like a short version of a male model, handsome with dark eyes and hair.

"Ma'am, I noticed you're working on this wonderful historic house and I was hoping we might help you out."

"I'd welcome help. What do you mean?"

"I have a paving company and I would like to pave that driveway for you. We've done quite a few in this area."

"You have?"

"Two on Virginia Avenue, and we just finished one downtown. Historic homes, just like this. We've learned to overcome the specific problems in these older driveways." He gave her his card:

East Texas Paving Excellence
13 years paving the way

She studied the card. "We were thinking of waiting until we've done all the rest..."

"Pave it now and you'll cut down on the dust and make it easier for your workers. *And* I can give you a discount because it's a historic property."

Peggy and the paving contractor haggled a little, then agreed on a price that seemed fair.

"We'll start right away," he said. "I'm going to have the materials delivered day after tomorrow, if that's all right with you."

"I'll let Scott McCullough know to expect you."

"I've heard a lot about Scott. You got yourself a good contractor there. It'll be nice to work on a project with him." He went to his car and came back with a clipboard.

"Just put your information here," he pointed to the multipage contract, "and here." Peggy signed.

"And now that you got my price down so low, your deposit is only...$5,000. And I'll go order the materials today."

"You need that now?"

"To cover the materials."

"Oh, okay, I've got to—I'm sure you take checks?"

"Of course. I trust you."

She wrote a check for $5,000 and waved as he drove away. She could hardly wait to tell Scott what she'd done. She hopped into her car and went home for lunch.

Scott and his crew were already working when she got back. When she told him about the paving contractor, he looked skeptical. "I haven't ever heard of East Texas Paving Excellence."

He looked hard at the card, which Peggy now realized had a phone number with an out-of-town area code and no address.

She tapped the card. "Well, Scott, he's heard of you, and he's looking forward to working with you."

Scott kind of harrumphed.

Peggy didn't like his attitude at all. "I know you wanted to wait till the end, but this is going to make it easier for you to get your work done."

"I'll just check around to see who's worked with them. Virginia Avenue and downtown, he said? He didn't say whose houses they did?"

"No, but I'm sure it'll be easy to figure out which ones they were." Peggy wished Scott had met the man; he wouldn't have felt so doubtful if he'd shaken hands with him.

On the day the materials were supposed to arrive, Peggy waited all day at the house. At 6 p.m., Scott came and stood beside her, knocking his dusty work gloves on his jeans.

Peggy didn't look up at him.

"I'm sure the materials will be here tomorrow."

Scott shook his head. "I called everybody in town who sells paving materials and nobody has heard of East Texas Paving Excellence. I checked Lufkin and Tyler; nobody there either."

The next day she dialed the number on the card over and over and never got an answer. And no materials arrived.

Peggy went to her bank. The check had already cleared. When she told the teller what had happened, she walked Peggy over to a bank officer. Reluctantly, she told him about the paving contractor. The officer put a fraud alert on her account but said it was too late to do anything about the check. He called the police and a young woman from the fraud unit came to the bank and sat down with her.

"I'm afraid this is a standard scam," the policewoman said. "We had two more in town last month."

"I feel so stupid." Tears stung Peggy's eyes.

"If these guys weren't good, nobody would give them money. They've got ways of sounding so reliable that people fall for this all the time. We can let people know what happened and that might stop them from trying this again here in Nacogdoches."

Peggy blinked and swallowed, trying not to cry. "I hate to be a cautionary tale."

The policewoman looked almost as sad as Peggy felt. "I hate that this happened to you. It's just not right."

"It serves me right for being so gullible."

"Being kind and trusting doesn't mean you should get scammed. That's on him, not you."

Peggy thought sadly that this was probably how people felt when Col. Wettermark made off with their money. It was terrible to lose the money, that was true. But Peggy felt it was also bad to be betrayed and to be left feeling like a fool for trusting. The newspaper articles Nona had given her showed the Wettermark bank scandal devastated the whole town, from working people who had small accounts of their hard-earned money to organizations like Nacogdoches Ice and Cold Storage that had elected Col. Wettermark treasurer.

Peggy had just thrown $5,000 down the drain. She sat in Erin and Jackson's living room while Erin fussed around in the kitchen. Peggy looked at the notebook with a list of all her expenses. Why was everything so much more expensive than she expected?

The doorbell rang and she flinched. Maybe it was the police with that paving contractor in handcuffs.

She was shocked to find William Calhoon at the door.

"William?"

"Thank you for inviting me for dinner." He handed her a bottle of wine. "You don't have to drink it; I just thought I ought to bring something. It's a white, I didn't know what you were having."

Erin came out of the kitchen, wearing an apron over her dress and a big smile.

"Mr. Calhoon! Thank you so much for coming. Please come in and have a seat in the living room. Mom, could you help me in the kitchen a minute?"

In the kitchen Peggy fixed Erin with a look. "Young lady, what have you done?"

"Shhhh! Mom, it's just dinner. I saw him up at the university today and, well, he's got to eat too."

"I can't believe you asked him here."

"Could you please set the table? Let's eat in the dining room."

Peggy, still shaking her head, grabbed a stack of plates. "Should I expect any other surprise guests?"

"No, just us. I made lasagna. I mean I bought one and heated it, so I'm pretty sure it will be okay."

Peggy put the plates on the table and sat with William in the living room.

"It's so nice to see you, William. I haven't got anything for you to sledge hammer yet, but your time is coming."

"I'm ready, just let me know."

"Erin said she saw you up at the university today."

"She was at the alumni office. They're going to honor me at some dinner during Homecoming," he explained. "I guess all you have to do is live long enough."

"Good for you! And good for them for recognizing how important to Nac you are."

Jackson came in through the garage and didn't seem surprised to see their guest.

"Mr. Calhoon! Nice to see you." They shook hands. "I hear the university is going to honor you!"

William smiled at Peggy. "It's a special award for longevity."

Erin announced dinner was ready and they all filed into the dining room. Peggy made sure to put Jackson between William and her so that it didn't seem like such a set up.

It was actually a very nice, very comfortable dinner. They all chatted like old friends, discussing everything from the weather to college football.

Of course talk turned to the Wettermark house and she told them they were making progress. She didn't mention she had been tricked out of $5,000 because she was too gullible to check references before she threw her money out the window. Or on the driveway.

"My guys went over to the house today," William said. "They seemed pretty impressed with the work you're doing over there."

"You were right about Scott McCullough," she said. "He is a fine person and a good contractor."

"They told me you've been right there working every day. Scraping off that old wallpaper. That's a tough job."

"Well, I got myself into this. I better be willing to work."

"The boys said you've barely got electric and what is there wasn't in-stalled by a credible electrician. Those wires are a mess. It looks like a den of snakes in some of the walls. One spark and that whole place could go up in smoke."

For a moment Peggy said nothing as she imagined that awful possibility. "I appreciate you having them look at it. Electric's not something we can mess around with. Even Scott doesn't work on it."

"That's the truth, electric's a special skill." He took a deep breath. "I've been thinking about it. I looked at their report and I believe in what you're doing and how you're doing it. I feel like you and I've got the same values: hard work, historic homes and this town. What I'd like to do is provide the labor for the electric on this project of yours."

Peggy was not sure what he was saying. "What do you mean?"

"I would be honored if you would let Calhoun Electric do the wiring for you. We'll donate all the labor. You just pay for the parts."

Erin jumped in, "Mr. Calhoon! That would be wonderful. What an incredible offer. That could take months and thousands of dollars off the project!" She looked at her mother, waiting for her response, hoping it would be positive.

Peggy shook her head in disbelief; "William! Oh no. That's too much."

He looked down at the table. "It's important to save the history, if we're going to brag about being the oldest town in Texas."

Erin and Jackson sputtered about how excited they felt. They had a lot more to say than Peggy.

"Mom?" Erin nudged her.

William finally looked at her. "I would personally appreciate it if you would let Calhoon Electric help restore the Wettermark home."

"I—I made a bad decision today. I guess this is the world righting itself. All right, it would be wonderful to have your company do the electric."

"Thank you." He didn't smile or look smug.

Erin, though, was smug enough for all of them. She jumped to her feet.

"Who wants dessert? I bought an all-American apple pie, just right for this occasion."

And Erin cut Mr. Calhoon the biggest piece.

22. VENTURING OUT AGAIN

1901

It had been almost a year and she was still grieving.

Mornings were the hardest. Ben went to work, the children went to school and all Daisy wanted to do was lie in bed. She could hear Mrs. Hamlin in the kitchen and Alita sweeping.

Everything ached. Especially her heart.

Most people thought her sorrow was for her mother, and that was part of it. Her mother, who was finally coming to Texas after eight years. That was a terrible loss. Maybe if her mother were here...but now her mother would never see the life she and Ben had made. The mayor, the mayor's wife, the most incredible house in town. She had been so happy her mother and father were coming.

Eight years was significant. It had been eight years since she left New York and everyone she had ever known. Eight years since she had seen her family. And in eight years, this was the first time she and Ben had created a baby.

Of course it was the baby that broke her heart. It felt like it was literally shattered and Daisy didn't know if it would ever heal.

She was so still that Alita peeked in to see if she could eat breakfast, then backed out and closed the door. She was in bed when school ended.

Minnie knocked tentatively on her door. At 17, Minnie was quiet and unerringly kind. When Daisy didn't answer, she gently opened the door and entered with a tray.

"Mama, Mrs. Hamlin made you a little tea. She's worried if you don't eat you'll just fade away. And I couldn't stand it if you faded away. I would miss you too much."

Daisy barely opened her eyes. "Minnie. I can't eat anything. Everything looks terrible to me."

"Maybe just try this sugar cookie. You love her sugar cookies. Please."

Daisy sighed. She slowly sat up. Minnie handed her a cup of tea with a sugar cookie on the saucer. She took a little bite then drank a little tea. Then she drank a little more tea.

It tasted good. Hot. Strong.

"She made some bread with butter too."

Minnie broke off a little piece of the bread and handed it to her. It was better than the sugar cookie. Not so sweet.

She drank a little more tea.

"Mama, I'm sorry but I need your help."

"Oh, Minnie. I just need to rest."

"I know. But it's my senior year. And there's a Christmas Ball at the Old University Building…"

Minnie sat on the edge of the bed. She put the cup and saucer on the tray.

"All the girls are getting dresses…"

"And you don't have anything."

"Mrs. Schmidt offered to take me to their shop but I really want you. You're always so beautiful and your dresses are just right…"

Daisy slipped back down into the bed. "What day is it?"

"Uh, Wednesday."

"Friday. Friday I'll get the dressmaker to come here."

Minnie kissed her cheek. "Thank, you, thank you!" She pulled the quilt up around Daisy, and danced the tray out of the room.

On Friday, Daisy got up and got dressed. She slowly went down to breakfast. She hadn't been there in many days. Benny and Carl were eating oatmeal and Mrs. Hamlin hurried to get her a bowl.

"We're glad to see you, aren't we, boys?" Mrs. Hamlin put a chunk of butter and some brown sugar on top of her bowl.

"Yes, ma'am!" Carl pulled out a spoon and presented it to Daisy with a flourish. "Our breakfasts are sad and dreary without you!"

"Yes, they are." Benny chimed in.

She got a little teary-eyed. These really were lovely children.

Her dressmaker came in the afternoon, carrying bolts of fabric and a basket of trim. When Minnie came home, Daisy sat in a parlor chair and helped make choices. She told Minnie she loved seeing blue tones with her blonde hair and that she did not think red or yellow suited her.

The dressmaker measured Minnie and they were all surprised she'd gotten three inches taller since the last time they'd had a dress made. That seemed so long ago, before they started building the house.

They chose deep blue satin and tiny pink rosebuds for trim. The dress would show her shoulders and fit tightly around her narrow waist. It would be beautiful on her.

Minnie was so pitifully grateful that Daisy felt bad she hadn't thought about her lately.

"All right, my dear girl, let's spend some time together, you and I. Maybe next week we can go downtown." Daisy hoped by then she wouldn't feel like she'd been run over by a train.

"Thank you. I would love that."

Slowly, slowly, Daisy came back to the land of the living. She still cried before she went down to breakfast, and sometimes before the children came home. And usually when Ben came to bed. But she was able to eat and walk around, and she found the list Matty had made for her before that really, really bad day.

One day she felt well enough to get out of the house. She told Ben she was going to buy furniture.

"Buy anything you want, my love." He took her face in his hands. "I want you to be happy."

She and Minnie looked at all the furniture makers in Nacogdoches and bought what they could. But the really fine things she wanted weren't available locally.

Every day she felt better and stronger. When she realized she could finally breathe without being knocked down by sorrow, she met Minnie at the door after school.

"I'm afraid we're going to have to go shop in New Orleans, Minnie."

"New Orleans? Really? New Orleans! I haven't ever been there."

"Well, neither have I, but we'll learn our way around."

Ben wanted to come with them but this wasn't a good time to leave the bank. Sweet Matty Goodson had been there before and offered to go with them.

They took the train to Houston then another to New Orleans. It took all day and they arrived in the early evening. Matty found a buggy to take them to the hotel.

Even in the dusk, New Orleans was colorful and exciting. There were more than 280,000 people living in the Louisiana city and most of them seemed to be out in the streets. The buggy crossed the electrified St. Charles Streetcar Line and they could see people hanging out the sides.

Over the next two days, Daisy, Matty and Minnie explored the heart of the city. They bought the Picayune's Little Guide to New Orleans and gaped at the wonderful buildings. Daisy yearned to see a performance at the French Opera House on Bourbon Street but there wasn't anything playing while they were there.

They took the streetcar to the Garden District. Matty said that was where the "nouveau riche" lived. Daisy realized the large, elegant mansions were a lot like her new house. The houses were Greek Revival or Italianate and some looked very much like her Queen Anne Victorian.

Minnie had never been anywhere but Nacogdoches. The 17-year old was excited about the streetcar, dazzled by the people of New Orleans, astonished by the rich velvet drapes of the hotel. And when they ate beignets, Minnie was beside herself. She wanted to take some home to Benny and Carl, but Daisy convinced her they wouldn't be very tasty by the time they got back.

There were furniture stores everywhere they looked. There were some that carried antiques from France and some that had the latest from New York. The three of them sat in everything, felt every piece of fabric, giggled about pieces that looked absurd and useless. With 12 rooms to fill, it took all of three days to find everything. Matty was the best friend a shopper could have. She wrote down everything they bought, noted the colors, and checked off the rooms where Daisy planned to put them.

The lamps were especially lovely, and Daisy couldn't resist buying one for each room. Twelve lamps! That might have been a little excessive, but each one was like a piece of art that would light up their lives.

The shopkeepers had no problem guaranteeing to ship the furniture, rugs and lamps to Nacogdoches so Daisy bought whatever she wanted. It was certainly nice not to worry about money.

When they visited a dressmaker, they saw elegant gowns for the New Orleans debutantes. It was just too bad Nacogdoches didn't have anything like that.

Right then and there Daisy decided Minnie should have a big coming-out party. They would fill their ballroom with young people and declare it Nacogdoches' first debutante ball. Who better to host it than the mayor and his wife?

Daisy vowed she would do this for Minnie. And she would spend more time with Benny and Carl. They deserved to experience the good things in life that she and Ben could afford to show them.

Since they were there, they had a dressmaker begin something spectacular for Nacogdoches' first debutante.

"How about fabric more delicate than satin?" Daisy looked through the bolts of material and held up a pale, pale green silk.

The dressmaker, an expert at flattery, said Daisy had a wonderful eye for fashion, and Minnie agreed. Together they decided on a décolletage of petals constructed of cut-lace openwork, repeated on the sleeve edges and the three tiers of the skirt. They had her fitted for an S corset with a sheer chemisette to keep the corset stays from poking her and they ordered a rustling silk petticoat.

"This will set Nacogdoches on fire!" Matty exclaimed and Minnie blushed.

The dressmaker would send Minnie's finery by train. Ah, life in New Orleans was so simple.

⁓

By the time they got back on the train, Daisy was completely worn out. She nodded off before they had pulled out of the station and slept almost all the way back home.

It took her a couple days to recover from the trip. Alita told the children Daisy "took to bed," but that she'd be all right after a little rest. And she was.

When her purchases started arriving, Daisy sat downstairs and directed the deliverymen. Everything was elegant and looked expensive. Well, Daisy had to admit, everything <u>was</u> expensive. There was nothing like it in town.

Each room got a deep richly-patterned Brussels carpet so that every step confirmed that this was luxury. She had purchased gold chairs for the parlor and a French mahogany *tete-a-tete* couch covered with gold velvet. She said it was to keep the boys at arms length when they came courting Minnie. This made Benny and Carl laugh, but Ben thought it was a very sensible idea.

There were so many small tables and lamps that she admitted she had gotten a little carried away. They put some of them in the ballroom so there would be places for punch cups at Minnie's coming out party.

"About that party," Ben cleared his throat and tried to put this delicately. "Are you sure we need that? Nobody around here has debutante balls."

"Then who will start it if not us?" She put her hand on Ben's chest and looked up into his eyes. "This is for Minnie. She needs this."

"Minnie does?" He started to say something else but thought better of it. "If that's what you want, that's what we'll do."

Honestly, that was all he said to her in the days after New Orleans. He seemed harried and preoccupied. Sometimes he was very sharp with Benny and Carl, who wanted him to look at their schoolwork or hear about their day.

She told Ben that Benny wanted to be a banker and suggested that he take the boy to visit the bank. Maybe he could have a small job as a helper in the summer.

"He's 15, Ben. Old enough to think about what he wants to do. And he says he wants to be just like you."

Ben shook his head. "We're too busy now for that kind of distraction." And that was the end of that.

Daisy scheduled the Debutante Ball for Saturday, May 31, 1902. That gave the seniors something to look forward to. And time to have gorgeous dresses made.

She and Minnie wrote personal invitations to every young person over the age of 15.

"Fifteen's a little young, but the ballroom is so big and we don't want it to look empty."

Minnie thought it was nice that Benny and his friends could come. "I imagine Carl will find a way to get in, and he'll probably give a speech to anyone who will listen."

"That's our Carl," Daisy agreed.

Daisy and Mrs. Hamlin and Alita had many planning sessions about food. There was so much to do that they invited Alita's sister to help them. She was known for the delicious food she prepared for the Cum Concilio meetings, and Daisy knew the word would get around town that she was cooking for the Debutante Ball.

Almost every day one woman or another stopped by the house to talk about the ball. They wanted to know how they could help, what Minnie or Daisy would be wearing, or if their sons needed to know how to waltz.

She was glad to get everyone involved. She agreed to those who wanted to bring bouquets from their gardens or loan their punch cups. She showed women around the house, and when she opened the pocket doors to the ballroom, they always gasped.

"Oh, Daisy," they often said. "There's nothing like this in Nacogdoches," and she would smile and say, "Why, thank you."

Sometimes she thought of those lonely days when she first arrived. The disappointment when Ben didn't meet her at the train station, the struggle to get into the women's club. She thought of Lenore and her own little lost baby and the old sadness came back to her.

She told herself she had three fine children and a husband who loved her so much he let her do anything she wanted. There was nothing like her house in Nacogdoches. She would give the community the first ever Debutante Ball.

No one could blame her for being proud of what she had. She had worked hard for it. And no one could take it away from her.

23. GETTING A GRANT

Peggy was standing in a pile of wallpaper scraps when Scott and his crew arrived. The end was in sight; this was her final wall on the main floor. Bits of wallpaper stuck out from her grey hair and the plastic goggles over her bifocals were so dusty it was a wonder she could see at all.

Scott knelt in front of her and handed her a battered scraper. "Morning, Miss Peggy! You get a special award for dedication to a task. We call it the Silver Scraper Award."

"I'm flabbergasted, Mr. McCullough. This is indeed an honor."

"No one in Nacogdoches has proven themselves better at wallpaper removal!"

Scott's crewmembers stopped and gave her a round of applause. Then they all headed to their appointed tasks.

"No driveway yet, I see."

"I've given up. The policewoman called to let me know I'm not the only gullible old woman he tricked."

"You did the right thing reporting it. Maybe the police can stop him."

"That would be good news. Oh, speaking of good news-- Calhoon Electric is coming today to start work on the electrical wiring."

"That'll be a big expense. You prepared for that?"

"Mr. Calhoon is donating all the labor. All I'm paying for is the parts."

"What? He's donating the labor? Those electricians charge a fortune. Whoa, Peggy. how'd you blackmail him? I didn't think you'd been in town long enough to do much damage."

"I snared him with his love of historic houses."

"Aha. Very incriminating."

"He says he cares about hard work, historic houses and this town. In that order."

"Hmmm, that sounds like he has the same priorities you do."

"Have you seen his house? He and his wife did a good bit of the work themselves. It's fantastic."

"Someday people will say that about this house."

"That's the dream."

"I don't know, Miss Peggy, it seems like you dream big. Next step--do you know anyone who'll show up with galvanized pipe slung over his shoulder, ready to help you out?"

Peggy shook her grey, curly hair. "I don't, but I'll keep my eyes open for pipefitters wandering down Wettermark Street!"

When the electricians came, they spread out all over the house pulling old dead wire, examining outlets and tracking wiring through the house. A lot of the time Peggy saw them shaking their heads; a couple of times the men called each other to come see the mess inside the walls. This was apparently the Guinness Book of World Records holder for the worst wiring ever.

The foreman of the electricians approached her while she was prying old linoleum from the kitchen floor. After a few pleasantries, he said. "I'll let Mr. Calhoon know our estimate for the labor. But we're going to have to replace every single piece of the electric. My best guess is that the parts will be about this much..."

He handed her a hand-written estimate that was so high she gasped. "Oh, my stars," she said. "And that's without labor?"

"Yes ma'am. This place is big and old and it looks like it was wired by people feeling their way in the dark. And I guess that might be what they did."

"I understand. By all means, go ahead and get started. It's only money, right?"

She didn't add, *"Money that I didn't budget enough for."*

Peggy would rather peel off linoleum with a Popsicle stick than give a speech, but here she sat, about to go in front of the board of the Nacogdoches County Historical Society. Her hands were sweaty and she cleared her throat a dozen or so times. She took off her glasses, cleaned them on a tissue, put them back on. If she hadn't needed a grant to help cover expenses, she would never have considered speaking to this group.

There were 12 people in the meeting room at the Convention and Visitors Bureau, most of them grey-headed like Peggy, all history-lovers, some history professors from the university. Most were women, three or four or were men.

"*Breathe,*" she told herself, and too late she added silently, *"Leave!"*

The president, Robbie Warwick, introduced her as the mother of Jackson Vance from the Chamber of Commerce.

She stood up and walked to the front of the room. "Thank you, but I have to tell you I'm not Jackson's mother, I'm his mother-in-law. Perhaps that's why I'm so eager to fix up a house and move out of his!"

The laugh she got was very reassuring.

"I didn't move to Nacogdoches intending to take up renovation. In fact I haven't ever done anything this big in my life. But when I walked into this beautiful historic home, I knew I had to get involved before it was gone. I feel like I have to try to bring it back to its former glory, if it's the last thing I do. And some people think it might be!"

Another laugh, and a hand went up.

"Now which house is it?"

"It's the old Wettermark house, on Wettermark Street by the university."

She saw the board members exchange looks.

"That's an interesting choice," Robbie Warwick said.

"I know it has a scandalous past, but it's part of history. Nacogdoches history."

Another hand went up.

"What year was it built?"

"1900."

"And Colonel Wettermark left town, when?"

"1903."

Again, the board members looked at each other. Peggy told them she'd been doing research with the reference librarian and that she had a general contractor. After she talked awhile, another hand went up.

"Can we come see it?"

"You want to come see the house?" Heads nodded. "Well, the contractor and his men are there and the electrical workers are pulling out the old wiring, and we don't have the flooring in..."

The president spoke up. "Mrs. Jensen, I know you would like to apply for a historic grant. To even consider it, we need to know what we're talking about."

"Of course. I would love for you to see it. Please just let me know when you want to come. I can have donuts..."

They laughed again. Goodness, this was an easily-amused group.

Warwick said, "You don't have to feed us. Most of us are too well fed as it is. But can we get back to you with a date and time?"

"Absolutely. I would be glad to have you. Just let me know."

A week later 11 of the 12 board members trooped into her house. She thought of them as jurors, weighing evidence to decide her fate. They all seemed to be wearing sensible shoes and comfortable clothes. Most greeted her with smiles, except for a couple of the men who looked grumpy and badly put-upon.

Scott's crew had cleaned up as much as they could and moved things out of the center of the rooms so there was a decent pathway. Boxes of wooden flooring had been pushed to the periphery of the rooms.

The crew didn't stop working for the tour; they had so much to do and only worked during daylight hours. Peggy thought the industrious workers made the project seem like it was progressing nicely.

Peggy led the tour, telling them everything she knew about the house. How it had been situated on 14 acres on the far north edge of town; how Wettermark Street used to come right up to the door; that there were 12 rooms including a big ballroom on the second floor.

"Obviously a Rulfs design," said Warwick, and at least five people nodded.

She showed them where the bathrooms would go on the main floor but she didn't take them upstairs. The railing was so rickety and some of the steps looked as if they might break. All she needed was to have a member of the Historical Commission break a leg. Then she'd have to shoot him.

The board members spread out and roamed around, looking closely at the windows and inspecting the flimsy front door. One of the men told her long, involved stories about what Nacogdoches was like when he was a child. The board members looked at her wallpaper removal and seemed to note that it didn't go all the way to the ceiling.

She thought, "This is how those poor high school students feel when they show their prize pigs," and smiled at the idea of her house as a fatted sow.

She hadn't gotten donuts but she didn't think anyone missed them. These people, of all the people in town, were the most interested in history. In fact, they seemed to be entranced by her house. She couldn't decide if they were glad she was restoring it or wished they'd had the idea themselves.

It seemed like hours until they all left. Warwick handed her a sheaf of papers and said, "Fill these out and get them back to us as soon as you can. We're going into the next grant cycle right away and if you miss it you'll have to wait a full year to apply. "

There was nothing easy about filling out the grant form. She had to put in a detailed budget, even though there were many things she didn't know. There was a section called "In Kind" and she put William Calhoon's donation of electrical workers there. She even put Nona's help with research as In-Kind, because it was valuable but Nona didn't charge for it.

She didn't have a tax ID, so she wrote her social security number. She put Erin and Jackson's address as hers, because it would be a long time and a lot of work before she could live in this house.

She asked for $25,000. Certainly that would be a lot of money, but realistically she knew they would probably cut a little off. She listed the specific things that would cover such as the driveway, some of the paint and antique glass for the windows.

There was a large box for a narrative. She had heard that this was the most important part of a grant application. Capture their imagination with the narrative, someone had told her. So she wrote:

> The story of the Wettermark House is one of the most intriguing in the history of Nacogdoches. The beautiful 12-room mansion was built in 1900 for the mayor of Nacogdoches and his family. Master architect Diedrich Rulfs incorporated the most distinctive features from other houses he designed for Nacogdoches' wealthy families.
>
> In January 1903, Colonel Wettermark cleaned out the coffers of his bank and skipped town, leaving his wife, three children and his mansion behind. The house passed hands several times but seemed to be unable to thrive. On the brink of deterioration, the home is now being restored in the Queen Ann style Rulfs intended. It will be the kind of home visitors expect to see when they visit the oldest town in Texas.

Erin read over the grant application and thought it sounded good. Jackson took a calculator to all of the numbers.

"Nice work, Peg," he said. "You might have a career as a grant writer!"

"I'd rather scrape wallpaper," she told him.

Two weeks later the president of the Historical Society called her.

"We were very impressed with what you're doing. This did come in at the very end of our grant consideration cycle. It was a rush job, something we don't usually do, but we've decided to give you a grant."

"That's wonderful!"

"Of course it comes with caveats. We have some regulations about the work, and I'm sure you'll be able to comply."

What Peggy wanted to say was, "How much and when can I get it?" But what she said was, "Can I come pick up the paperwork? I have some time this afternoon."

Here was the surprise of the day: the Nacogdoches Historical Commission had granted her $2,500, only a tenth of what she had asked. The caveats were that they had to approve anything that deviated from the original plan of the house and that she needed to give them time to assess the workmanship before they signed off on it.

Peggy took the papers and said she would read over them.

SAVING THE OLDEST TOWN IN TEXAS   149

Warwick had the good grace to look slightly embarrassed. "We wish it could have been more but so much of our budget had already been allotted when we got your application."

It seemed to her that they were asking too much for what they were giving. If she turned down the money, would they ever consider her again? If she accepted the money, would they be looking over her shoulder at everything she did?

Was $2,500 enough money for her to allow the Historical Commission to be a part of her house?

24. EVERYTHING IS PERFECT

1902

There had never been a better party in Nacogdoches, as far as Daisy knew. The Debutante Ball was her finest moment.

Everybody came—not just the young people, but also their parents who wanted to look around the house. The new furniture from New Orleans was perfect. Daisy was glad she had chosen the golden color for the drapes and upholstery on the furniture for every room on the main floor. It looked so elegant and rich. The parents all followed their children upstairs to look at the ballroom then came back downstairs to admire her gold chairs and the lush carpets.

Alita had polished everything to a high sheen so that the floors and the furniture seemed to glow in the light from the acetylene lamps. Mrs. Hamlin and Alita's sister had created two feasts, one for the young guests and one for their parents. By the end of the evening both tables were nearly empty.

Ben had an incredible memory and greeted each adult by name.

"Roland and Esme. How nice that you could come." Ben hadn't spoken to Roland Jones since he withdrew the money for Christ Episcopal Church. Ben could have gloated about the trouble the church had building its new sanctuary, but he was so gracious they probably doubly regretted their decision to work with Commercial Bank. He never once said aloud, "Serves you right."

Minnie was the belle of the ball. Daisy stood at the door of the ballroom and watched her whirling from one dance partner to the other. Daisy was so glad they had Minnie's dress made in New Orleans; there was nothing like it in all of Nacogdoches. Beside Minnie's pale green silk, the other girls looked garish and overdone.

Matty squeezed her arm. "Best trip we ever made. Everything you got in

New Orleans is just right."

"It was good for Minnie and for me. It was a turning point after all the bad things that happened."

"It was that. I look at Minnie and I can see she just blossomed."

Daisy caught Matty's hand. "Thank you for going with us. Guiding us. We couldn't have made it without you."

Lizzie Schmidt walked between them. She had inspected every room in the house and had what Alita called "her lemon-squeezing face."

"Daisy, you certainly have done a nice job with the house. Pocket doors, running water, acetylene lamps. How—how nice for you."

"Thank you for being the inspiration for some of our best ideas, Lizzie. We admired your house so much and we appreciate the lead you took here in Nacogdoches."

Lizzie looked surprised. Apparently she didn't expect an acknowledgment. "We, well, we worked closely with Mr. Rulfs..."

"Isn't he amazing? What a brilliant man. We're so lucky he's in Nacogdoches."

"My husband tries to keep him busy so he won't run off anywhere else."

"Please thank Mr. Schmidt for us. Mr. Rulfs has made such a difference in this town."

Mollified, Lizzie nodded her way back down the hall.

"I think she's going to count the number of rooms," Daisy whispered to Matty. "She'll be glad we've only got 12 and she has 13."

"Oh, but one of yours is a ballroom. I'm sure that counts as two!" Matty whispered back.

Ben came and stood beside Daisy and she leaned her head against him. They watched their daughter.

Minnie's dance card was so full she didn't have a repeat dance the entire evening. Boys rushed to bring her punch, vied to stand next to her and flattered her unmercifully, each boy trying to top the one before him. She looked flushed and happy--and honestly, quite dazzling.

"This is a beautiful ball for our beautiful Minnie," Ben said. "Thank you for the incredible job you did making it happen."

"I don't think I've ever been happier."

"My Daisy."

"My Ben. I wish this moment could last forever."

In September, Minnie sat beside Daisy in the parlor.

"Mama." She hesitated.

"Minnie?"

"Clifford Witherspoon has asked me to marry him."

"Oh, my gracious, Minnie! How wonderful! But you're so young."

"I'm two years older than Cliff, but we don't care. We graduated at the same time."

"Witherspoon? That's your mother's family."

"Yes."

"He is a handsome young man. But he's your cousin?"

"Second cousin. I've known him all my life. But lately..."

"Oh, Minnie, I see that smile when you talk about him. I'm so happy for you. I just want you to be happy. But you know he'll have to talk to your father."

"I wanted you to know first. If it hadn't been for the ball, he might not have asked me. He said he didn't know there were so many boys who liked me!"

Ben was so busy they could barely find an evening for Cliff to come ask for Minnie's hand. Ben counted his obligations on his fingers for Daisy: treasurer of Nacogdoches Ice and Cold Storage, secretary and treasurer of Nacogdoches Compress Company, treasurer for the Cotton Seed Oil Company AND treasurer of several benevolent associations.

Daisy pushed him to find an evening he could be available. "I know how busy you are, Ben, but you must meet with the boy if you intend to marry off our Minnie."

"I'd like to see her settled," he said.

"Pick an evening, then. And soon! We'll have a beautiful wedding." Daisy was already envisioning another trip to New Orleans for a fantastic wedding dress.

"Maybe not as extravagant as the Debutante Ball?"

"This is your only daughter, Ben. We'll have to do it right."

He sighed. His handsome face looked clouded for a minute, as if he might say NO to the whole idea. He put his face into his hand and rubbed his eyes.

"Ben? Are you all right?"

"I'm fine. Everything's so—busy lately. This is just one more thing. But making Minnie happy—and making you happy—" Ben dropped his hand and looked into Daisy's eyes. "Fine, Daisy. Do what you will."

Minnie didn't come into the parlor when Cliff and his parents came to visit. His father Clifford Sr. and his mother Martha reminisced with Ben about his first wife Lenore Witherspoon and her family. Daisy found it very uncomfortable but she poured tea and nodded. Cliff's father had many happy memories of his lovely cousin Lenore and the family gatherings the Witherspoon family hosted.

"Yes, yes, yes," she wanted to say. *"Get on with it."* But of course she didn't.

Another topic of conversation was Lenore's father, who Mr. Witherspoon said was one of the most successful cotton brokers in town. Daisy couldn't understand why Cliff's father would talk about Lenore's family while she sat right here beside Ben.

When the elder Witherspoon *finally* nodded at Cliff, the young man stood up and cleared his throat.

"Could I talk to you alone, sir?"

Ben and Cliff went out on the porch while Daisy and Mr. and Mrs. Witherspoon sat smiling inanely at each other.

"More tea?" She couldn't think of anything else to say to them.

When they came back in, Ben asked her to go get Minnie. It took about two seconds, because Minnie had apparently been listening at the stairwell. She bounded into the parlor and went out the front door with the young man.

"Yes!" they could hear her exclaim.

Planning a wedding for next year, 1903, was as much fun as the ball. Minnie and Daisy spent many happy hours together.

Of course they planned to go to New Orleans for the dress, and of course they'd ask Matty to come with them again. They clipped pages out of magazines and made sketches, each one more elegant than the last.

They had quite a debate about whether they should have it at the First Presbyterian Church or their house. In 1899 the Presbyterians had built a one-story rectangular building with a steep gabled roof and a small bay window on the east side. On the north and south walls of the sanctuary, Rulfs had placed four arched Gothic windows. There were no towers or gables; in fact there were no fancy frills at all.

Daisy thought it was too modest and plain for their wedding. Minnie, who hardly argued about anything, said she wanted to start her married life in the church. So they reserved the church for Saturday, April 11. The Farmers' Almanac said there would be a partial eclipse on Sunday, and they thought it would be nice to have such an historic event the day after the wedding.

Daisy convinced Ben to make a donation to the Presbytery. Even though there was no charge for the ceremony it just seemed right.

At dinner one night Benny and Carl complained that they weren't the least bit interested in planning the wedding.

"Imagine two teenage boys not interested in flowers and altars! Benny and Carl, you know you'll have to be all dressed up yourselves, while all the young girls in town make eyes at you!"

Benny blushed and Carl laughed, "We'd rather do anything than stand up there getting ogled by the girls!"

"I guess it is a little tedious for the two of you." Daisy was serving one of

Mrs. Hamlin's two-layer chocolate cakes. "Ben, why don't you and the boys do something fun? Maybe you could all go fishing?"

Ben stood up from the table. His frown froze her in place.

"Do I seem like someone who has time to go fishing? You two are big enough, why don't you go fishing on your own? Or do something, anything, rather than sit around and complain?"

And he threw down his napkin and stomped out of the room.

Daisy and the three children looked at each other.

Daisy said, "He is awfully busy. We probably shouldn't ask him to do anything extra right now."

Carl, ever the pragmatist, said, "Can I have his piece of cake?"

One evening just as they finished dinner, there was a knock at the front door. Alita opened it and stood back.

"Mrs. Wettermark, it's Mr. Clark."

Daisy looked at Ben. He nodded. "You can invite him in, Alita."

Mr. Junius Clark Harris was the most prominent attorney in Nacogdoches. He had seldom shown up at their door, except for the election party and the ball.

Both Ben and Daisy went to the foyer.

"Come on in, June. Thanks for coming over." Ben took the lawyer's hat and hung it on the coat tree.

Daisy would not have been more surprised if a locomotive had pulled off the tracks and chugged up to their door. "Mr. Harris, we were just finishing dinner. Have you eaten? We have plenty of roast and potatoes. Would you like to sit down with us?"

"I'm so sorry to have interrupted your meal. I've already eaten, but it does smell delicious."

Ben turned to Daisy. "I invited Mr. Harris over tonight to do a little business. You all go ahead and finish up. We'll be in the study; you can come join us a little later if you want."

Daisy certainly did want to pop her head in; that much was sure. Why would an attorney, the best attorney in Nacogdoches, come to their house at night? She sat back down with the children as they finished. She tried not to rush them but her mind was already bustling through the door of the study.

She hustled them off to their rooms, told them to get into their night-clothes and read. She kissed each one good night, even though they were getting a little too old for that.

Then she headed to the study.

The two men were leaning over a paper on the desk and looked up when she knocked lightly on the door.

Mr. Clark nodded to her. "Mrs. Wettermark. I should tell you again how much my wife and I like your beautiful house."

"Your house is so lovely that I'm honored you like ours. That location on Virginia—you must be able to see the whole town from your top floor. "

"We have a wonderful view, and wonderful breezes. You know two of our ten children had gotten ill and the doctor thought it might be from the water downtown. I had to move them up and out of there."

"And they recovered?"

"They did. Good as new."

Ben decided he'd had enough of the chitchat.

"Daisy, I asked Mr. Harris over because I'd like him to help me make a will."

"A will! Good heavens, Ben, what's wrong?"

"Nothing's wrong. I just want to be sure you and the children are taken care of if anything happens to me."

She sat down, shocked.

Mr. Harris said in a comforting tone, "I wish everyone was wise enough to make a will while they're still young and hearty. Why should we wait to be prepared?"

"Ben?"

"I guess all this talk about Minnie getting married, it's just made me feel, well, mortal. Nothing's going to happen to me, Daisy. But I've got assets scattered all over, and nothing set up for you…"

Mr. Harris looked kindly at her. "And I ran into Ben downtown and we just both said, why don't we get those affairs in order while we've got extra time? So here I am."

Daisy still felt off-kilter. She looked at Mr. Harris' comforting face, then at Ben.

"I just love you so much, Ben. I couldn't stand it if anything happened to you."

She hadn't ever made such a declaration out loud before.

Junius Clark Harris looked down at the desk, studiously reading the paper he'd brought.

Ben took Daisy's hand and kissed it. "And I love you Daisy. More than anything. That's why I'm doing this. I want to be sure you're always taken care of."

25. PLANNING A WORKDAY

If there was one thing Peggy was grateful for, it was the speed of the Nacogdoches historical commission's reply. Two weeks was a very quick turn-around, but she understood she had squeaked in at the very end of their granting cycle.

At breakfast, Erin and Jackson weighed in on their thoughts. Or rather, debated what she should do.

Erin was indignant. "I can't believe the commission thinks they can regulate what you do for only $2,500."

"On the other hand, this is a first-pass. You do this and prove you're worth more." Jackson pointed his spoon emphatically.

"I think I need to find out what the rules are for historic preservation." Peggy was already planning to spend the morning with Nona.

"You're right, Mom. That's the best way to go. Be prepared. So they don't push you around."

Jackson stirred cream in his coffee. "Erin, it's a historic commission, not a schoolyard bully."

"Isn't it, Jackson? Isn't it?"

Peggy had emailed Nona that she needed help finding grants to offset the steadily rising costs of the renovation. Nona had plenty of time to work with her after the library's morning meeting.

"Researcher at the ready, Miss Peggy!" she said as Peggy approached her desk, a paper plate of millionaire cookies held out as an offering.

The first thing Nona pulled up was from the Federal Register of Historic Houses. It said:

"From the Federal perspective a property owner can do whatever they want with their property as long as there are no Federal monies attached to the property. If Federal monies are attached to the property then any changes to the property have to allow the Advisory Council on Historic Preservation to comment on the project."

That made sense. Peggy figured that anybody who would give her money wanted a say in how it was used. The question, of course, was how much say they would have.

Nona looked up from the computer screen. "Maybe you can be really specific about what the local commission's money will go toward. Then they can regulate that, not your entire project."

"That's a brilliant idea."

Nona pointed out the National Trust for Historic Preservation gives small matching grants that fund professional services for preservation planning, education programs, and preservation emergencies.

Then they looked at the Preserve America information. That was a federal grant for community efforts for the sustainable use of historic sites that promote the economic and educational benefits of heritage tourism. She could check to see if the local historical society or tourism bureau had applied for a Preserve America designation. That would be another reason to work with the local group.

Nona asked, "Do you think you can get the house on the national register? Here's the information:

"The National Register is an authoritative guide to be used by Federal, State, and local governments, private groups and citizens to identify the Nation's cultural resources and to indicate what properties should be considered for protection from destruction or impairment."

Nona continued, "It says that getting private property listed on the National Register doesn't prohibit any actions the property owner might take."

"I can give it a try. I think the house is a cultural resource, don't you?"

"I surely do."

They put together a list of programs she could contact for grants. There were quite a few other federal and state possibilities and she would work on them from home. There was no harm reading over the application forms to see if she could get some funding.

She was not afraid to try. She had, after all, been afraid to give a speech to the historical commission and she earned $2,500 for it. That was the most she'd ever been offered per hour. And she had thought she wasn't good at giving speeches.

Nona handed her the list she'd printed.

Peggy felt like it was a list of marching orders.

"Thank you so much, Nona. You're the best research librarian in town!"

"The only one, you mean. And you're welcome."

As Peggy gathered up her things to go, Nona stopped her.

"One more thing, Miss Peggy, I talked to my service sorority and they would love to have a workday at your house."

"Oh, my gosh, Nona, that would be wonderful. When do you want to come?"

"Next month we have our National Day of Service. We could do it any Saturday. There are a lot of us, though. You and I would have to figure out all the tasks and I can have them each pick what they want to do. Some of them don't like to get their hands dirty and some do. A few of us have all sorts of experience from helping Habitat for Humanity and Zion Hill."

"I'll furnish lunch."

"No need. One of our committees shows up at noon with food when we do service projects. You just lead the way and we'll swarm all over that house like a plague of locust. But good locusts, that leave a place better than they found it."

Peggy spent the next week filling out application forms for national grants. She found a few state agencies and applied to those too. It took some doing but she was getting the hang of it. She learned that each form had a different order and questions and formats for the budget. Once she wrote the narrative, did a budget and schedule, she cut and pasted the information into the forms.

This was just one more thing she was learning she could do.

Most of the grants required a commitment from a local organization. She knew she had to go back to the Nacogdoches Historical Society. She called the president, Robbie Warwick, and set up a meeting time at the Convention and Visitors Bureau.

She took the papers with her. Warwick was already in the meeting room and stood when she walked in. He pulled out a chair for her and she sat down.

"How's the house coming?" he said.

"It's a huge job, but it's gratifying. We're starting to see progress. And when the electricity comes on, we'll see even more."

"We were very impressed with what you're doing. I'm glad we can help you out."

"I wanted to talk to you about that. I'm concerned about having to pass everything I do on the house through the historical society. It just seems like it would slow the work down so much."

Warwick looked deflated. "That's just what we do."

"Is it possible that perhaps you could inspect and sign off on the things you're paying for? For instance, we could designate your grant for the antique glass that's so important for the windows. Then you all could make sure it's the right kind, the right density, and so on. "

"I don't know..."

"That would help so much. There are ten million things we have to do, and I'm sure you don't want to sign off on all of them. I'll bet one of your members could be the advisor on the historic windows."

"Well, the Fergusons did redo their windows and they did a lot of research on them."

"It would be wonderful if you could talk to them. I wondered, too, if you have applied for a Preserve America grant. I could apply for one, if a community organization endorsed the project."

He looked steadily at her. "We haven't applied, but if we did that, we'd have to be much more involved with the renovation." She couldn't tell if it was a warning or a simple statement.

"Certainly. That would be a necessity, I'm sure."

Warwick looked at the papers in her hand. "If we applied for the Preserve America grant, it would be a separate discussion. Are you signing these grant papers today?"

"I'd rather wait till we can find out about narrowing the scope, if that's at all possible."

He nodded. "I'll talk to the board. To the Fergusons. We think what you're doing is important for Nacogdoches. I'll see what we can do."

Peggy walked back to the car feeling like she had negotiated peace for the free world. She hadn't ever bargained for such high stakes. The most she'd negotiated in recent years was trying to get Bill into the car to go the VA hospital, his least favorite place. She walked out of the Convention & Visitors Bureau feeling very good.

Scott McCullough met her at the house to talk about the workday for Nona's sorority. He pointed out possibilities as they walked through the house.

"The wooden window frames can be sanded and any hardware taken off and saved. Any baseboards that are left can be taken off. They don't have to save them; we'll get all new throughout the house. Somebody could pull out nails anywhere we're going to use the shiplap. Old linoleum can be scraped off."

He went on and on pointing out things on the main floor.

"How about the upstairs? Do we dare let anyone up there?"

Scott walked over to the railing and jiggled it. "We can get these stairs done right away and that'll open the upstairs. I want to rip these out and put in new."

"Isn't there anyway to save them? That seems so expensive."

He put his weight on the second stair and it gave slightly. "These stairs are over 100 years old. I just don't trust them."

"All right. Nona said she's bringing a pretty big group so it would be nice if some of them could work upstairs."

"We'll do it tomorrow."

"Wow, you are good."

"Best in the west. Or in East Texas, more like it. What kind of railing you want? Wrought iron looks nice."

"No, we need the rails to look just like these old ones. Wooden, turned, and we'll polish them till they glow."

"All right, add sand the railings to the sorority list."

They spent another hour walking through the house. They didn't even get started on the outside; there was so much to do inside. Scott said his crew would hold off putting in the new flooring until after the workday. If there was any painting done, and Scott wasn't sure that was a good idea for a big group, he didn't want it on the new wooden floors.

Peggy took the list to the library. She waited while Nona helped a collector figure out how to find prices for comic books. As soon as she finished, Nona called her over.

"Everybody's getting real excited about helping at your house. We can come the last Saturday of the month," she said.

"This is the best thing to happen to us! Scott and I wrote this list of projects for you. It's a lot but you can pick anything you want to do."

Nona read the list and then started putting initials beside the tasks.

"Uh huh. Well, that's Kendra. Oh, Jazzmine for sure."

When Nona looked up she was smiling. "This is going to put us to the test. We'll see who's got mad skills and who's just frontin."

"I haven't ever done anything like this. Do we need to have tools for each of you? Or do you bring that sort of thing?"

"Some of us have our own tools like hammers and screwdrivers, but you need sandpaper and caulk and paint and nails and scrapers and products that are, I don't know, perishable."

"I'll have that ready for you the last Saturday of the month. But not lunch, you said."

"Not lunch. We'll have the lunch crew feed you!"

"Would it be all right to include my daughter Erin and son-in-law Jackson? And maybe even Mr. Calhoon? And of course Scott the contractor. He'll be there for sure. He's putting in new stairs in honor of your workday."

"They're welcome if they're willing to work as hard as a Tau Alpha Sigma."

"What time can you start?"

"I said early and everybody said 9 a.m. was as early as they can possibly make it on a Saturday. Well, they said 10 a.m. but I shamed them into 9."

"9 a.m. it is. Thank you, Nona. On behalf of the historic Wettermark house, thank you."

The cars started arriving at 8:45 and by 9:15 there were 35 women in the Wettermark parlor. They wore matching turquoise T-shirts with Tau Alpha Sigma Chapter in big letters on the back. Some of them were drinking coffee and eating the donuts Erin was serving. Some had Camelbak water bottles. All of them were ready to work.

They looked to Nona for their assignments. Nona nodded to Peggy.

Peggy stood in the middle of the room. "I want to thank you so much for coming to help. I know history is important to all of us and when we lose the artifacts of history, like this house, we lose part of who we are. I'm honored that you have chosen to spend a workday here. Thank you, Nona, for all of your help, your research and your willingness to share your expertise with me. And thank you for persuading the members of Tau Alpha Sigma Chapter to pitch in and help save this house."

Everybody whistled, stomped or applauded Peggy's speech. Nona began to call out names and assignments. As she did, the women went to the pile of materials and Scott and Jackson helped them find what they needed. They handed each woman a pair of work gloves, too, and thanked each one as they did.

William Calhoon, who always prided himself on being early, came about 30 minutes later and looked astonished to find the house full of people. Nona found him a job and he got right to work.

It was an amazing day as 35 women worked and laughed and sang. Peggy, Erin, Jackson and Mr. Calhoon took assignments and found working in a group made the time go faster. Scott supervised, moving from one work area to another, showing how to use the power sander, how to get leverage to pull off a baseboard. There were a few hotly contested races, as sanding window frames became a competition, or sorority sisters vied to see who would be first to pull out all the old nails on opposite walls.

Just at the time they were breaking for lunch, Peggy's phone rang.

"Mrs. Jensen, this is Robbie Warwick. We have decided to revise our contract for the grant. We'll grant you $2,500 and we'll limit our input to the windows. And the Fergusons are going to work with you on that."

Peggy put her hand over her eyes as they filled with tears. What a day this had been.

26. BEN PACKS A TRUNK

1902-1903

Daisy felt like Christmas had been sweet and sad because Minnie and Clifford Witherspoon were getting married in April. Ben was so melancholy that the boys got very silly, trying to cheer him up.

All Daisy and Minnie had talked about for months was the wedding so they hadn't spent a lot of time shopping for Christmas presents. Daisy realized, as they sat around the tree, she should have bought something for Ben, but he had told her he absolutely did not want anything and she took him at his word. He sat glumly drinking a whiskey in a heavy crystal glass, watching the boys unwrap their presents.

Daisy leaned her head against him. She was surprised he was taking Minnie's upcoming marriage so hard.

"Ben, she's not leaving forever. She'll be right here in Nacogdoches. Minnie, you'll bring your family here for our Christmases, won't you?"

Minnie reached over and patted his hand. "Father, we'll be close enough we can run over every night for Mrs. Hamlin's dinners."

Everyone laughed except Ben. He shook his head and took another drink. "I hate to think of this as our last Christmas together."

Daisy kissed him on the cheek. "Ben Wettermark, you are a sentimental sweetheart. Stop that moping. Let's just enjoy this time while we're all together."

Thursday, January 1: New Year's Day in Nacogdoches was cool and lovely, the perfect start for 1903. Ben and Daisy had a nice dinner together and toasted to another year of joy and happiness.

On Saturday, Nacogdoches was still celebrating the dawn of the New Year. Minnie was at the Witherspoon's house and the boys had gone off to their own party. Ben had some work to do downtown but in the evening when he got back Daisy went to the icebox and got the bottle of champagne she had been chilling. She took the champagne upstairs for Ben to open.

When she walked into the bedroom he was packing a steamer trunk.

"Ben? What are you doing?"

He didn't stop packing. "I have to go on a little trip."

"Where are you going? Why?"

He stopped and seemed to think about his answer. Then he sat down on the bed and patted the spot next to him.

Daisy sat.

"This has been a bad year for the bank." He took her hand and looked at her. "The cotton farmers have been defaulting on their loans. That's left us short. And we haven't been able to collect from some of the lumber companies."

She nodded.

"I'm going to have to go down to Houston to see if I can secure some funds to cover the shortfall."

"Tonight? Saturday night?"

"That'll give me some travel time. Our bank has been closed this week for the holiday. I'll be able to get down there and take care of business and get right back before anybody misses me."

"I'll come with you."

He pulled his hand away and looked shocked. "Absolutely not. You've got to take care of the children..."

"They have Alita and Mrs. Hamlin. They can spare me for a day or two."

"No, if you come with me people will get suspicious and think something's wrong."

"I don't see why. Many women travel with their husbands. It'll seem like a New Year's holiday together."

"It's no holiday, I'll tell you that. No, Daisy, I can't take you with me now. But when this is all straightened out maybe we can have a holiday together." He stood back up and put a suit and shirts in the trunk.

"When did you decide to do this?"

"I met with June Harris earlier today and we went over the books. We looked at the accounts from every angle. We had so many shortfalls on loans that the books look bad. I told June I could get some investors in Houston. I'll meet with some of my father's big accounts and get them to tide us over."

"Why didn't you tell me?"

"You're so busy with the wedding and your women's club and the children. I didn't want to worry you."

A horse and buggy pulled up outside and they both turned to the window.

"That's my ride to the station. I'd better hurry." Ben started shoving clothes into the trunk. He grabbed his toiletries, stuffed them in, closed and locked the trunk.

"Could you ask the driver to come help me carry this downstairs?"

"Ben, surely, you don't need to take everything you own."

"I don't know how many meetings I'll have to go to in Houston. It might take some convincing."

When the buggy rattled off, Daisy sat in the parlor, stunned. She felt terrible that Ben didn't think he could confide in her. She felt terrible that his bank was in trouble. She just felt terrible as her husband rushed off to catch a train. Then it was so quiet and he was gone.

She looked around her beautiful parlor with the golden chairs, shining lamps and thick rug. She shivered in the cold realization that they might be in trouble.

On Monday morning when the cashiers came to open Wettermark Bank, they were locked out. There was a bulletin posted on the door:

CLOSED FOR LIQUIDATION

The news flashed through Nacogdoches faster than a runaway mule. The cashiers bemoaned the fact that they hadn't been paid, but that was nothing compared to the outcry from people who couldn't get to their money. William Patton, one of the cashiers left standing on the sidewalk, told everyone he didn't know anything about it. He was sure Col. Wettermark would explain it as soon as he came in.

Within 20 minutes, Sheriff A.J. Spradley knocked at Daisy's door. She had hardly slept; she pulled on her dressing gown and tried to look composed.

"Mrs. Wettermark, is your husband here?"

She shook her head.

"May I come in?"

She opened the door to him and peeked out to see if he was alone.

They sat in the parlor. The sheriff seemed to be studying her. She looked miserable.

"Can you tell me where Col. Wettermark is?"

"He's gone to Houston to raise some money for the bank. He...he said there was some trouble with the loans..."

"When did he leave?"

"Saturday...Saturday night. As soon as he gets some investors he'll be back."

"Yes, ma'am. I know he will. Would you let me know when he's back home? I imagine he can clear everything up just fine."

"I will. I'm sure he will take care of everything. He just went down to straighten things out. He just works so hard and he wants everything to be right..."

Minnie stood at the door of the parlor. "Mama, what's wrong?"

"Your father...the sheriff..."

The sheriff cleared his throat. "There's a little trouble at the bank. I'm sure it's nothing for you to worry about. But I need to talk to your father as soon as he gets back."

Lizzie Schmidt knocked at the door and called out, "Daisy? Are you here?"

Sheriff Spradley thanked Daisy. When he opened the door to leave, Lizzie rushed in.

"Oh, my dear Daisy, what has happened at the bank?"

Minnie sank down beside Daisy. "Mama, what's happened at the bank?"

"Your father has gone to get help...some of the loans, the cotton farmers, they haven't paid...he's going to get some investors to cover the loans..."

"It's all anybody's talking about," Lizzie fluttered around the parlor. "The bank closed for liquidation, a sign on the door and not a word to anyone. The cashiers locked out, the assets frozen. Well, I don't know if they're frozen, but that's what everyone is saying."

Minnie, who was the sweetest, quietest girl in town, stood up and faced Lizzie.

"You are upsetting my mother. Can you please leave now?"

Lizzie sputtered then left as suddenly as she had arrived. Later Daisy thought she should have thanked her; Lizzie was responsible for spreading the news that the Colonel had gone to get money to save the bank. That gave them a couple of days for Ben to come back.

That afternoon the attorney June Harris came to the house. He wanted to know if Daisy had heard from Ben.

"Mrs. Wettermark, I don't know how much the Colonel told you."

"Just that he's gone to get investors to cover the loans at the bank."

"Ben asked me to meet him Saturday afternoon to go over the books. His father was sending someone from Henderson to meet with us."

Daisy was surprised. "Alfred Wettermark? His father? This is Ben's bank."

"Alfred still holds a major interest in the bank," Harris said "I don't know that I got that impression from Ben, and apparently you hadn't either. Alfred sent Judge Buford here from Henderson and Hulen Crane joined us. When we went over the books we found the bank is in unsatisfactory shape. It was shocking to see such trouble in the books."

"My poor Ben. He must have been devastated."

"Judge Buford went back to Henderson on the northbound train that night. When Hulen left, Ben asked me to stay. He told me he was going to Houston to get money to tide him over. He said if he succeeded he would wire back to open the bank this morning. If I didn't hear from him I was to close it up. I was hoping maybe he'd contacted you."

"He needs time to talk to people who want to invest."

"I know, but I got this telegram this morning and Alfred Wettermark asked me to post it at the bank today."

Daisy read:

> "I have been forced to suspend banking business on account of conditions at Nacogdoches. As soon as the assets and liabilities at both Nacogdoches and Henderson can be ascertained a meeting of all the creditors will be called and the matter submitted to them. No assignment, deed of trust, or petition in bankruptcy has been filed because I wish to save all expense possible for the benefit of creditors. Mr. June C. Harris is in charge at Nacogdoches and Mr. E.B. Alford at Henderson."
>
> Signed with regret,
> A. Wettermark

Daisy looked up, aghast. "He's not giving Ben enough time to take care of this."

"I got the feeling Alfred might not have much patience." Mr. Harris looked sad. Daisy thought he seemed like a very kind man who cared about Ben.

On Tuesday, Daisy kept the children home from school. Matty Goodson brought her a loaf of fresh baked bread and some homemade mayhaw jelly.

She threw her arms around Daisy. "My dear sweet friend. I just want you to know we support you, and we'll help anyway we can."

"Oh, Matty, it's so hard. Ben is trying to take care of everything and his father closed the bank, it's just awful."

"It is. It is. I want to help you anyway I can. I don't know if I should give you the Houston Post or if it will make you feel worse. Do you think you want to see it?"

"When did it come?"

"Today. On the train."

"I need to know what everybody else is seeing."

Matty reluctantly handed her the January 6 Houston Post, turned to page 4. At the top of the page was the headline:

A Failure in East Texas

The Wettermark Firms Have Gone Into Liquidation

Liabilities and Assets are Believed to Be

About $400,000—A Statement Issued
by the Head of the Firm.

The story included the telegram that Alfred Wettermark had Mr. Harris post at the bank.

Daisy groaned. "His father sent this to the paper? How can he expect Ben to raise the money when this runs in Houston, where Ben is trying to get investors?"

"You just have to have faith, Daisy. Everything will be all right."

As Matty hugged her again, Daisy wondered if everything would ever be all right again.

27. A SNAKE IN THE GRASS

The new wooden plank flooring was the most beautiful thing Peggy had ever seen. It flowed through every room in the house, from the downstairs to the upstairs. Scott had used the same wood on the stairs and they looked as if they were installed the day the house was built.

After the big workday, Calhoon Electric finished the wiring and the foreman flipped the switch on the lights. Peggy thought they were brilliant. Literally and figuratively.

The foreman handed Peggy the receipt. There was a long list of parts and hours the crew worked. At the bottom, the total was 0.

Peggy turned the receipt over, looking for the total.

"I'm sorry, I can't figure out what I owe."

"It's right there. Zero. Mr. Calhoon decided to donate the parts."

"What? The parts *and* the labor? I can't imagine..."

"He said to tell you he'll use it as a charitable donation. He's like that about Nacogdoches, you know."

"Oh, my, oh thank you. Please thank Mr. Calhoon. I'm just... I don't even have words to express it."

"All I know is he loved that workday. Said he hasn't had that much fun since he finished his own house."

Peggy could hardly believe it. The electrical work was such a big part of the house and now it was completely donated. The wire, the parts, the workers on this huge house that had nothing but ruined electrical wiring. The foreman had said it looked like it was put in by people working in the dark. And now, her house was full of light.

What an incredible gift from William. She almost laughed out loud. She couldn't wait to tell Erin, who would take this as an endorsement of her tactics for getting William involved in the project.

Dan and Frances Ferguson met her at the house to talk about the windows. They had restored a historic house in Nacogdoches and were sent by the historical commission. Peggy thought they were the cutest couple, about her own age and they sounded like they might be from somewhere up east.

"This house is so much bigger than ours," Frances said. "But I do love our house, Dan."

"I do too, sweetheart." Dan was writing in a pocket notebook where he had made a lot of hash marks. "I counted 24 windows. There may be some I haven't seen yet."

"There are some that are still usable," Peggy pointed out some windows on the second floor. "I don't think they'll have to be replaced."

When they entered the main room, it looked fresh and finished and Peggy was proud to show it off. She flipped a light switch, just because she could, and the floors were lustrous. Nona's sorority sisters had painted the walls with the creamy white Peggy and Scott had chosen. They looked flawless.

They stood in the middle of the room.

"This is beautiful," Frances said quietly. "Nacogdoches history, right here."

"The oldest town in Texas," Dan said.

"So many of these wonderful houses get torn down. Like they're nothing." Frances walked slowly around the room.

Frances tapped on the hollow-cord door and creaked it back and forth.

"Dan, didn't one of the banks downtown have an old bank door donated --I think it's way too big for this spot but I wonder if they would let us have it and we could figure out how to use it."

She took out her measuring tape and she and Dan measured it.

Peggy was surprised that now she and Frances were "us," but not displeased. She was glad for an ally.

"Dan, can you ask the bank if we can have that antique door? They seem to like you there," Frances smiled so sweetly at her husband that they all knew he wouldn't be able to say no.

Peggy felt the way she had when she first entered this house, before she even knew its history. Like restoring it was possible.

"Thank you. I'm glad you're involved in this project. The house is part of the history of this town. It's a story of trust, betrayal, forgery and disappearance, and that's part of Nacogdoches."

"That IS a story," Frances smiled at her. "And we've got to get this story told."

Dan said, "We can use the grant money for the windows. But of course you'll have to find someone to put them in."

"Probably not something my contractor does."

Dan looked appraisingly at Peggy. To him she looked short, kind of on the skinny side, grey-haired, wearing faded khaki pants and a T-shirt. "This is a mighty big project. You in this all by yourself?"

"In a way, yes. But I've had help at every step of the way."

"How's your money holding out?"

Frances looked appalled. "Dan! Who are you, Geraldo Rivera?"

"I'm sorry, hon, but I've got to ask these things if we're going to help her. We're not just supposed to drop by, impress her with our knowledge of glass and drive away."

"Forgive him, Mrs. Jensen. The historic council chose us as their representatives and we take that seriously."

"Yes, we do. Here's what I'm thinking: Robbie Warlick was talking about that Preservation Grant. Maybe we can look into that."

Now it was Frances' turn to look cautiously at Peggy. "Do you want us to see about that? We don't want to do anything you don't want. But Dan and I want to help."

"I wouldn't mind some help. I want to restore this house the way it needs to be restored." Peggy decided to level with them. "This is a bigger project than I ever imagined. Every bit of this is so expensive and I'm not going to spend money I don't have. That's what got the Wettermarks in trouble over a hundred years ago."

Frances looked at her husband. "We're honored to be a part of saving this wonderful house."

Dan grinned. "Mrs. Jensen, we will look at that grant and see what we can do for you."

Peggy had already paid for the fixtures for the bathrooms. She hadn't found a generous purveyor of galvanized pipe, but Scott and his crew were ready to install the bathrooms.

She went home and went through all the bills. She totaled everything, and then looked at the amount she had from the bank loan and her savings account.

The highest amount was for Scott. He had bought materials and listed hours for his crew. And he noted that he had given her discounts throughout his work.

But oh my gosh it was high. She realized she had not added the amount she spent on the bathroom fixtures and that she was already $20,000 more than she'd budgeted. Even with William's donation of the electrical parts, she had miscalculated.

She added the totals, then added them again. She felt sick. Where would she get that money?

She called and left a message. "Scott, I'm paying your bill today. But I'm going to have to stop awhile on the construction. That's all the money I have right now."

He called back immediately. "I can let you pay on account."

"What does that mean?"

"We keep on working and you pay small amounts as you can. You catch up when you get the money."

"I can't, Scott, I just can't. That's not the way I need to do this. I can't spend more than I have—and I'm already way over my budget."

"I hate to lose the momentum."

"I know, and I'm sorry. You're the best and you're doing an incredible job. But I've got to be careful."

He said gently, "This from a woman who bought this house because it spoke to her?"

"I'm sick about this, Scott. We've come so far and I can almost see the end. And to stop breaks my heart. I just can't, I can't spend money I don't have."

Scott sounded as disappointed as she felt. "Oh, well, Miss Peggy, it's all right. I've got a couple jobs we can do until you're ready."

"Thank you. You'll be the first person I'll call when we can go at it again."

She went to the library and sat down at Nona's desk.

Nona looked up from her screen. "What's wrong, Miss Peggy?"

"I wondered if you could talk a few minutes, Nona. I need some advice."

Nona turned away from her screen and faced Peggy. "I am here to help. Shoot."

"I just totaled up the expenses for the house. I'm way over where I thought I would be, even with a big donation of electrical work. My outgo exceeds my income."

"Whoo, like I haven't been there. What are you going to do?"

"I called the contractor and asked him to stop for a while. I'm hoping for a grant, but so far there's nothing beside the $2,500 from the historical society for the window glass. But I don't even have enough to have it installed."

"Your house is a treasure. All my sorority sisters are still talking about it, about how important it is to save Nacogdoches history."

"Their work made a huge impact. I can stand in the middle of the house and imagine how wonderful it will be."

"I can double down on researching grants." Nona looked worried.

"The historical society is looking at the Preserve America grant."

"I'll look it up again and check the criteria. That would be the saving grace, right there."

Talking with Nona made her feel there was hope on the horizon. Peggy went back through the bills and decided to cut anything that could be spared for now.

She called the big appliance store and told them she had to cancel the order of bathroom fixtures. She had already put them on her credit card and the store was just waiting for a delivery date. The manager was reluctant but he said he would make sure they went back into stock.

There went the beautiful historical-looking bathroom fixtures she'd picked out. She hadn't thought that would make her so sad but she felt like it was a major blow to the project.

That night she let Erin and Jackson know she was putting the renovation on hold for a while. They did not say, "I told you so," for which she was grateful. Then she told them firmly she didn't want them to loan her money.

"Uh, all right," Jackson said.

"We were about to order windows using the historical commission's grant. I've got to hold off now."

Erin looked concerned. "That's true. You don't want to have them sitting around here waiting to get broken."

Peggy called Frances Ferguson and told her the situation.

Frances agreed. "We can look at samples but you're right, if they're piled up here they're vulnerable. Let's wait to order. But I have to tell you, the grant money has to be used within this calendar year."

Peggy thanked her for being so understanding.

"Of course," Frances said. "When we did our house we had more delays than we'd like to remember. I know you must hate to wait. That made me whacky."

Peggy laughed. "I'm already whacky or I wouldn't have started this project."

Peggy was feeling whacky. She was impatient and aggravated, thinking of her house sitting idle while there should be work going on. She decided there was one thing she could do alone, and that was yard work.

The outside of the house was a mess, with riotous bushes and tangled vines. All the grass and flowers had been strangled by weeds and neglect long ago. The few trees on the property hadn't seen pruning in a long, long time, and bare ground showed around their trunks.

When Scott's crew came back, they would start working on the outside of the house. She would take the pro-active step to cut back the mess crowding the porch.

She put on a long-sleeved shirt and jeans and pulled an old baseball cap over her curly hair. In the garage, she looked at Jackson's tools and picked long-handled clippers, a pair of little clippers that looked like scissors, a shovel and a rake. She picked out a pair of clear plastic goggles to wear over her glasses. She decided not to take the chainsaw because it was too dangerous. She piled everything into the trunk of her car.

When she pulled up in front of the house, she felt certain she had made the right decision. The inside of the house was a thing of beauty but the outside looked as bad as the day she had first walked in. She opened the trunk and took out all the tools, silently promising Jackson she would bring back every one in good shape.

She started with the bushes right in front of the porch. A clean line across the top might make them look better. She took the long clippers and began to cut. There were a few branches at the top that were easy, but the branches were so gnarled and thick it was very hard to break them. She clipped as hard as she could and worked until her shoulders ached. This was why chainsaws were invented, she thought.

"Tomorrow I'll learn how to use the chainsaw," she vowed. How hard could it be? She thought about the Lumberjack mascot of the university, and decided she would become one. Yes, tomorrow she'd learn to be a chain-sawing lumberjack.

Maybe she could just dig up the bushes instead of clipping them. One by one, she'd get them out. Then she'd get some lovely heritage azaleas and the front of the house would come alive.

She picked up the shovel and used her foot to jam it into the dirt in front of a bush. She put her weight on the metal and worked her way across the front of the bush, digging into the dirt as deeply as she could. This wasn't easy but it was better than trying to clip the branches using those long-handled clippers.

She couldn't get to the back of the bush but made a real impact in the front. She pushed on the bush from the top and felt it give a little. She knelt down in front of the bush and reached both hands in to push it back and forth. There. She had made it looser; she could move the bush back and forth.

Then she had a searing pain in her right hand. She put her head down below the lowest branches and peered into the eyes of a snake, a snake that had sunk its fangs into her hand.

She screamed and pulled her hand away. The snake looked stunned, too, then jerked back and slithered away from her, away from the bush and under the porch.

Peggy sat back on the ground. She had been bitten by a snake.

It took her breath away. She literally could not breathe for a second, then she drew in a deep breath.

She screamed. "Help!"

There was no one there to help her. At first the pain felt like she had been hit with a hammer, now it was like an ice pick was being jammed into her hand.

She had locked her purse in the car and she used her left hand to take her key out of her pocket. She cradled her right hand with her left and carefully went to the car. She didn't know if she would pass out so she had to get her phone as quickly as she could.

She opened the passenger side, climbed inside and dialed 911.

"I've been bitten by a snake." She gasped. "A snake."

She gave the address and slumped back on the seat, her purse in her lap. The operator kept her talking

"I don't know what kind of a snake. It was gray or brown. It had marks on its back. My hand. I…I, yes, I'm sitting in my car in front of the house."

Around the bite the skin looked like a dark blue bruise. Her hand was swollen and as she watched, the swelling expanded up to her wrist.

The ambulance came so quickly she had barely begun crying. Now she sobbed as the stabbing pain ran from her hand to her elbow. The EMTs put her on a stretcher, took her purse, locked her car and drove her to the emergency room, the siren wailing.

28. CHANGING SENTIMENT

January 6-10, 1903

On Tuesday there was a steady stream of people dropping by the house to console Daisy. Or at least that's how they always started. They said they respected Col. Wettermark and knew he was trying to do the right thing.

Then they wanted to know if she'd heard from the Colonel. They asked her to let her husband know how they had put their life savings in the bank and they couldn't get it out.

It was humiliating.

Neither of the boys wanted to go to school but she sent them out the door in the morning with the words, "Hold your heads up, boys. Your father is doing his best to save the bank."

Minnie stayed with her, answering the door, sending people away when Daisy had had too much.

Earlier, Mr. June Harris posted a note on the door of the bank that ran in the Houston Post and the *New Orleans Times-Democrat* that same day:

> To local creditors...I am working with three clerks in the preparation of the statement of the condition of A. Wettermark & Son. This work, for obvious reasons, will consume several days. Until this is done, no other matter will be considered. I shall at all times endeavor to give an audience to enquiring creditors and extend perfect courtesy to each. After the statement from both banks have been completed, a meeting of all creditors will be called and permanent plans effected. Until then, so long as I have control of the Nacogdoches bank, not one entry will be made in conditions existing at the time the doors were

closed, but all things will remain just as I found them, except that all papers sent the bank for collection will be returned to the owners. Neither threats nor persuasion will alter these plans.

Respectfully,
June C. Harris

Apparently there actually were "threats and persuasions" that caused Mr. Harris to write the posting.

Newspapers across the US trumpeted that the Wettermark Bank was the strongest and largest in Nacogdoches, an "old Texas Banking House," that had sufficient resources to make final settlement and that there had been about $400,000 in assets.

A reporter for the Nacogdoches *Daily Sentinel* wrote:

> The entire community greatly deplores the embarrass-ment that has fallen the Wettermark bank. Their many years of work have given them very great prominence and popularity. Public confidence remains strong, and public sympathy is unbounded, both at home and abroad. Col. B.S. Wettermark's unlimited devotion to the public, especially to this town and country is proverbial. His big-heartedness is beyond question. His creditors all have faith in his father, too, and so they will stand by these noble men to the end, trusting in their paying dollar for dollar.

The New Orleans paper added that no one in Nacogdoches knew that the bank was in trouble in any way and the whole community was dumbfounded.

Not, of course, as dumbfounded as Daisy and the children.

"I feel so stupid that I didn't know anything," she told Minnie. "I want to do anything I can to defend your father but I don't know anything."

Alita and Mrs. Hamlin had heard the news on the street and they both tiptoed around the family, doing their work silently while sneaking sidelong looks at them.

Matty Goodson was the only person they let into the house. Daisy read all the papers that Matty could bring to her.

"Daisy, I don't know if it hurts or helps for me to bring you these news-papers."

"There's so much gossip; I feel like I have to know what people are saying. It's comforting that everyone in town is feeling sorry about this 'embarrass-ment' to the bank."

"You and Ben have been so devoted to Nacogdoches. People are standing up for you."

"I think everybody feels like I do, that Ben will fix this…this embarrassment."

On Wednesday, everything changed.

Nobody felt sorry for the Colonel anymore. It was as if the man they had known, the mayor they had elected, was suddenly someone else, a shadowy figure, the forger who robbed them in the night.

The Nacogdoches reporter wrote:

> The outlook concerning the affairs of the Wettermark bank has a gloomier appearance today, and many who spoke kindly of Col. Wettermark yesterday, expressing confidence in him, have changed their verdict. The younger Wettermark has fled, leaving high and dry a number of farmers who had entrusted his bank with what little cash they had, as well as merchants who had deposited Christmas sales receipts but hadn't paid their bills yet.

Matty read the last line aloud: "It is feared the worst is yet to come."

Daisy did not want to believe that.

Matty had brought three other papers. The Houston Post newspaper wrote,

> The failure of the bank is decidedly worse than at first thought. The books are in such condition that no intelligent statement can be made without the presence of B.S. Wettermark, who is still absent and whose whereabouts since Saturday night are unknown.

The *New Orleans Times-Democrat* ran the same article.

The Wall Street Journal was still on Ben's side. The paper had an article that Wednesday that said *"The failure was due to the bad crops and the inability of farmers to pay loans."* But that was the last day the newspapers repeated that line. The articles began to say that Ben had forged checks and embezzled from the bank.

W.D. Lambert of Chireno, a town near Nacogdoches, was notified by a firm in St. Louis that a note was in their hands from him for $3,500. It was endorsed by A. Wettermark and Son. Lambert said he had never heard of this note until he was notified by the firm that it was due.

The president of the Whitney bank, James T. Hayden, said his bank held a note from $10,000 from A. Wettermark and Son. It was supposedly secured by cotton press receipts for 350 bales of cotton, stored in a Texas warehouse. There were no cotton bales securing the note.

The papers carried new specific information about forged notes. The

New Orleans paper had names and numbers that added up to $188,898 and included forgeries of two notes to T B. Hardeman for $8,280 and to the Nacogdoches Oil Mill for notes adding up to $53,550. The article said, "*Every mail is bringing in these forged instruments, and the end is not reached yet.*"

Benny and Carl came home from school Thursday and said they had heard there was a mass meeting downtown. Ben's former friends raised $500 as a reward for "*the apprehension of a member of the firm, who has disappeared and against whom a warrant has been sworn out charging him with forgery.*"

"Those aren't his friends," Daisy said indignantly. "Those must be people who don't really know your father."

That was the day the out-of-town newspaper reporters arrived in Nacogdoches and the headlines announced, "*Forgeries Caused It.*" Now if there was a knock on the door, Daisy and the children cowered in rooms where they couldn't be seen from the windows. Alita answered the door if the pounding went on too long, and told the newspapermen the family had nothing to say and wouldn't come to the door.

"I just want to give Mrs. Wettermark a chance to tell her husband's side of the story," Daisy heard the reporter from the Nashville Tennessean newspaper drawl.

She buried her head in a quilt. Daisy didn't know her husband's side of the story. There was nothing she could tell, even if she would. She hadn't heard a word from Ben since Saturday when he climbed into the buggy and left for the train station.

The *St. Louis Post Dispatch* wrote about the downfall:

> A series of stock investments had turned sour, and Wettermark began selling notes he had made to local businessmen at a discount to other banks across the country—including in St. Louis. He pocketed the payments made by the original creditor in a Ponzi scheme that, as most do, collapsed. A Garrison merchant, who had borrowed $6,000 from Wettermark, was contracted by a distant banking house that now held his note and wanted its money—even though the merchant had paid off the note to Wettermark and had proof of it.

Alita brought them many pots of tea. She was as worried as Daisy; she had been with the Wettermark family for over 15 years. This was the only family she'd ever worked for.

It might have been the $500 reward that got everyone excited but this was suddenly the hottest story in America.

"I'm terrified that Ben has gone from being a banker seeking to save the bank to being hunted like an outlaw," Daisy told Matty. "How can he come back here now?"

The *Times-Democrat* said:

> The sensation created in regard to the Wettermark bank failure has seldom been equaled. It may be truthfully said that the people are wild. The man accused has always been regarded, next to his father, as being the leading citizen of the town, always ready to do more than his part toward public enterprise of all kinds, sociable, agreeable, known and liked by nearly everybody. He commanded the utmost confidence of the people.

It was interesting that the reporters wrote as if Alfred Wettermark were a leading citizen in Nacogdoches, where he was hardly known. Most of the papers called Ben "the young man," as if he was not already 45 years old. They seemed to think of Ben as a runaway boy who was still beholden to his father.

The Times-Democrat had a story about the hunt for the forger and speculated that the "absconding Texas Banker" was thought to be New Orleans. A search was made of all ships in the harbor. A long feature told about a sheriff who intercepted the huge ships and searched *"every nook and cranny but unless he was disguised as a stoker or sailor or deckhand, or perhaps stowed away in a packing case or trunk as a piece of luggage,"* Wettermark was not aboard.

Daisy and the children felt more alone every day. No one from her women's club or even the church came to see them. It was as if their house was a ship surrounded by angry waters and they were hiding inside.

The only people who came to the door were reporters and her friend Matty, who brought her more newspapers. Daisy would have liked to keep everything from the children, but they reached for the papers Matty brought and read every word. Their school friends stayed away from the storm-tossed house, where the family clung together for support.

Daisy's father-in-law Alfred Wettermark did not contact her. He had closed his banks, A. Wettermark and Co., the same day he closed the Nacogdoches bank. As far as she knew he hadn't come to Nacogdoches. She had heard that he had rushed down to Houston, but she didn't know if he was trying to find Ben or save himself.

On Thursday, Alfred was arrested in Houston on the charge of receiving deposits knowing his bank to be insolvent. He proclaimed his innocence and said he knew nothing about the Nacogdoches bank. He was put on the train with a sheriff and sent to Henderson.

When the train arrived in Henderson at 1 a.m., the town's businessmen had made arrangements for his bond and met Alfred and the sheriff at the station.

Two district judges were at the courthouse waiting and they opened the court and fixed the bond at $1,000, which was immediately made and accepted.

The editor of the Henderson paper wrote, "The people here do not believe Mr. Wettermark guilty of willful or premeditated criminality and deplore his arrest. They are confident that he will be able to make a satisfactory showing of the condition of his banking institution at this place."

A Deputy Marshall had been sent to take possession of Alfred's Henderson house, where his wife Alice was very ill in bed. Their home was a historic Henderson building, the large brick school building where Alice's parents had raised her and her ten brothers and sisters.

Alfred and his supporters in Henderson claimed the bank was separate from the Nacogdoches bank and "if contention holds they will not lose very heavily."

The next day Alfred came into the Henderson bank and worked with the Deputy US Marshall George Eason who had been put in charge of the bank. Mr. Wettermark was, the Henderson reporter said, "Utterly cast down." The reporter added, "The sympathy for him is deep and sincere."

Ben's bank failure ended his father's 50-year career in banking. Although he proclaimed his innocence, Alfred never reopened his Henderson bank.

People in Henderson may have been sympathetic to Alfred Wettermark but no such sympathy existed for Ben anymore.

Saturday was the worst day for Daisy and the children. The editor of the Nacogdoches *Daily Sentinel* brought a copy of the editorial he wrote that ran in his paper and the *Houston Post*. He wondered if Daisy would like to comment on it. He stood on the porch while Daisy read it. It said:

> It is believed here that by the majority of citizens that Benjamin S. Wettermark will never be captured. He is a haughty man and before he would humiliate himself to face these people whose confidence he has grossly betrayed he will probably take his own life. A great many surmises have been printed as to the cause of his downfall, but the principal cause is whiskey and neglect of business. By his most intimate associates it is said that for many years he has been a constant plunger, dealing in cotton futures, wheat, oats and corn, hog products, oil and mining stock.

Daisy slammed the door in his face, sat in the parlor and cried.

The next person at the door was Sheriff A.J. Spradley. Daisy had heard he had lost a lot of money at the bank and she was afraid to open the door. Minnie stepped up and allowed him in.

He took off his hat and held it in his hands. "Mrs. Wettermark, I just came to offer you some comfort. I know how the town has turned against you."

She looked up at him, her eyes filled with tears.

"I know people are ready to class Ben Wettermark as a wanton criminal. Often men are driven to desperation and commit rash acts by force of circumstances unavoidable. I understand Ben Wettermark made bad bets of speculation and lost. Now some men, some commit suicide, some murder trying to cover their shame."

Daisy sobbed.

He kneeled down beside her. "Not your husband. Mr Wettermark is charged with forgery, I believe, with the hopes that he would save his name and his creditors. But instead he lost. It was suicide or flee; and he chose the latter."

The sheriff put his hand on her shoulder. "When Ben Wettermark went down, the business interests of Nacogdoches lost their best friend."

He straightened up.

"I just wanted to say that, ma'am. I just want you to know some people here understand what he was trying to do."

The sheriff nodded to Daisy and to Minnie, put on his hat and left.

Daisy and Minnie sat in the parlor, grateful for a lawman who didn't think Ben was an outlaw.

29. TALK OF THE TOWN

The ambulance pulled up to the emergency room, siren still blaring. Ray, the head of the Nacogdoches Fire & Rescue's Venom Response Team, had been with her in the ambulance and was still by her side. The EMTs wheeled her through the door, a narrow oxygen tube in her nose.

Ray stepped aside as the nurses cut off her long-sleeved shirt and put a hospital gown on her. They moved her from the stretcher onto a bed in a small room and pulled the curtain. They attached a blood pressure cuff and took her temperature.

"Can you see me? Can you talk?" An administrative clerk was right in Peggy's face.

"Yes," she gasped.

Ray was holding her purse. "Ma'am, is it all right if we give them your billfold? They need to check you in."

The pain was excruciating, all the way to her elbow. She nodded and the clerk took out her billfold out and started filling out a form. "Mrs. Jensen?"

She nodded, her teeth clamped together.

Ray took her other hand. "Now, ma'am, you said the snake was brown or gray and had marks on its back. Do you remember what those marks looked like?"

While he leaned over her, a nurse took a marker and drew circles around the two holes on her swollen hand.

Tears squeezed out of her eyes. "Maybe like an hourglass. All over its back."

"That's good. We're looking at those fang marks and the size of them looks like it was not a very big snake, maybe 12-14 inches long. We're going to watch that ecchymosis for just a few minutes. That's like a bruise, there, and we can tell a lot by that."

Sweat broke out on her forehead and the nurse put a wet cloth on it.

"Can you call my daughter?"

The clerk found the phone and Peggy told her Erin's name. She couldn't remember the number, not now.

"She's coming," the clerk said.

A doctor came in and started talking quietly with Ray. He then examined her arm.

A wave of nausea flooded over her. The nurse wiped her forehead again and said, "Here you go, now, Mrs. Jensen, here you go."

The doctor seemed to be poking her swollen arm but it already hurt so much she couldn't tell.

"You had the head of the venom unit for your ride-along," he said. "You're a pretty lucky lady."

If this is lucky, Peggy thought to herself, I don't want to see unlucky.

"Ray tells me he thinks this was the work of a copperhead," the doctor nodded. "That's one of the better snakes to be bitten by, if you've got to be bitten."

Peggy looked at Ray. He nodded. "That's true, ma'am. The copperhead's the mildest of the poisonous snakes. Of course none of the bites are good. But the way you feel now, that's probably the worst you'll feel."

The doctor shared a subtle look at the nurse, who hurried out of the room. "We're going to start an anti-venom on you and that'll prevent this from spreading, and you'll start to level off pretty soon."

Ray must have thought she wanted more information because he came back over beside the bed.

"Anti-venom is made from venom of the same snake that bit you. It's going to reduce your pain, reduce the digestion of tissue and blood; it's gonna help all the way around."

While Ray was talking, a nurse drew blood from her good arm and hurried away with it.

Ray took her left hand again. "They're gonna do some lab work. That'll give us a real idea of how you're doing."

"I was afraid—I thought it was a rattlesnake," Peggy hadn't heard a rattle but those marks on the snake's back…

"We can tell it's not a timber rattler because its venom usually does neurological damage; your eyes would flutter and your face muscles and eyelids would be drooping."

By the time Erin and Jackson found her in the emergency room, the doctor had administered the anti-venom. Her arm was huge, swollen and black and blue. But her blood pressure wasn't soaring and she was able to convince herself she wouldn't die.

"Mama!" Erin rushed in, crying as she hugged Peggy. Jackson put his arms around them both, leaning awkwardly over the bed.

Then Jackson cornered the doctor to get every detail and left to arrange for her room in the hospital.

Erin pulled up a chair. "Mom, you just cannot take chances like this. Bitten by a copperhead. I was terrified. What were you doing?"

"I was clipping the hedge."

"That's not a hedge, it's a forest of weeds. You just can't do things like that. If anything happened to you, I couldn't stand it."

"I have to do something. I can't let the house just sit there, unfinished."

"I think you'll have to. Obviously this is a dangerous, dangerous thing to do."

"Oh no!" Peggy cried out.

Erin jumped to her feet. "What? What is it, Mom?"

"I just remembered, I left Jackson's tools in front of the house. Oh, he'll be so upset!"

"His tools aren't near as important as you are."

"Do you have to tell him? Could you go by and see if you can get them?"

"He'll be fine." Erin straightened the thin blanket. "He can drive by and pick them up when we get you settled in."

The doctor insisted on a tetanus shot that hurt almost as much as the snakebite. It just wasn't as terrifying. Then they took her up to a room.

Erin stayed beside her bed all night, crunched in a recliner that was a size too small. All night long, the nurses checked Peggy's vital signs. She would just doze off and in they would come again. Erin was able to immediately go back to sleep after each nurse left.

Every time Peggy woke up, she revisited the snakebite scene, feeling alternately stupid and horrified before going back to sleep.

Apparently the jungle drums signaled all of Nacogdoches about her snakebite. There was a steady stream of visitors before her first sip of the lukewarm coffee.

The first person through the door, much to her surprise, was the man who steadied her foundation.

He had his cap in his hand and he looked as sad as she'd ever seen a man look. "Miz Jenson, I'm Tanner Elroy, remember me?"

"I do. You straightened up my foundation."

"I just feel so bad, ma'am. I told you there wasn't no snakes around because the raccoons or possums probably scared them away."

She looked at his sunburned face, his hangdog, shamefaced look. "I do remember that."

"I feel responsible for you getting bit crawling under the porch."

"It's not your fault. I shouldn't have been reaching under the bushes."

"Everybody said you wuz under the house and I felt so bad about giving you a false sense of security."

Erin, who had been sitting quietly, spoke up. "My mother, a false sense of security? There's nothing false about it. She's so secure she tackled that copperhead all by herself."

Peggy barely had time to brush her teeth before the next visitors descended— Neil, the banker; Robbie, president of historical foundation and Scott, her contractor.

Neil passed around donuts and said she was the talk of the town. Scott and Robbie agreed.

"I'd be surprised if you didn't get a proclamation from the mayor," Scott said, picking out a cream-filled donut. "Braved a den of vipers to restore Nacogdoches' history."

She'd have laughed if her arm and her head didn't ache so much. She couldn't tell if her arm was that swollen or if that was just the huge bandage.

While people came and went bringing flowers and good wishes, Erin rode herd on the visitors, making sure Peggy was not suffering more from the visits than the bites. She kept her mother's plastic mug filled with ice water and encouraged Peggy to drink it.

At about 10 a.m., the doctor and a nurse came in and shooed everyone out. He thoroughly checked her and very carefully removed the bandage.

Her arm actually was that swollen. It looked awful, dark blue and puffed up. "That's looking good," he said.

Peggy thought he must have been kidding. She looked at Erin, who had her hand over her mouth, her eyes wide.

"It's a clean bite, and your circulation is starting to come back. How do you feel?"

"I ache all over, not just in my arm. But that's still where it hurts the most."

"You're how old?"

"78."

"Well you certainly look good for 78. We'll keep you a couple days. This has been a shock to your system, and you might as well let us take care of you. The swelling will go down gradually and that arm will be back to normal soon and by next month you'll hardly even remember it happened."

Erin had picked up the hospital menu and seemed very interested in it. "Can she eat? Can we order lunch?"

"Absolutely. My prescription is for everyone to be well-fed."

Peggy slept awhile and woke to a little knock at the door. Erin opened it to William Calhoon, who peeked around her to see Peggy.

"Mrs. Jensen? Peggy? Can I come in?" He stood in the door with a bouquet of flowers in his hand.

Erin opened the door and took the flowers, stuck them in the water pitcher. "Mr. Calhoon! Please come right in; I was just going for coffee." She closed the door behind her.

William stepped over to her bed. "Peggy. I had to come see you. You were bit by a rattler?"

"A copperhead, which apparently is the best of all possible snakebites."

"There aren't any good snakebites, from what I've seen. I'm so sorry that happened to you."

"I guess I shouldn't have been crawling around trying to do the yard work. I was just trying to get things done."

"I admire that about you, doing so much alone. You have got some gumption, for sure."

"Gumption gets me into trouble all the time," she said with a smile. "Thank you again for donating the electrical work. That was the best surprise I've had in the whole project."

"My guys like a challenge. And that was a challenge, all right. They were pretty proud of themselves when they got all the lights working."

"You'll have to go over and see it. It looks brilliant."

"Are you going to do another work day? That was such so much fun."

"The doctor said my arm will feel normal someday, and I hope he meant someday soon."

"Then we'll go back and work again. You shouldn't be over there trying to do the work all by yourself."

Dan and Frances Ferguson eased open the door.

"Yoo-hoo!" Frances trilled. "Anybody home? William! You know Peggy?"

"We installed her electric," William said as the couple came in and crowded next to the bed.

"Donated all the electrical," Peggy amended.

Dan and Frances looked impressed.

"We're getting her a door to make sure nobody damages anything," Dan said. "We were going to come over today to tell you the bank decided to donate it. Then we heard you were crawling under the house and got snakes all over you."

"One snake, and I was attempting to garden." Peggy leaned back on the pillow. She was so tired.

Dan turned to William and the two moved aside, engaging in a deep conversation worthy of historians. Dan began, "The big carved wooden door had been on the original First National Bank in 1886. The bank liquidated its assets in 1899, leaving Wettermark the only bank in town until Commercial Bank came into Nacogdoches in 1901 and challenged it."

While the two men talked, Frances fussed over Peggy, checking her water cup and smoothing her blanket, "My goodness, you are brave. I think if a snake bit me I would faint dead away."

"I thought about it but I had to call the ambulance."

"You're amazing. I've never known anyone who survived snakebite. Well, I've never known anyone bitten by a snake, but still…"

Dan turned back to Peggy, "Would you mind if we met the carpenter over there to get the door in?"

"Please, make yourself at home. Frances, can you pass my purse? I have the key in there." Peggy fumbled around with her left hand and handed the key to Frances.

William looked hopefully at Peggy.

"William, maybe you'd like to go with them? You haven't seen the house lighted up."

William looked delighted, and she was glad he would see the good work his crew had done.

Dan stepped toward her; his look told her he didn't have good news. "I'm so sorry to tell you but it doesn't look like we'll be able to get a Preserve America grant. We've been looking at their criteria and we don't meet it."

She tried not to look devastated. "Thank you for trying."

Frances, Dan and William left together, making plans.

Peggy closed her eyes and even the sadness about the grant wasn't enough to keep her from falling asleep.

When she awoke, Nona was standing at the door of her room.

"Miss Peggy! First you tackle our history, now you're taking on the snakes?"

"Oh, Nona! I'm so glad to see you."

"I'd rather not see you under these circumstances, but you look mighty good for having fought a viper and won."

"I haven't won yet. You know I'm at a stopping place."

"Most people don't tempt snakes after they've stopped working."

"I thought maybe there was something I could do without any money."

Nona spoke quietly and held up a stack of printouts from her computer. "Miss Peggy, I think I may have a solution. At least, I want to see what you think."

Peggy immediately felt wide-awake. She could hardly wait to hear what Nona had to say.

30. MAKING DO

1903

Every day Daisy heard "absolutely certain" rumors that Ben had been captured on a ship, in a seedy hotel room, hiding behind a bar. The bank's estimate of loss was now half a million dollars.

On Friday, Jan. 9, attorney E.W. Smith announced that most bankruptcy proceedings were simple but that the Wettermark bankruptcy was enormous and intricate with a lot of conflicting interests. "*There are questions of offsets, counter claims, agency, suretyship, partnership etc which will take time and patience, thought and work to solve,*" he said.

The New Orleans paper said photographs and descriptions of B.S. Wettermark, "a junior member of the firm," had been sent all over the country. Ben, or the fugitive, as they called him, was described as:

> **Height six feet, weight about 200 pounds, of fairly well-proportioned build, dark hair and beard (close cropped), a white scar on the right cheek having the appearance of a scar; much space between the teeth which are fairly good; age about 42 years; generally good looking, a good dresser, deliberate in movements, easy swinging gate in walking, general appearance that of a man who might be deserving of overconfidence.**

On Monday, Jan. 12, Smith announced that he would be in the County Clerk's office from 10 a.m.-4 p.m. everyday and that he would pay "the closest and most careful attention to all claims." His consultation and advice would be free of charge. He had a steady stream of farmers, businesspeople and laborers filing claims to get their money back.

Daisy couldn't even shop for groceries without being approached.

"Mizz Wettermark, have you heard from the Colonel?"

"Daisy, at club we were just wondering if you're planning to stay in town?"

"Mrs. Wettermark. When you talk to your husband, tell him I put every paycheck I made in the bank and now I can't get anything out."

She came home in tears each time. Mrs. Hamlin volunteered to do the shopping, but Daisy didn't know how much longer she could pay her. Daisy's bank account, of course, was frozen inside the bank like everyone else's. Or, as some people speculated, in Ben's pocket.

Like everybody else in town, she couldn't believe she hadn't heard from Ben.

Benny, 17, had it worst at school because his name was the same as the now famous forger, Benjamin Wettermark. Carl, 15, had always been able to think on his feet and was able to talk his way out of most problems with his classmates.

Daisy was heartsick for 19-year-old Minnie. All their plans of a glorious wedding evaporated when her father left town. The wedding dress from New Orleans, the lavish feast at their house, the guest list they had already started making.

Minnie didn't break down until she went to the Presbyterian Church and found her wedding ceremony had been cancelled.

"We didn't dream you'd still want to be married in the church," the Reverend said. "I would imagine some other venue would be more appropriate."

As she sat in a pew and cried, the pastor looked uncomfortable. "Of course, we're praying for you," he said.

A heavy question on Minnie's mind was if Cliff Witherspoon still wanted to marry her. Daisy had Alita deliver a note inviting Cliff and his parents to the Wettermark house. She was relieved when they wrote back, "We would be glad to come over tomorrow evening."

Minnie and Daisy sat in the parlor with Cliff, his father Clifford and his mother Martha. They all drank tea but none of them touched the sugar cookies Mrs. Hamlin had made.

"Thank you for coming over," Daisy started. "It's hard for us to get out right now."

The three Witherspoons nodded. They looked at each other, then Clifford spoke.

"It's a terrible thing that's happened. For a man to leave his family like this..."

"Clifford." Martha gave him a sharp look. "We feel awful for you all. We keep hoping this will pass, and Ben will come home again and make everything right."

"We keep hoping that too." Daisy tried very hard not to get weepy.

"We're related to you, so it's hit us, of course." Clifford received another sharp look from his wife. "Well, it's true. Everybody knows the Witherspoons and Wettermarks are kin. Even if Lenore died after having these children."

Cliff looked at Minnie, who had kept her eyes downcast since they arrived.

"Minnie, I still feel the same about you. You're the person I want to be my wife."

She looked up. "Are you sure, Cliff?"

"I guess I got to make an honest woman of you now."

Minnie laughed and gave him a slap on the arm. Cliff's parents' whipped their heads toward him, and Daisy's mouth fell open.

Seeing the children smiling at each other, they laughed, but just a little.

"We had been planning a big wedding," Daisy said. "But now..."

"A nice little ceremony might be better," Martha said. "Our house isn't as fancy as this one, but we could have the wedding and reception there."

"In April, just like we planned," Cliff said.

Daisy wondered if she would have enough money to live on until the wedding, but she didn't say that out loud.

When they left, Minnie threw her arms around Daisy. "Everything's going to be all right," she sighed.

Daisy returned her hug. "Let's go upstairs and see if I have anything you can wear for your wedding."

Mr. June Harris came right away when Daisy contacted him. He had been pursued by reporters and by creditors and he knew what Daisy was going through.

He hurried into the house, glancing around to be sure none of the reporters had followed him.

Daisy didn't know how to ask Mr. Harris how she should live now that Ben was gone. "Thank you for coming. I just need to talk to someone about...about what I should do."

"I assume you haven't heard from the Colonel?"

"Not since the night he left. You helped him write his will...I thought he was taking care of us. I didn't know..."

"I didn't know either. Even the day we saw how bad the books were. Well, I knew he was going to try to get help, but I didn't imagine he wouldn't come back."

Daisy spoke in a whisper. "He's coming back."

Mr. Harris looked at her sadly. "I suppose he might."

"The will...is there any money for us?"

"Anything he left isn't available until he passes away and we have verifiable proof of that. And even then the creditors will seize his assets and you'll have to fight for them."

"Fight for them?"

"In court. And believe me, there are a lot of people who will put a claim on any assets he leaves."

"How will we live?"

"Do you have anything of your own?"

"Everything I have is ours, Ben's and mine."

"Do you have any family, besides the Wettermarks?"

"My father, in New York."

"If he were to give you some funds, the courts could not seize them."

"I haven't told my father anything about this."

"I would imagine he's heard about it by now; it's been in the Wall Street Journal and probably the *New York Times*."

"Oh, this is awful."

Mr. Harris was sympathetic. He had a family; he would never put them in this position. "You can sell the house."

"When Ben comes back, if the house is gone…"

"That would be one less economic burden he would have to face."

She bowed her head. "If we sold it, would the creditors take that money?"

"Probably. But I'll find out for you. I'll talk to the federal marshal."

When he left, Daisy sat down and wrote to one of the New Orleans decorating firms where she'd bought many of her most beautiful lamps and pieces of furniture.

> *Dear Sirs,*
>
> *I have purchased many fine items from your shop and have proudly displayed each of them. However, we find ourselves in changed circumstances and can no longer afford to enjoy them.*
>
> *Is it possible that you would consider buying some things back from us? They are still in exceptional condition and have been greatly admired by everyone who has seen them."*
>
> *Sincerely,*
>
> *Mrs. Daisy Sutton Wettermark*

She sent Alita to the post office with the letter. That would give people something to talk about. Every bit of mail she sent or received was scrutinized to see if Ben was writing her to reveal the whereabouts of his hidden treasure.

Alas, he was not. But a letter to New Orleans? That would seem like pure gold to the town gossips. They might think it was from Ben, but when they saw the address they would know Daisy was trying to resell her New Orleans purchases.

Daisy's father sent her a modest amount of money along with a strongly worded letter:

> *Dear Daisy,*
>
> *I am sorry that you have gotten mixed up in this terrible scandal. Of course I have heard about it in every newspaper, and I wondered when you would contact me. Perhaps you recall your mother and I said you should not move to Texas, where things like this happen all the time.*
>
> *I hope this sum will tide you over until you get your affairs in order. I cannot invite you and the children to New York right now because I have recently remarried and my life is much too hectic. Bess Richmond Sutton is a lovely woman and I'm sure you will like her very much.*
>
> *Perhaps in a year or so, we will be able to accommodate you.*
>
> *Sincerely,*
>
> *Father*

The New Orleans shop sent some men who paid her pennies on the dollar. She sold back all the lamps, some of the furniture and most of the rugs. She couldn't part with the golden chairs in the parlor or the rug that had been in the house when she moved to Nacogdoches. They wouldn't take the custom drapes. The men packed her things in crates and took them to the train.

The house felt as empty as her life. She was so lonesome she went to one meeting of the Cum Concilio. Once there, she couldn't imagine why she thought this a good idea. She had never felt colder as when the women inched away from her.

In February US Deputy Marshal George W. Eason from Tyler finished compiling his report on the bank. There was approximately $278,000 in assets and $319,500 in liabilities missing. In addition to that, Eason announced, there was nearly $200,000 in forgeries. Forgeries, obviously, by Col. B.S. Wettermark.

In March there was a big meeting of the creditors and people came to Nacogdoches from all over the state. At that meeting Eason was appointed trustee of the bank funds.

The people who attended had suffered the disappointment in losing their money to the foreclosure. Now, they had a second disappointment. They learned there was a little-known law that required them to place in Wettermark Bank the amount they had in their account four months ago when the doors closed.

Some of them didn't have enough to put more money in; some didn't trust the bank enough to want to. Therefore many of the creditors couldn't get the money they had lost.

Easton announced that winnowing people out with this regulation was good because now Wettermark Bank could pay a larger percentage to those people who could still submit claims.

This did not endear Daisy to anyone in town. Although she did not attend the meeting, those who saw her walking, with her head down, pointed her out to the out-of-towners as if she had destroyed their lives herself. She wore her plainest clothes, no jewelry. In fact, her black dresses and hats looked like widow's weeds. She walked and talked and felt like a widow.

In April Minnie and Cliff got married. The Witherspoons' house was not a mansion, but it was very nice. In fact, it was just the right size for the very, very small group of people who came to the wedding. Mostly it was Witherspoon relatives, a few school friends, Matty Goodson, and the three Wettermarks. Mrs. Hamlin and Alita, who came to serve food, joined everyone in the parlor for the ceremony.

April was the most beautiful month in Nacogdoches, and the Witherspoon house was filled with yellow heritage azaleas and buttercup jonquils. Minnie wore the pale green silk dress she had gotten for the debutant ball. It was perfect on her and, as Minnie said, why would anyone have a dress that could only be worn once? She had borrowed a long lace veil from a school friend and it transformed the dress. Her bouquet was jonquils, lovely with her blonde hair.

It was a bittersweet ceremony. Almost everyone cried, including Daisy who could not stop once she got started. Benny and Carl were on either side with their arms around her. Daisy and Minnie had eliminated "Who gives this woman away," and the couple went right up to the pastor. When he proclaimed them man and wife, Minnie had the most glorious smile on her face and Cliff looked like he was the luckiest man in the world.

Throughout the wedding and reception, Daisy silently repeated over and over: "What should I do? What should I do? What should I do?"

As usual, there was no answer.

31. OUT OF THE BOX

Nona pulled the chair up to Peggy's hospital bed. "Miss Peggy, how are you? I was heartsick when I heard you were bitten by a snake."

"I keep thinking about when it bit me. I can't stop seeing it."

"Snakes have been bad, bad creatures ever since the Garden of Eden. Well, I know some of them are good, but not this one that bit you. Are you hurting?"

"I feel like I've been run over by a truck. But other than that, I'm glad to know I'm going to live."

"Thank the Lord for that."

"I am sick to have stopped work on the house, but apparently I am not fit to even do the yard work. That thought is almost as bad as the snakebite."

"I've been thinking about you ever since you came in the library," Nona said. "All of my sorority sisters keep talking about our work day. It was wonderful. It just felt right."

Peggy's arm had started to ache and she thought they'd better talk fast before the nurse came back with a pain pill.

"William Calhoon said it was the most fun he's had in a long time," Peggy almost smiled at the memory of everyone working, laughing and singing.

"I've been looking for grants and I may have found something that might work." Nona tapped the papers in her hand.

Peggy looked doubtful. "I already heard I'm not eligible for the Preserve America grant."

"I read over their website and I'd come to that conclusion myself. There are some of the basics that don't fit this house and this situation."

"I don't want to give up, but I wonder if there is anything this project is eligible for."

Nona seemed hesitant. She was quiet a moment then said, "This is completely out of the box. Out of the ballpark. Out of the..."

"Nona--tell me now before the nurse come in and I get looped on pain medicine!"

"All right. It's this." She handed some papers to Peggy. "It's a clearing-house for money and programs for service organizations. They give major grants to service fraternities and sororities every year."

"You think they'd give us money to finish the house?"

"Well, here's the deal. I think the Wettermark house would make an incredible home for the state office of Tau Alpha Sigma."

"What?"

"The head office of our service organization is looking for a place to put the headquarters, and I'd like to propose Nacogdoches. We've got a good university with 13,000 students and 600 faculty members. We're midway between Houston and Dallas and close enough to Louisiana that they could go to regional meetings in New Orleans."

"My house?" Peggy looked puzzled and Nona hurried on.

"Your house is an incredible piece of Texas history, over 100 years old. The sorority could get the grant and finish fixing it up. From here Tau Alpha Sigma could organize all the activities in the state, award scholarships and set up campus tours to Texas universities for historically underserved students."

"So it would be a sorority house? Would I live there? I've never been in a sorority, much less a house where they live. I got married before I even had a chance to go to college."

"We're not that kind of a sorority. Tau Alpha Sigma's primary purpose is service for African American students. It's a non-profit organization. We're not a sorority where college girls live and college boys stage panty raids."

Peggy looked even more surprised.

"I don't reckon there are still panty raids, but you know what I mean." Nona looked anxiously at her. "It would be the state organization office. We help college students—like single mothers who want to succeed in college. And we connect first generation African American students with faculty mentors. We even have seminars that help students learn to manage their money, something that Mr. Wettermark would have benefitted from."

"Where is the state organization now?"

"They're in a downtown office building in Houston, short of parking and office space. They're looking to move right now. And I can just imagine what they would see if they looked right here."

"Well, one thing they would see is snakes..."

"Oh, Miss Peggy, I'm so sorry. I'm just jabbering on and you are lying here all wounded and agonized."

"You've certainly given me something to think about, rather than remembering how I ended up in the hospital. I just don't know. Where would I go? Where would I live?"

"I'm thinking the organization could buy the house from you and pay a fair price for what you've done already. And you could get your own house— something that doesn't have a ballroom."

"It is a huge house. What possessed me to think it would the place for me to live?"

"You were thinking that this house needed to be saved from deteriorating more and more everyday."

"Maybe when the house spoke to me, it was saying 'Save me! Save me!' not 'Come fix me up and live here!'"

Nona patted her good hand. "You're gonna have to learn to speak *house*."

Peggy squeaked, "Save me! Save me!"

And Nona responded in a deep voice, "Save yourself! And keep your hands off my snakes!"

They were laughing so hard that the nurse popped her head in the door.

"Mrs. Jensen, you should probably get some rest."

"I do need rest. I'm hearing voices," Peggy laughed.

"I'll call the doctor!"

Nona put her hand up. "I'm hearing them too!"

The nurse looked from one to another, at their smiling faces.

"Uh huh. Well, we'll be in soon and you can tell me if you're still hearing those voices." She nodded and closed the door behind her.

Nona put the papers on a little table.

"Thank you for hearing me out. It might be a crazy idea, but it's the best I've come up with."

"And thank you for giving me a new crazy idea. I wouldn't have imagined it, but now it's going around in my head."

"Maybe we could make you an honorary sorority sister."

"Only if you swear there won't be panty raids."

"I can't promise anything. You know those frat boys. Always looking for excitement at historic houses…"

"Thank you, Nona. This is the most fun I've had since just before I reached under that bush."

Nona leaned over and gave Peggy a hug. "You are a sweet, sweet lady. And that snake sure better hope I never get my hands on him!"

As she lay in the hospital bed, Peggy couldn't stop thinking that Nacogdoches' richest people bought the house, then sold the house. Then it sold again and again, until it did not sell anymore. There was just something wrong with it, something that wouldn't let it thrive.

She knew people thought the house would never be revitalized again, that it was too far gone. They didn't think it was worth saving, if they thought about it at all.

Before Peggy was bitten by the snake, she had the highest hopes that the Wettermark house would flourish under her tender care. She had seen setback after setback—the driveway fiasco, the snakebite, miscalculating expenses, running out of money.

But she was still determined to save the Wettermark house.

Each day her arm recovered and every day she liked Nona's idea more and more. She could visualize exactly what the house would look like, active, alive, making a difference.

Erin wasn't opposed to the idea; but she didn't want her mother working on the Wettermark house anymore. She liked the idea of Peggy safely ensconced in her living room, watching Let's Make a Deal. Or anywhere deadly reptiles were not slinking around.

"Please, Mom, don't go anywhere while I'm at work. Just sit right here and recover," Erin would say every day.

"Erin, I am not in my dotage," Peggy would reply. "I won't do anything I don't feel good enough to do."

Although she did admit to herself she would not be doing yard work anytime soon.

Peggy and Nona worked on the grant application together, sometimes at the library and sometimes at Erin and Jackson's house. One day Peggy had a revelation about the restrooms.

"Nona, I just thought how lucky it is that the hardware store took back the bathroom fixtures. The house won't need showers and bathtubs because they'll be working in it, not living there. There should be more stalls and you know everything will need to be ADA compliant."

Nona thought that was a sign of divine intervention. "I see what you mean. You think the spirit of Daisy Wettermark interceded on behalf of the women who will use the restrooms in the house? She must not have liked to stand in line."

"I think probably she waited in the line to an outhouse—that was 1903, after all."

"Let's not get that authentic."

Peggy asked Tyler Pate, the young real estate agent, to meet her at the house.

"Remember how surprised I was when you wanted to look at this house? Then when you decided to buy it?" He crinkled up his forehead as he recalled that day.

"You were worried Jackson would have your hide," Peggy grinned at him. "I remember."

"You wish you hadn't gotten involved with it?"

"No, I've loved every minute of restoring it. I learned a lot, I had a lot of good luck and I had some bad luck."

"Attacked by snakes," Tyler nodded sagely.

"One snake, when I practically stuck my hand in its mouth. But I'm feeling really good now, and I need your help."

"I don't like snakes either."

"I need get an estimate of what the house is worth. There might be an opportunity to sell it to someone who could finish it and then move in."

Tyler promised to find a "good, not-too-expensive appraiser" and hurried off, glad not to be called upon to be a snake handler.

The day Mrs. Lydia Whitehouse, executive director of Tau Alpha Sigma, came to visit, Nona brought her to the house. She and Peggy knew the outside didn't look good, so they rushed her up the steps. Peggy unlocked the heavy antique door the Fergusons had installed and flipped on the lights.

It looked beautiful inside and she felt proud to show it.

Nona was either excited or nervous, because she was talking fast and saying a lot. "We painted all these walls. And some of the sisters helped prep the flooring for these gorgeous boards. And we sanded the stair rails, and did all the wood trim around the windows."

Peggy added, "It was a wonderful work day. There were over 30 women here, working like mad."

"And this was a service project?" Mrs. Whitehouse asked, looking around.

"It was during our month of service," Nona confirmed. "There were actually 35 of us, 31 members and four alums."

"But this is not a non-profit."

"No, but it's a historic house and we were unanimous in wanting to help."

The director walked slowly around, looking at everything.

"Tell me the history of the house."

Nona and Peggy looked at each other and for the first time, Nona seemed to be considering what she should say.

"It's a long story," Peggy began. "It was built in 1900 by Diedrich Rulfs, the most important architect in Nacogdoches history. "

"And wait till you hear the story behind it," Nona took a deep breath. "It's, well, it's part of what made Nacogdoches what it is today. And I can just picture Tau Alpha Sigma here in the oldest town in Texas representing us throughout the whole state."

32. A LETTER

May 1903--January 1904

Daisy missed Minnie.

Mrs. Minnie Wettermark Witherspoon lived in a little house on her in-laws' property. Daisy was happy for her but she missed gentle Minnie every morning and every evening.

She talked to Alita about it. "I miss how brave Minnie was. She always stepped right up and answered the door even when it was people who had lost their life savings and hated every one of us."

"Yes ma'am, and she has such sweet face that most people forgot all their venom when they looked at her. I miss that. My face don't seem to have that effect on people."

"Mine neither, Alita. They seem to just build up a head of steam when they get started with me."

"Yes, ma'am. I surely do miss our Minnie."

In fact, Daisy missed Minnie more than she missed Ben. Minnie hadn't snuck off as a thief in the night, leaving her family impoverished and despised. Minnie would never do that.

Ben, on the other hand, had disappeared completely. Even rumors about sightings had almost stopped.

Almost. An article in the *Daily Sentinel* said:

> People have about ceased to talk about the recent bank wreck, and business again has settled in its old time ruts. It is a matter of general congratulations that in consequence of the bank suspension, not a single mercantile house in Nacogdoches was compelled to go out of business.

It had been five months since Daisy had heard from Ben. Months she saw what little money she had dwindle, months when people turned their backs as she walked by. Or stared at her, which was even worse.

Some days she missed Ben and the love they used to have. Some days she hated him, as she doubted he had ever loved her, to leave her this way. She felt frozen in place, not sure what she and the children should do or where they could go.

Every once and awhile the sheriff or Mr. Harris stopped by the house to see if she had heard from Ben. No, of course she hadn't. Apparently she and the children did not matter to him.

Mr. Harris suggested Daisy try to establish that she and the children still owned some land. She couldn't imagine that the courts would allow that, but she let Mr. Harris take their claim to court.

On September 28 Carl, Ben Jr. Minnie and Daisy were plaintiffs in the court case. It involved "a settlement of possession of some land southeast of Nacogdoches in the J.M. Mora Survey that was jointly owned by Wettermark and others." The defendant was "George W. Eason, Trustee of A. Wettermark & Son, bankruptcy."

It was horribly embarrassing going to court. And painful. She was reminded every moment in court of the way Ben had betrayed her and what he had done to the people of this town. Daisy knew it was the main topic of conversation throughout Nacogdoches.

With Mr. Harris as their attorney, the court awarded the Wettermarks one-sixth of the property, and Eason, the trustee, one-sixth. The other two-thirds went to the other plaintiffs. The one-sixth interest Eason was awarded as trustee was used in settling more claims against the bank's assets.

Daisy was relieved to receive anything from the case. That meant she and the children got to keep some land that they didn't have to share with the claimants.

"Thank you, Mr. Harris. I don't imagine it was easy representing us in court."

"Mrs. Wettermark, I am your attorney. I am one of the few people who saw the colonel the day he left. In some ways I feel party to his departure. I wish I had given him alternatives, something besides becoming a fugitive."

"I feel the same way. If only he had talked to me. I would have sold the house, sold the furniture, turned everything over to the bank, just to keep him here."

"I don't think that would have been enough. This was bigger than us, Mrs. Wettermark. A half a million dollars bigger than us."

On September 17, there was a story in the Nacogdoches newspaper with a New Orleans byline. It listed several "noted fugitives from justice from the United States" in Spanish Honduras." Among them was "Wettermark, the Nacogdoches bank wrecker." Daisy read with interest: *"The greatest contrast of them all is seen in the life which Wettermark is living. From the rich, distinguished citizen, he has turned into a sunburned, hardened cattle puncher in the tropics."*

Could she imagine Ben as a cattle puncher? Sunburned, certainly. But living like a ranch hand? No, but she never imagined him as a bank wrecker, either. She didn't know if this was just the product of a journalist's imagination or if Ben was truly living in another country.

Two weeks later Mr. Harris knocked on her door.

"No, I haven't heard from him," she said reflexively as she stepped out onto the porch. It was her standard response, the answer to everyone's question.

"Could I come in?"

Something about his tone made her wary. She nodded and opened the door. He walked in front of her to the parlor. When she sat down, he sat too.

"Are we alone?"

This was making her very uncomfortable. "Alita just stepped out but she'll be back in a minute. And the boys are due home from school very soon."

"Then I'll make this quick." He unbuckled his briefcase and pulled out an envelope. It had her name written on the front. No address, no return address.

"This was inside an envelope sent to me, postmarked Houston. I haven't opened it."

She felt like her heart stopped. She couldn't make herself reach out for it. The attorney stood up and handed it to her.

"It's best if I am not here when you open it. Whatever it says, I don't need to know."

She clasped the letter to her heart. "Thank you," she said.

He nodded and let himself out the door.

Ben wrote:

> *My own little Daisy,*
>
> *I love you. I have never regretted anything as much as not letting you come with me when I left. But that night I still believed I could save the bank. I'm so sorry. I couldn't find any other solution but to leave Nacogdoches.*
>
> *I know now, I cannot live without you. Will you come to me? We can make a new life together. It will be very different from our life in Nacogdoches. But when we are together, life will be good.*

Daisy read those lines over and over. She was angry. She was confused. She didn't think she could ever forgive him.

She asked herself the same question she had been asking all long, "What should I do?" She had nowhere to go, no assets except some land south of town and this huge house. She had two children at home. The money her father had given her was almost gone.

> Here is enough money for train tickets to Houston, then New Orleans then a berth on a steamer to the Spanish Republic of Costa Rica.

> I hope you will come to me as soon as possible. I will wait for you and the children at the dock every day in January. Each day when the steamship from New Orleans pulls into Puerto Limón, I will be hoping to see your beautiful face.

> Please forgive me. I will never stop asking your forgiveness.

> Your humble husband,
> Col. Benjamin S. Wettermark

She threw the letter on the floor. She cried. She picked it up and read it again.

How could he ask her to sneak out of Nacogdoches and meet him in his hideout in some Spanish republic?

He had left her, deserted her in the middle of the scandal he created. He didn't trust her enough to tell her what he was going through. She and his children bore a disgrace they had not earned, alone and friendless. She had left everything and everyone she had ever known and moved to this little town in Texas. She had loved him and trusted him and he had left her.

And now he said he loved her. He loved her. And she cursed the day she had begun to love him.

He loved her. He could not live without her.

What was there for her here, in this mansion in a town that hated her? Where could she go, where she could not be hunted and asked the same old question, "Have you heard from the colonel?"

What kind of a life was there here for their children who bore the mark of his betrayal every day?

But where else could she go? She had come to Texas because of him, and now--now could she leave Texas and follow him?

She sat very still. Was Ben a sunburned cattle puncher? Was he a rich man, living on money from his bank? What would it be like to have him ask her forgiveness every day of his life?

What did she have to lose if she took a steamer to Costa Rica? She would lose the house, a mansion that had once been the most beautiful home in town. The courts already had a claim on it. She had sold all the beautiful lamps and furniture that had been the envy of all who saw them.

She would lose her friends, Matty especially. She would never see Alita and Mrs. Hudson again, and they had supported her through everything.

She would not miss the women of the club who moved away from her rather than offer comfort. She wouldn't miss the church that had closed its doors to Minnie's wedding. Or the school friends of her boys, who no longer came to visit.

She would not be stared at as the wife of a man who went from mayor to embezzler. She would not be asked a thousand times a day if she had heard from the colonel.

She took a deep breath. She sat very still and thought of her options. That was a brief train of thought. She did not have money to move to another town and start over. Her father could not take her in. The small plot of land the courts had granted her would not become hers until Ben was dead. And unless he came forward and proved he was alive, it would be impossible to prove him dead.

This man who said he loved her forced her to endure this year. He had so little love for her he left her to grasp at rumors of where he had gone. And the children! Surely they didn't deserve what their father had done to them.

But Ben said he loved her and could not live without her. He sent money for his children to come with her. He could have disappeared forever but he would be waiting for them on the dock, hoping to see their faces.

He was her first true love, and she felt she would never love again. Rather, she would never trust enough to love again. Could she learn to trust him if she took that steamer to Costa Rico and saw him waiting on the dock? She had no answers.

She closed her eyes and bowed her head. What were her options?

She could think of only one. She would escape from Nacogdoches and take a steamer to Costa Rica.

That night she sat Benny and Carl down and talked to them. She made them swear to secrecy. She knew Benny wouldn't say anything, as cruelly treated as he had been by his classmates, but Carl was her little talker.

"Carl, you have to swear on this Bible you will NOT say a word of this to anyone."

"Really, Mama, is that appropriate? I thought we weren't supposed to swear."

"Young man, you do this now or leave the room and you won't hear a word of what we're saying."

"All right. I swear, by the power invested in me..."

"Carl!"

"I solemnly swear I will not say a word of this to anyone."

She looked at them both for a minute. Then:

"I got a letter from your father today."

Benny whooped. "I knew it!"

Carl was more subdued. "What does he want?"

"He wrote that he misses us so much he can't stand it without us."

"That's why he's been gone almost a year with no word." Carl said bitterly.

"He regrets not taking us with him."

"But he doesn't regret embezzling from the bank?"

Benny slugged Carl's arm. "He can't stand it without us!"

Daisy looked from one boy to the other. "He's sent money for tickets and he wants us to join him."

Carl was indignant. "You're not thinking of running after him, are you, Mother? He destroyed the bank, practically ruined Nacogdoches, left us sitting here in the mess he made."

"I'd go in a minute," Benny said. "You've been lucky, Carl. You're not named Benjamin S. Wettermark, Jr. Your friends haven't reminded you of that every single day. In fact, I don't even have any friends left because of all this."

Carl shrugged. "So that means you'd go to him?"

Benny straightened up. "In a minute. I would do anything to get out of here."

"Not me. I won't go anywhere with that cheating forger."

"Carl," Daisy was aghast. "You are talking about your father."

"I'm sorry. I'm not leaving here."

"If you won't go, I'll have to stay." Daisy felt her eyes fill with tears.

"No you won't. Sell the house. The court's going to ask for it anyway. Get rid of everything. I'll go live with Minnie."

Daisy was shocked.

Benny looked as if he was ready to pack. "When does he want us to come? How soon can we leave?"

"Please do not say anything to anyone. At all. Let me think this through and we'll talk about it tomorrow." Daisy rose slowly and headed to her room. "I just want you to know, I love you both very much. And I know your father loves you too."

On Nov. 24, 1903, Daisy signed a power of attorney authorizing Mr. June C. Harris to handle any and all legal dealings for her. She gave Alita and Mrs. Hamlin the most valuable pieces of her jewelry and told them to take anything that was left in the house that they might want. Everyone cried—Alita and Mrs.

Hamlin were the most loyal members of their family and it broke her heart to leave them. They had taken care of the children before Daisy was their Mother.

On December 28 in the darkness of night she, Carl and Benny pulled their trunks onto the porch. Minnie and Cliff quietly brought their buggy up to the house.

Minnie and Daisy cried and hugged each other in the darkness as the boys loaded the trunks. There wasn't room for Carl's trunk; the buggy would come back for it after they unloaded Daisy and Benny at the train station. Then Minnie would take Carl into their home.

When they got to the train station, Daisy tried to dry her streaming eyes. "Minnie. You have been the best daughter I could ever have."

"And you've been a wonderful mother. I'll miss you so much."

Daisy handed her the money that would have covered Carl's ticket. "This is all I have to give you."

"It's enough. Carl will be fine with us."

Benny said, "If he gives you any trouble, pack him up and put him on the train to us. He'll make a fine cattle puncher."

Carl heard that. "In that case, I will never give them any trouble."

Daisy threw her arms around him. "Carl, how can we live without you?"

"You'll be fine. I'll be fine. We'll all live through this. Tell Father I said 'Hello, you old reprobate.' And keep Benny from sniveling too much."

They hugged until Daisy stopped crying and released her hold.

"I love you Carl. You're a brave boy to stay here."

"And you're brave yourself, heading out to the unknown. I hope my father appreciates what a wonderful person you are and how lucky he is you're willing to leave everything behind."

"I think we can make a new life with him."

Carl rolled his eyes. " A new life? He gave you no choice because he destroyed this one. You're much more generous than you should be, not to close him off forever. As far as I'm concerned, he is a despicable cheat who doesn't deserve you. And you can tell him I said so when you see him. Wherever you're going."

"You understand why I can't tell you and Minnie where we're going?"

"I don't want to know, anyhow."

Carl and Benny hugged then she and Benny stepped up to the station where she bought two tickets to Houston. She would wait until she got there to buy the tickets to New Orleans, then buy the final destination tickets in New Orleans.

One last long hug from Minnie, a short one from Cliff, and they climbed on the train and left Nacogdoches behind in the dark.

The big house, Ben's dream house, stood empty on Wettermark Street. When the neighbors saw it was empty, the word spread around town. Daisy and Benny were gone; Ben Wettermark would never be coming back. If any of the townspeople harbored hope that they would see their money again, they gave it up. Not that many of them still had that hope.

When the year became 1904, Daisy and Benny were on the ship headed for Costa Rico.

Harris used the power of attorney to sell the Wettermark house and 12 acres on North Street to J.J. Hayter on Jan 28. The money was added to the funds to be divided by the claimants.

There was nothing left inside the house but four gold chairs and a deep, plush Brussels carpet.

33. A New Day for an Old House

Peggy wished the picture that ran in the newspaper had shown her inside the house, instead of standing on the porch. But she was glad they had done a story to tell about the announcement she was going to make at the house.

"You look nice," Erin said. "That dress looks lovely on you."

Jackson looked at the front-page photo. "You do look nice. You have on lipstick. And you look almost normal."

"Thank you, Jackson. Almost normal. High praise!"

"You know what I mean. It's getting hard to tell your bad arm from your good one."

Erin laughed. "You are a master of the compliment, Jackson. Mom, are you ready?"

"I am. I wish I could have gotten that front yard looking better." Erin shot her a warning look. "I don't mean by myself. I just wish it looked better for the big event."

There were lots of things Peggy wished. She wished the outside of the house had been scraped and painted and the heritage azaleas planted. She wished she had more time and more money and knew how to do construction work herself.

But on the short drive to the house, Peggy stopped wishing and felt honestly, totally grateful.

When they drove up, Nona was already at the Wettermark house with all the Tau Alpha Sigma members and alumni. Like Peggy, they were wearing their Sunday best.

"You all look wonderful," Peggy told the smiling women who rushed to crowd around and hug her.

"We decided against our T-shirts," Nona said. "They do make a statement, but we wanted to say something besides how paint-splattered we could get."

"I liked that look too! If it hadn't been for this group splattering the paint around, none of this would have happened."

"Now Miss Peggy, you know that's not true. You single-handedly started this project—"

"Is that a snake bite joke?"

"Sorry!" Nona laughed. "You opened the door to this project and without you this house would still be falling apart."

The townspeople began to arrive—the workmen, Scott, the real estate people, even Ray, the head of the Venom Response Team. William Calhoon came and stood beside her. They gathered around the house, on the porch, by the front door. If they hadn't already known about the event, they had read it about in today's newspaper.

When the car with the Tau Alpha Sigma staff pulled up, the sorority sisters started to cheer, then everybody was clapping and cheering. The staff of the state organization got out, waving and smiling. If they were surprised by the turnout, they didn't show it.

When the camera crew from the Tyler TV station was set up, Erin nudged Peggy. "Mom, are you ready to say something?"

"Jackson first," she whispered back.

Jackson nodded and stepped forward. "I'm a lucky man," he said. "As the executive director of the Chamber of Commerce, I know what it means to have our history saved and a beautiful building like this renovated. But beyond that, I'm lucky to have the best mother-in-law a man could ever have."

He gestured for her to step forward. "Peggy Jensen saw a wreck of a house and instead of driving by, like most of us do, she stopped to save it. She put her own money, even her own safety, on the line. She shook up the snakes and put all of us on notice. This strong woman standing here reminds us we can do more to save the oldest town in Texas. This house tells a story, and Peggy Jensen breathed life into it for us. And today, the story continues."

Peggy stepped forward in the applause. "Thank you. When Col. Ben Wettermark stole away in the night in 1903, he left Nacogdoches devastated and his wife and children alone in this big house. But this isn't just any house. It was built by the great architect Diedrich Rulfs. It has the story of Nacogdoches in its bones and that includes a scandal, a bank failure and heartbreak. Some of your grandparents or great grandparents may still be mad at Col. Wettermark."

Some people nodded.

"I understand that. But that's where I come in. I just couldn't let this house die. And I haven't gotten to this point alone. I'd like to acknowledge the people who helped me on the renovation."

She called for applause for them all: Scott McCullough and his crew, the banker who that had faith in her, William Calhoon and Calhoon Electric who brought electricity to the house, and the members of the Nacogdoches Historical Society.

Then she turned to Nona.

"I want to give a personal thank you to Nona Hopkins, the reference librarian who just kept digging and digging until we got the whole story. She enlisted the women of Tau Alpha Sigma for a day of service, and their work transformed the interior of the house."

The sorority sisters put their hands in the air and whooped and hollered. They got applause from the crowd.

Peggy continued, "And Nona came up with the most brilliant idea of all— to bring the state office of Tau Alpha Sigma to Nacogdoches. To this house. To turn the page for a new day of history. Nona, come on up here and tell the rest of the story."

Peggy stepped back to let her speak and Nona squeezed Peggy's hand as she went by. They both got a little weepy.

"When Miss Peggy first told me the house she was looking at, I didn't know much more of its history than she did. The more I dug into it, the more I got worried that she'd picked the wrong house. Col. Wettermark took off with almost a half a million dollars that belonged to the people of East Texas. He was a scoundrel, and that's no lie. But she was insistent about saving this house. And gradually, I got to thinking—some history is bad, but that doesn't mean it's not true. And if it's true, we shouldn't be afraid to acknowledge it."

Like a well-trained cheering section, the sorority sisters applauded loudly.

"Tell it, sister," one of them hollered.

"Our social sorority, Tau Alpha Sigma, is a positive force for good. We like turning bad news into good news, especially for college students. We've got that hands-on approach that makes all the difference. And that's the way Miss Peggy has worked. She put her heart into this house and she started bringing it back to life. We found a grant and worked the hardest I've ever worked—you and I both, Miss Peggy—to write an application that would persuade the state office to move here to Nacogdoches."

Nona paused, took a big breath. "And we got word last week that the answer is YES. The grant will fund the continuation of the renovation of the Wettermark House so Tau Alpha Sigma can move here. They've got plans for each and every room of this historic house. The big ballroom upstairs will be the conference room where volunteers like Miss Peggy and I can help strategize the good works Tau Alpha Sigma will do from here. So today I'm proud to introduce Mrs. Lydia Whitehouse, the executive director of the state organization."

While Mrs. Whitehouse talked about the way the service sorority helps minority college students find their way to success with scholarships, mentorships and involvement, Peggy looked around at the faces of the crowd. There were more smiles than she'd seen the whole time she'd lived in Nacogdoches.

A year ago she wasn't sure if she could leave everything behind and move to her daughter's home. She was afraid she'd never again find a place where she fit in. Now she felt like she was right where she should be.

When the executive director finished her remarks, Peggy handed her the key to the antique front door. Everyone surged forward and when the door opened, they pushed into the room and spread out, pointing and exclaiming, complimenting everything that glowed in the brightness of the lights.

Frances and Dan Ferguson had personally funded the installation of the glass windows. They stood by a window, explaining how the Historical Foundation paid for the glass and pointing out the little bubbles and flaws that made the windows look authentic.

Frances looked so happy. She turned to Peggy. "It's all here, isn't it? History is all around us, just waiting for us to find it."

William Calhoon caught her eye from across the room. When she smiled, he walked over. "Very impressive, Peggy. You did good."

"Thank you for your help, William. It never would have come together without your gift of the electrical work."

"What's next? Where are you going to put your spoon collection and your miniature buffaloes?"

She laughed, remembering when she was so cocky she thought she needed a house with 12 rooms.

"I'm going to stay with Erin and Jackson a while longer. Then I'm going to start looking for another wreck to renovate. But this time, it will be a smaller house that fits my budget and abilities."

"I hope you'll let me help. I do swing a mean sledge hammer."

"Of course, William. You'll be the first one I'll call."

Then people surged around Peggy to congratulate her and thank her. She and William smiled at each other as she was swept away.

She could hardly wait to get started on her next renovation.

34. AN OLD REPROBATE

1904

Daisy and Benny stood at the rail looking west across the Caribbean toward Costa Rica. It had been a long journey, and they had both been seasick much of the time.

Daisy had been so sick, in fact, she had vowed that if she made it to Costa Rica alive she would never leave.

Now she and Benny scanned the coastline, both nervous and anxious.

"Do you think he'll come?" Benny didn't look at her as he asked. It hurt her heart to hear him. Benny was almost 18, but in that moment he sounded like a little boy, wondering if his father had forgotten him.

"He'll be here," Daisy answered. "He will be here." And she prayed she was right.

The coastline was rugged and the wild tropical forest seemed to come right down to the water's edge. Beyond the coast, dark mountains loomed, some of them volcanic. The towns on the coast looked small and shabby. Would they live in a little hut by the ocean? Would they eat coconuts and fish from this deep sea?

The steward had told them they would be landing in Puerto Limon today and she and Benny had gotten their trunks packed and left them by their doors. As ready as she was to get off the ship, she knew she was not prepared to see Ben. She had rehearsed speeches ranging from strident to magnanimous, and still didn't know what she should say.

If she was certain how she felt about Ben, she would know what to say to him. If she had anywhere else to go, she would not be on this boat right now.

"*You've had a year to think about it,*" she told herself. "*And now you don't know what to say?*"

Benny was apparently thinking the same thing. "What should I tell him?

He doesn't know Carl didn't come. Should we tell him Carl called him an old reprobate?"

Daisy laughed at that. "Probably. But not the first thing off the ship."

When the port came into view, they bustled around, making sure the steward had their trunks. Daisy put on her coat and gloves and then took them off again. She fiddled with her hat and tried breathing deeply. The closer the ship got, the more intently she scanned the shore, looking for Ben.

They were close now. She gripped the railing, staring at the gathered crowd. The gangplank was lowered and still she didn't see him. As they hung on the handrails and moved slowly off the ship, she looked around, side to side, into the crowd. People pushed past them, eager to get off the ship. Vendors crowded forward, waving bananas and woven fabrics. They called out in a language that was a mix of African and Spanish and she didn't understand a word.

What had she been thinking? What was she doing here? She must have been a fool to leave the United States.

Benny took Daisy's arm to steady her, or perhaps to steady himself.

Still, no Ben.

The crowd swept them toward where the crew was piling trunks. Benny elbowed his way in and pulled first her trunk then his out of the pile.

"Help you with your bags, ma'am?"

She whirled around, right into Ben. She was so startled she flung herself at him, crying and burying herself in his chest. Benny grabbed hold and they stood in a three-person hug, all crying, but no one as hard as Daisy. Not one word of any of her rehearsed speeches came back to her. She and Benny just clung to Ben.

Ben looked around and then patted her on the back and stepped back. She looked at him through her tears. Who was this man, why wasn't he apologizing? Why was he smiling? He hadn't seen them for a year. And now all he said was, "Help you with your bags, ma'am?"

He was ruddy, as sunburned as the newspaper article had said. He had a big hat and his mustache was gone. He wore khaki pants and a lightweight linen jacket, slightly wrinkled and sweat-stained. But he was unmistakably her blue-eyed Ben, here to take them to their new home.

His voice was a hoarse whisper. "Where are the other children? Where's Carl? Is Minnie coming?"

"Carl's living with Minnie and Clifford in their new little house." Daisy said it firmly, hoping Ben could hear the disappointment in her voice.

"Carl said to tell you you're an old reprobate," Benny blurted.

Ben glanced around to be sure no one had understood that. "I guess I am! I guess I am. Well, Benny, I'm glad you came. Look at you, you're a foot taller, my boy."

Benny grinned but Ben was looking around at the people crowding up to the stack of bags. "Let's get out of this crowd," he said. He grabbed Daisy's trunk and Benny got his own. They dragged them to a buggy and loaded them in.

Ben turned to help Daisy up and whispered, "Daisy, you look beautiful. Even more beautiful that the day we got married."

Her eyes welled up again. "I didn't know if we'd ever see you again."

He seemed artificially hearty. "Of course you'd see me! I said I'd meet you at the dock."

As they rode slowly away from the dock, Ben kept up a narrative: "It's a bit rundown from all the earthquakes that have hit it, but Puerto Limon has some fascinating architecture and open air markets. Sometime when we come back to the main market in the center of town, you can buy woodcarvings and other things as souvenirs."

"Souvenirs?" Daisy could not imagine sending anyone a wood carving from Costa Rica.

"Benny, you'll like this. We'll come back to Puerto Limon for Columbus Day. They have this huge carnival with parades, loud music and wild parties. You'll have the time of your life down here."

Benny and Daisy looked at each other. Parades? Wild parties? Did Ben think they were here for a party?

Daisy stared at him. He sounded like a tour guide, not a repentant husband.

"Do you have the impression we have left everything, that is everything we hadn't already sold, to come here for parades and parties?"

Benny was silent and looked at them both.

"Daisy, let's get out of Limon. Then we'll talk."

The buggy jostled on a bumpy road surrounded by lush tropical greenery. "Where are we going?" Daisy was cold as ice.

"Home. To our new home. We're going right into the mountains." Then he was the tour guide again. "The mountains really are the heart of Costa Rica. You can see some of the most diverse and beautiful forests in the world. Wait till you see the breath-taking land and the ocean views from the mountains."

They bumped along, Ben narrating the scenery, Daisy and Benny stunned to silence. Finally they passed the last bungalow of Limon. The jungle seemed to come right up around the road and close them off from the rest of the world.

Ben pulled the horse to a stop in a clearing and silence surrounded them.

He took a second to collect himself. Daisy and Benny weren't sure what was coming.

Ben turned to them both and said, "I am so sorry. I am so sorry for leaving you. And I'm sorry I couldn't say that back in Limon. I couldn't take a chance on anyone hearing us, or hearing my name. It's still not safe for me, even here."

Daisy turned to look him right in the eyes. "A year. We have lived a year with what you did to the bank. Alone."

"I know. What I did was terrible. I panicked. It was wrong, but I couldn't see a way out."

"You could have told me, I could have helped. I would have gone with you."

"Me too," Benny said.

"That would have been worse, to pull you into my problem. You were all innocent."

Daisy shook her head, still not taking her eyes from him. "It certainly didn't feel that way, sitting alone in Nacogdoches."

Ben lowered his eyes. "I did the wrong thing and I feel awful. Daisy, I've had a year to think about what I did. I thought I could fix it and no one would ever know. I see now how self-centered I was. I was ruthless, thoughtless, without compassion."

Daisy spoke softly. "Every day someone asked me, 'Have you heard from the Colonel yet?' and every day I had to admit, 'No.' And I would say to myself, no, my husband abandoned me and the children and does not care enough to even send word that he is alive."

"There were some days I thought I would be better dead," Ben admitted. "I've been in agony, afraid that every person I saw was a bounty hunter, coming to take me back dead or alive. And I missed home so much it was like a stabbing pain."

Benny said, "I'll bet if you came back home with us and gave back the money..."

Ben turned and looked directly at his son. He looked pained. "I can't go back, I can't ever step foot in America. They would hang me."

Benny and Daisy gasped.

"I have to live with that every day for the rest of my life." He shook his head. "I've had plenty of time to think and the main thing I learned is that the big house doesn't matter. Being mayor or colonel or president of the bank. None of that matters. The only thing that remains when everything is gone is the love I have for you Daisy, and for our family."

Ben started to tear up.

"I wrote that I will ask you every day to forgive me. And that starts today." He took her hand and she did not pull away.

"Forgive me Daisy. I was wrong, I betrayed you. You don't have to forgive me today, but today I need to thank you for coming here. I love you. Forgive me, Daisy, I was wrong. Thank you for taking a chance on this old reprobate."

He smiled a little and looked at Benny. "And you, son. I'm sorry. I will teach you to ride a horse, and climb a mountain, and fish in the ocean. And with everything I do I hope you'll understand that I am saying, 'Forgive me, Benny. Forgive me and give me a chance to be the father you deserve.'"

They heard a noise behind them and they all froze. A large bird burst out of the trees and swept away above them.

"How will we live, Ben? You are a hunted man. Now I'm afraid too."

Ben glanced at her then back at the road. "First, we have a new name. We are now the Wathens."

"The Wathens?"

"So we could still start with W."

Benny leaned forward from the back seat. "So my name is Benny Wathen?"

"Yes, and this is Señora Daisy Wathen. I'm not a colonel anymore, I'm just Señor Burton Wathen."

"Oh, Ben." Daisy's voice held all the sorrow of his desertion, her shame, her loss and her tears.

"Daisy, in this new life I am a new man. I don't spend all day in the bank like the old days. I don't covet the neighbors' house, I don't seek to have people call my name."

"They don't even know your name," Benny interjected.

Ben smiled at Benny. "They only know me by my new name. And you'll be a new man too, Benny. We'll ride together and we'll repair fences and ride herd. We'll be caballeros, you and I."

"Caballeros," Benny echoed.

"The señoritas are going to love you, Benny Wathen. I can guarantee you that."

"We have fences? And a herd?"

"We do. We have a little ranch with a house that is just the right size for our family. No ballroom," he said apologetically to Daisy.

"I've already had a ballroom, and in the end it was just a big, empty room."

"Our new house is never going to be empty again. I love you. Please forgive me, Daisy, I was wrong." Ben kissed her hand, then she leaned forward and let him kiss her.

After a long, long ride on a road that got progressively more primitive, they pulled out of the rainforest into a small clearing and stopped in front of a colonial ranch house. It had been left by an Englishman who went back to Great Britain. It had stood empty five years before Ben bought it.

"The Wathen house," Ben said as they pulled up.

"Wathen Drive is pretty rocky," Benny said.

"Not as rocky as the road we've traveled to get here," Daisy added.

In the house in Costa Rica, gradually Daisy discovered Ben was still the man she had fallen in love with years ago when he swept into New York and picked her out at the opera.

As he told her the truth about what he had done, Daisy slowly, slowly began to trust him again.

"At first I took some money from the bank to cover new construction and purchases I shouldn't have made. Instead of slowing down on our new house, I told Rulfs to add more. Then I funded two buildings downtown. And I took some money from the cotton loans to cover that."

Daisy nodded.

"I thought prosperity would continue and when some of the cotton farmers defaulted on their loans I covered that with money I had borrowed from organizations that had trusted me to be their treasurer."

Ben put his head in his hands and sat still a long time.

"I covered everything I could and I started to see a pattern. The money was pouring out and not enough was coming back in. I couldn't cover it all, no matter what I did. That's when I, when I started putting some away just in case I needed it. The day I left you, I cleaned out the safe at work. I don't know what I was thinking, that I could somehow make everything all right— or that it would be worse to be found out than to leave town…"

"You should have told me."

"I couldn't face you. You're the one person I love most in the world and I didn't want you to know what a failure I was."

"Ben."

He looked up at her and said, "I love you. Forgive me, Daisy, I was wrong. And I will say that every day the rest of my life."

Whenever they heard an American had gotten off the ship in Costa Rica, they were afraid it was a bounty hunter, come to drag Ben, and now her and Benny as accomplices, back to Texas to pay for his crime. Daisy never had a party or even fixed dinner for anyone but the ranch hands. They worried every time they went to Limon to shop. They never wrote to or heard from anyone they had left behind, not even Minnie or Carl.

They couldn't take that chance.

Every conversation held the threat that somehow one of them would slip and reveal that Señor Burton Wathen was the infamous scoundrel who destroyed the Wettermark Bank and caused his father's banks to fail. In any language, English, Spanish or lilting Caribbean, that was a fear that never left them.

One little miracle happened in Costa Rica. When Daisy was 35 years old, she and Ben had a baby. A beautiful baby boy. He was named after his father—rather, his father's assumed name—and her maiden name. He was Burton Sutton Wathen.

The baby was her joy. Daisy secretly thought of little Burton as her reward for leaving American civilization behind.

The señoritas of Costa Rica did love Benny Wathen. He married the beautiful Maria Luisa Valle and they had four children, who never knew their father's real name.

After Daisy had plenty of time to see him grow up, Burton married Maria Christina Ruiz. They had three wonderful Wathen Ruiz sons.

Daisy loved her seven grandchildren and sometimes hugged them so long that when they pulled away they saw her eyes filled with tears.

It was not the life Daisy had expected but it was the life she had. She had accepted the good with the bad, from the beginning.

And every day, Ben said, "I love you. Forgive me, Daisy, I was wrong."

And he said it every day for the rest of his life.

35. TRACES

Peggy hurried over to the library when she got Nona's message: "New info! Come see!"

She didn't even stop to watch Scott's crew working on the exterior of the Wettermark house. She had been there almost every day since Tau Alpha Sigma signed the papers to buy it from her.

Peggy was finding it a little hard to let it go.

Apparently, so did Nona. She was still researching the Wettermarks.

She had the papers spread out on a library table when Peggy rushed in.

"If we thought the story stopped when the family left Nacogdoches, we were way off," she exclaimed.

"Did we think that?"

"I found a court case in East Texas in 2006 that showed Burton Wathen's three children and Benny Wathen's four children fought Minnie's son for the land left behind by Ben Wettermark!"

"What?"

"In 1934, a document allegedly signed by Ben and Daisy granted Clifford Witherspoon power of attorney over the undivided one-half of the mineral estate in seven tracks of land. Carl sold his land to an oil company and Minnie and Clifford gave theirs to their son, Ford Witherspoon."

Nona looked at Peggy to make sure she was following. Peggy nodded and Nona continued, "In 2006 Burton and Benny's children claimed that power of attorney was a forgery. They took Ford and the oil company to court."

Nona tapped a paper and passed it to Peggy. "There were still people in Nacogdoches whose families lost money in the bank failure and they watched the case carefully. They had claims for as little as $7.50 and as high as $7,000. Seeing the new name of the Wettermark family got them all stirred up again."

"What happened?"

"The Witherspoons won the case and the Wathen families of Costa Rica did not. No one else got anything. Most people never saw a cent of the money they lost when the Wettermark Bank closed its doors forever. But it gave people one thing."

"What was that?"

"Now they know for sure where the Wettermarks went. Apparently both Daisy and Ben are buried in Costa Rica under the name Wathen."

"Costa Rica. Hmmm. The Costa Rica with beaches, mountains, and palm trees?"

Nona grinned, "Are you thinking what I'm thinking?"

Peggy looked at Nona and then back at the paper. "I'm not sure. Are you thinking we need to fly down to Costa Rica and do some hands-on research?"

"Why, yes, Miss Peggy. I am. We've got more work to do on the story of the Wettermarks."

"My thoughts exactly. Well, then, let's get packing."

ACKNOWLEDGMENTS

Saving the Oldest Town in Texas is based on the true story of Col. Benjamin S. Wettermark who broke the bank in Nacogdoches, Texas in 1903. His forgeries and embezzlement practically destroyed the oldest town in Texas. The former mayor emptied the vault of an estimated half a million dollars and skipped town, leaving his wife, his children and his mansion behind.

There is a wealth of information about the all too-true story of the night Wettermark took the train out of Nacogdoches and the search to bring him to justice.

The late Carolyn Reeves Ericson, author and historian, was a brilliant source for information about East Texas. She located historical data about the Wettermark family history in Sweden, Houston and Nacogdoches. She shared her own biographical directory, "Nacogdoches: Gateway to Texas" and even gave me a copy of a Wettermark Bank check dated 1898.

The Nacogdoches Daily Sentinel and the *Houston Chronicle* were rich sources of information. The Wettermark bank failure was reported in 1903 in over 30 newspapers nationwide. Records of court cases came from public records from Tyler, Texas.

The definitive book on Nacogdoches' most famous architect is "Diedrich Rulfs: Designing Modern Nacogdoches" by Dr. Jere Langdon Jackson. The modern-day photos by Christopher Talbot are spectacular, especially those of Zion Hill Baptist Church. The turn-of-the-century architectural details in this book came from Jackson's book. It contains the only photo I've seen of the Wettermark House, taken in 1910.

Gary B. Borders 2008 book, "A Hanging in Nacogdoches: Murder, Race, Politics, and Polemics in Texas's Oldest Town, 1870-1916" has captured the time period very well.

Dr. Scott Sosebee, a history professor at Stephen F. Austin State University, helped me understand 1900s elections.

Ray Cole, head of the Venom Response Team in Nacogdoches, was an excellent source of information about snakebites.

Karle Wilson Baker's writing is from her own books and the biography "Texas Woman of Letters" by Sarah Ragland Jackson.

The information about the Wettermark house is based on historic truth with one exception. The house did not thrive after the Wettermarks left and it burned down in 1924. There is no trace of it except the sign on the corner, Wettermark Street.

The names of the Wettermark family are unchanged; some other historic names have been changed in this book.

The character of Peggy Jensen is a composite of irrepressible women I've known who don't hesitate to do the hard thing. Like my own mother, Peggy is a woman who tackles projects that would terrify most people.

Thanks to Dr. Wanda Mouton and Ted Ringer for advice, suggestions and corrections.

My husband, sons and daughter-in-law are brilliant supporters and always encourage my desire to combine the present day with the historic.

Thanks to Sarah Johnson with SFA Press for the layout and editing of *Saving the Oldest Town in Texas*. Special thanks to Kimberly Verhines, the Director of the SFA Press. The cover image was drawn by Tristan Brewster, based on a photo of the Wettermark House taken in 1910.

Dr. Linda Thorsen Bond is a journalist, author, producer, and professor. She has written and produced over 20 original historic plays, including several in Nacogdoches, the oldest town in Texas. A television show she wrote and produced about the historic Hoverhome in Colorado won a national silver People's Choice Telly Award and a bronze award for historical production.

She is co-author of "Swingtime Canteen," a musical performed hundreds of times all around the world. Dr. Bond taught in the Department of Mass Communication at Stephen F. Austin State University in Nacogdoches since 2002.

CPSIA information can be obtained
at www.ICGtesting.com
Printed in the USA
BVHW030210210519
548865BV00004B/8/P